D1357229

Snobbery with Violence

by the same author

THE NAKED NUNS

BROOMSTICKS OVER FLAXBOROUGH

THE FLAXBOROUGH CRAB

CHARITY ENDS AT HOME

LONELYHEART 4122

HOPJOY WAS HERE

BUMP IN THE NIGHT

COFFIN SCARCELY USED

ONE MAN'S MEAT

BLUE MURDER

COLIN WATSON

Snobbery with Violence

ENGLISH CRIME STORIES AND THEIR AUDIENCE

THE DETECTIVE STORY.

EYRE METHUEN

First published 1971 by Eyre & Spottiswoode (Publishers) Ltd
Revised and reprinted 1979 by Eyre Methuen Ltd
11 New Fetter Lane, London EC4P 4EE
Copyright © 1971 Colin Watson
Set, printed and bound in Great Britain by
Fakenham Press Ltd, Fakenham, Norfolk

British Library Cataloguing in Publication Data

Watson, Colin, b. 1920
   Snobbery with violence.
   1. Detective and mystery stories, English
   – History and criticism
   I. Title
   823' .0872   PR830.D4

ISBN 0-413-46570-5

'that School of Snobbery with Violence that runs
like a thread of good-class tweed through
twentieth-century literature'

Alan Bennett, *Forty Years On*

Contents

Acknowledgements

Acknowledgements and thanks are due to the following authors and publishers for the use of copyright material:

To William Collins, Sons & Co. Ltd. for extracts from *The Deduction of Colonel Gore* by Lynn Brock;

To David Higham Associates for extracts from *Lord Peter Views the Body* (1928) and *Have His Carcase* (1932) by Dorothy L. Sayers (Victor Gollancz);

To Hodder & Stoughton Ltd. for extracts from *The Last Hero* (*The Saint Closes the Case*) by Leslie Charteris (1930), and for extracts from *Moran Chambers Smiled* by E. Phillips Oppenheim (1932);

To Lord Oxford and A. P. Watt & Son for extracts from *Solved by Inspection* by R. A. Knox (Methuen):

The cartoons are reproduced by kind permission of *Punch*.

Preface

This second edition has been revised only in as much as one 'revises' yesterday's date by adding one. Such is the durability of the public appetite for mysteries and thrillers, and such is the persistence of established forms, that in no other field of fiction is there so little risk of obsolescence.

Introduction

One of the most consistently busy of Britain's home industries during the past fifty years has been the manufacture of crime fiction. Some three hundred writers now contribute, more or less regularly, to the satisfaction of the public's appetite for books about murder, theft, fraud, espionage, arson, blackmail and kindred activities. The appetite appears to grow with the advance of what we call the standard of living.

More than half of these authors, one in four of whom is a woman, live in London or within a few miles of it. Their addresses include precious few manors or granges, but a host of numbered, semi-detached houses in Roads, Gardens, Avenues and Crescents. A handful of the most successful enjoy incomes comparable with those of chiefs of the Civil Service or of minor property dealers. But more than three quarters of the others depend for their living on wages from regular, non-literary, employment. They are authors only in their spare time.

These facts may seem odd to those who have been led to picture the typical thriller writer as a rich émigré, dictating his tales at luxurious remove beside some lido or lagoon. Yet the situation really has altered very little since the 1920s. Then, as now, the spectacularly successful crime novelist was a rarity. For every Phillips Oppenheim or Edgar Wallace, there were scores whose writing, even at a steady rate of a book every six months, brought in little better than pocket money.

It is doubtful if there has ever existed, outside the dairy industry, so large, so diligent and so easily contented a body of primary producers.

This book is not an attempt to catalogue them, to offer a Who's Who of authorship or a comprehensive survey of the *'genre'*. Its purpose is to explore some of the crime and mystery fiction of the past half century – characteristic samples, that is, and not necessarily the best known or most widely approved – for clues to the convictions and attitudes of the large section of British society for which it was written.

History's most frustrating pages are the many left empty of record of the thoughts and beliefs of ordinary men and women. Evidence of what ideas had common currency at this or that moment in the past is among the hardest to adduce. What a pity it is, from the social historian's point of view, that there was no Ronald Knox in the monastery of the Venerable Bede; no Dorothy L. Sayers looking over Holinshed's shoulder while he whitewashed the Tudors; no 'Sapper' to echo in hearty prose the solid citizenry's approval of Peterloo. Nothing would have been added to our knowledge of the old battles, usurpations and massacres, perhaps, but we should be much better informed about the tribal, class and religious dogmatism that motivated them.

CHAPTER I

'So many yards of stuff, sensation pattern'

More than two hundred years ago, Lady Mary Wortley Montagu declared of the writer of the popular fiction of her day:

> Perhaps you will say I should not take my ideas of the manners of the times from such trifling authors; but it is more truly to be found among them than from any historian: as they write merely to get money, they always fall into the notions that are most acceptable to the present taste.

'Trifling' is scarcely the word that would occur to us in connection with the enormous eighteenth-century novel, but it would have been understood and approved by the contemporaries of Pope and, indeed, by several succeeding generations. It was not until the later years of Victoria's reign – and then only with misgivings – that fiction, stories invented to entertain, was conceded to be anything other than a reprehensible invitation to waste time. It took the combined industry of Scott, Lytton, Trollope, Thackeray and Dickens to render the novel respectable. Their industry, that is, plus a shrewd appreciation of current taste, plus the good fortune to have been born to authorship at just the right moment to reap the benefit of cheap printing, big-scale serialization

(Dickens enjoyed periodical prints of 70,000 and more), and the direct marketing and wide distribution made possible by the growth of the railways.

Against the tide of fiction from the booksellers, the railway bookstalls and the ever-expanding circulating libraries, objections to its 'triviality' and to its degrading and enervating influence failed not because they were morally invalid but because they were economically inappropriate. Literature had joined the list of human products that the industrial revolution brought within the field of organized commercial exploitation. It had become a commodity.

There always had been profit in books, of course. Dr Johnson's famous disavowal of altruism is applicable to the entire post-Caxton era. But Lady Mary Wortley Montagu showed perception of something beyond the basic principle that 'they write merely to get money'. The interesting part of her statement is: 'they always fall into the notions that are most acceptable to the present taste'.

Was this true of the fiction writers of two centuries ago? Of some, undoubtedly. The prospect of strictly limited circulation must have prompted conformity to fashion and the choice of themes known to be approved by potential subscribers. The opinions of patrons were important, also; the authors of those slavish dedications knew better than to undo their good effect by giving offence in the text.

Yet the section of society involved was small. By 'the manners of the times', Lady Mary meant the manners of a literate minority, an isolated and privileged minority. She cannot have expected even the most 'trifling' author to reflect the ideas and attitudes of the bulk of the common people, the labourers, peasants and artisans.

It was only with the development of mass dissemination of books and periodicals in the second half of the nineteenth century that it became important for the ambitious author to acquaint himself with the views of classes of people other than his immediate social circle. And even then, there was no question of a writer seeking popularity at every level. What was later to be dignified in the language of the advertisers as 'mass response' would still, in Dickens's day, have been called 'the plaudits of the mob'. The mob did not buy books; it did not subscribe to libraries; it did not take *Household Words* or *Chambers' Weekly*. There was, in fact, nothing to be earned by exploring the tastes and aspirations of the amorphous millions of non-consumers unless it was to provide 'copy' to shock or amuse one's middle-class readers.

Dickens himself was an assiduous and gifted gatherer of copy. He was fascinated by squalor and depravity. His sense of the grotesque was perhaps the keenest of his age and allied with it was a gift for divining the curious mixture of guilt and complacency with which the Victorian middle class regarded the horrors spawned by the same industrial revolution that had created its own comfort and security.

It was reassuring for people who enjoyed the material benefits of the new age to be able to divide the poor neatly and without hesitation into three distinct categories: the brutalized, the comic, and the not-long-for-this-world.

For those such as Fagin and Sykes, there awaited the rope, an inevitable and satisfactory conclusion (though not in the view of Dickens himself, for he opposed capital punishment). Only the most fanciful would have disputed that 'going to the bad' was a purely voluntary exercise, albeit prompted in some cases by hereditary factors, that cast no reflection on society in general.

The comic poor, while not undeserving of sympathy judiciously expressed through approved agencies, were clearly happy folk on the whole. Their unconventionality, their bizarre tricks of speech and quaint mannerisms, lent colour to an otherwise dreary environment. They always had a cheery word and kept aloof, despite the deprivations natural to their situation in life, from the criminal classes. No problem there.

As for the third, the pathetic group, this also had its place in what a substantially religious community held to be the divine plan. It was an omnipresent example of fortitude in adversity and of suffering bravely borne. Noteworthy in the Dickens novels – and

in those of his less celebrated contemporaries – is the uncom-
plaining attitude of the sick and destitute. They seem to have
taken advice to make the best of a bad job with the literal-minded
determination of ham actors at an audition. Even their dying
becomes a demonstration so protracted as seriously to put diagnosis in doubt.

Not that the readers doubted. They knew what was coming to
Little Nell, to Smike, to Oliver Twist's mother, to Dora. It would
be extravagant to claim that these fictional deaths were relished in
a sadistic way, although there undoubtedly is a close relation between sentimentality and cruelty. What they did afford was a
sense of noble sublimation. The Victorians' capacity for being
sustained by abstract conceptions such as nobility, refinement,
virtue, redemption, and so on, was larger and more genuine than
we sometimes are prepared to credit. It was, to some degree, a
protective mechanism. The road society had taken was sign-
posted to heaven, but the scenery included notably satanic
stretches. The many who fell on that unattractive wayside had
perforce to be stepped over – or on – and it was less distressing to
do so in the persuasion that God was under firm contract to give
the stragglers a lift.

High-mindedness was not, of course, the only 'notion acceptable to the present taste' conveyed by the popular novelists of the
second half of the nineteenth century. The acquisition of money
was a preoccupation scarcely less constant. There were sound
reasons for this. Commercial and industrial expansion was pro-
ceeding at a pace that was immensely exciting to those whose
efforts were dedicated to it. Profits were pursued with a zeal
beyond mere cupidity; they were seen as a sign of progress, of
man's self-improvement. One of the significant features of Dic-
kensian popular literature is insistence on ascribing wealth other
than inherited possessions to the practice of virtues such as thrift,
inventiveness, energy. There is seldom any suggestion of un-
fairness or illogicality within the commercial system itself. Fraud,
theft, exploitation – these are featured as plot ingredients, but they
invariably are represented as the misdeeds of exceptional indi-

viduals. The frequency with which these rogues happen to be lawyers seems to have matched fully the expectations of the Victorian public.

One simple fact of Victorian England which the inhabitants of a welfare state can appreciate only with difficulty is that life without money was literally hell. Pauperdom was a terror that haunted whole multitudes. It was the terminal stage of the illness of poverty and as real a possibility for the school teacher, the shopkeeper or the government clerk as for the seamstress or the furnaceman. Revivals of Victorian melodrama win easy laughs when the villain announces the foreclosing of a mortgage, but the audiences of the time would have been harrowed, not amused; they knew well what being evicted meant. 'Ruin' was not a quaint euphemism for a girl's first tumble into sexual experience; it was a word no stronger than was justified by a system of economic servitude, iron-banded with moral strictures, that submerged scores of thousands into prostitution.

The most terrifying feature of being deprived, for whatever reason, of a means of livelihood was the high probability of the process being irreversible. Another phrase from the Victorians' vocabulary that evokes a superior smile today is 'station in life'. But it was a solemnly meaningful reference to what was felt to be a pre-ordained and permanent social structure. The optimists – and there were more of them about than pessimists – were convinced that things were getting a little better every day in every way for everybody, but only because society as a whole was allowed to progress slowly and steadily, undisturbed by any changing of places. Fortunes were to be made, of course, and men made them: sometimes in romantic circumstances, sometimes by dubious methods, most often by sheer diligence and the application of such advantages as technical education and ready capital. But the majority of people were to die very little richer than they had been born. They considered themselves fortunate if they achieved the modest ambition of always being able to 'pay their way'.

In this climate of stern realism, lightened only a little by the spritely unorthodoxy of Micawbers, there was one source of benefit that figured perpetually in the calculations of every family in the land. This was the legacy. A measure of the importance attached to inheritance by the Victorian public is the frequency of its use as a motive, often the main motive, in contemporary novels. If wills were expunged from the works of Dickens, three-quarters of his plots would be quite meaningless. The fiction of the period could almost be described as the literature of probate.

It would not be true to suggest that obsession with inheritance began in the Victorian era. Property and its disposition were already a well-established theme by the time Jane Austen took her first cool look at her heroines' financial prospects and set within the same descriptive paragraph a high, intelligent forehead and an income of twenty thousand a year. What had happened, though, in the forty-eight years between the publication of *Pride and Prejudice* and that of *Great Expectations* was a radical shift in what might be called the centre of gravity of the national wealth.

In 1813, it was still inconceivable that a Mrs Bennett would seek a profitable match for one of her daughters outside the ranks of the landed gentry. By 1861, the whole climate of social opportunity had changed. New wealth had been and continued to be created, and it was going into hands very different from Mr Darcy's. The capitalist principles of Mr Gradgrind now prevailed. The new rich were the manufacturers, the traders, the bankers, the steelmasters, the shipowners and railway directors. The ancient laws of apportionment by tribal title did not apply to winnings from mine and factory. A Hudson could be king, if only a railway king, and the credulity of readers was not strained by the tale of a convict who made his pile and bequeathed it to his penniless boy benefactor. Indeed, it was a story exactly attuned to the wishful thinking of the times.

The title *Great Expectations* is not only apt in the context of a single book. It epitomizes the attitude of a reading public that had seen wonders and believed them to presage continual social progress, with special bonuses in deserving cases, and every now and again a prize contributed directly by the deity as token of personal interest and approval.

The popular novelist's understanding and response to the sort of yearning that found satisfaction in accounts of secret bene-factors, long-lost heirs, frustrated frauds and the rest, did not remain uncriticized. As early as 1851 when a list of authors sell-ing most readily on W. H. Smith's bookstalls was headed by such unexceptionable names as Bulwer Lytton, Captain Marryatt, C. P. R. James and Mrs Trollope, *The Times* had complained :

'Every addition to the stock (of the bookstalls) was positively made on the assumption that persons of the better class who con-stitute the larger portion of railway readers lose their accustomed taste the moment they enter the station.'

In 1863, two years after the success of *Great Expectations*, the following onslaught was made in a leading review, the *Quar-terly*:

A class of literature has grown up around us . . . playing no inconsiderable part in moulding the minds and forming the habits and tastes of its generation; and doing so principally, we had almost said exclusively, by 'preaching to the nerves'. . . . Excitement, and excitement alone, seems to be the great end at which they aim . . . A commercial atmosphere floats around works of this class, redolent of the manufactory and the shop. The public wants novels, and novels must be made – so many yards of printed stuff, sensation pattern, to be ready at the beginning of the season . . . Various causes have been at work to produce this phenomenon of our literature. Three principal ones may be named as having had a large share in it – period-icals, circulating libraries, and railway bookstalls.

By 1880, Matthew Arnold felt himself constrained to apply the description 'cheap, hideous and ignoble of aspect' to 'the tawdry novels which flare in the bookshelves of our railway stations, and which seem designed, as so much else that is produced for the use of our middle-class seems designed, for people with a low standard of life'.

The occurrence of the word 'class' is to be noted in all three of these attacks. One might wonder if there was not at the root of the writers' irritation a sense of outrage that people able to afford books, and therefore a cut above the plebeian masses, had neglected to show discrimination proper to their social standing.

What every critic failed in some measure to understand was that the production of books – their writing, printing and selling – had become a commercial operation, subject to commercial laws and pressures, and that their character was no longer likely to be determinable by enlightened arbiters. In literature, as in all else that was bought and sold, it was now needful to conform to the ethos of the market place, the principle that the customer was always right.

Later, in 1889, Arnold showed himself aware of what had happened and of what it portended. He wrote:

> If literature is to be judged by a plebiscite, and if the plebiscite recognizes its power, it will certainly by degrees cease to support reputations which give it no pleasure and which it cannot comprehend.

Which then, were the reputations that were to command the support of the 'plebiscite', by which Arnold meant that growing section of society placed between an aristocracy too contemptuous of culture to read books and a proletariat too impecunious to buy them? Who but the authors of the 'novel of sensation', the vendors of excitement, the 'preachers to the nerves'? The *Quarterly*'s definition was wide enough to catch a Mrs Gaskell, a Thackeray and a whole parsonage of Brontës, but such was the accommodating nature of the English puritan tradition. What it was doubtless intended to indict in particular was fiction that pandered to the 'non-serious' public by offering vicarious experience in contrived and self-resolving situations – a sort of literary fairground ride. This was the reading matter that subsequently would be categorized as 'escapist' literature. It was fated never to become quite respectable, and although by the turn of the century the tradition of regarding all but expressly educative or morally improving books as time-wasters was virtually dead, censure was still reserved for those novels of sensation whose theme was crime and for which the handy terms 'thriller' or 'shocker' had been coined.

Like most things that excite disapproval, the thriller was popular. It was to become addictive, even if it could not yet be so described at the time when Dickens, emulating his friend Wilkie Collins, began work on *The Mystery of Edwin Drood*. This unfinished essay in detective fiction followed Collins's *The Moonstone* on a road away from the Gothic fantasy world that had served to scare the readers of a line of authors from Walpole to Sheridan le Fanu. The development was towards sensationalism relevant to contemporary life and its line had been indicated as early as the 1840s by Edgar Allen Poe's brief excursion from his graveyard to create the Dupin trilogy and earn thereby the title of Father of the Detective Story.

An increasing number of writers after 1870, the year of Dickens's death, turned their ingenuity and energy to the construction of crime stories. The market widened steadily. It seemed almost as if human waywardness were a newly invented commodity, like oilcloth or soda-water, and that the public could not have enough of it.

Then, in 1887, a Scottish doctor practising in Southsea scored a modest success with a book he had written in hope of adding a few pounds to his income. Subsequently serialized in the *Strand* magazine, the tale was called *A Study in Scarlet* and featured an eccentric private detective of phenomenal intellect who lodged in an unfashionable London street with a companion whose loyalty and stoutness of heart were matched only by the ordinariness of his opinions and the thickness of his comprehension. The Holmes–Watson combination was a formula that succeeded almost at once and its inventor, Arthur Conan Doyle, was to expand it in the next forty years into a myth that seized the imagination of the world.

So much analysis, speculation, commentary and spoof biography have been produced by the worshippers at the Baker

Street shrine as to convey the impression that Doyle was the sole patentee not only of Sherlock Holmes but of gaslight, the hansom cab, telegraphy, Scotland Yard, perhaps even of Victorian London itself, fogs and all. Is this a tribute to the man's gift for imparting a sense of period and of atmosphere? Dickens had a greater descriptive skill, for he was a very much more accomplished writer, and yet one is reluctant, somehow, to give his pictures absolute credence, perhaps because they are frightening. The London of Holmes commends itself at once and unconditionally. It is quaint enough to make nostalgic appeal. It is exceedingly well-ordered: those telegraphic offices are never closed, no cab is ever otherwise than within instant hail. Its population is unfailingly obliging: half-a-crown will secure from the nearest stranger the immediate execution of whatever task or errand one cares to name. It is a city whose every crime is soluble and whose vices are sealed within narrow and defined areas. It is a cosy place. It is, for as long as a hawk-eyed man broods in Baker Street, a safe place. It does not exist. It never did. But Doyle managed to build it in the minds of his readers.

And here we have the real achievement of Conan Doyle. He successfully transplanted from the big, solid, slow-paced novel of social relationships to his own piquant and immediately enthralling crime fiction that element of illusory reassurance, that echo of the reader's private wishes and opinions, which is the germ of every bestseller. He was an outstanding example of the sort of author who was destined first to capture, then to be imprisoned by, the mass readership of the new century. Long after he had tired of his own creation, public insistence upon repeat performance was too strong to be denied. Not even Doyle's desperate attempt to kill off his hero – a precursor of the 'writing out' of characters in television series – persuaded the public to abate its appetite for Holmesian adventure and allow Doyle to concentrate on work he considered much more important. In any case, where Holmes was, there was the money also, and Doyle's generosity in the causes he espoused was dependent on it. So despite failing enthusiasm, evidenced by carelessness of style and increasing artificiality of plot, new stories continued to be published right up to 1927, three years before his death.

Conan Doyle opened his literary career as a Victorian, prepared to take just enough time off from serious matters to earn an extra guinea or two by means of a relatively frivolous device. At its close, he was rich, and enormously respected by a generation that already used Victorianism as a term of scorn. He was openly imitated by a large proportion of crime fiction's great catering corps of the 1920s. The device had made his fortune and his reputation, and Doyle reflected that it had mastered him in the process. He lived long enough to have the comfort of seeing himself in the company of plenty of other writers for whom success was also a sort of servitude.

"EXCUSE ME—DO YOU HAPPEN TO HAVE COME ACROSS A PORTION OF *THE EVENING GAZETTE* CONTAINING THE THIRD INSTAL-
MENT OF 'THIRTEEN CROOKS'?"

CHAPTER 2

Mr Smith, Mr Boot
and others

The 1870 Education Act that formally decreed schooling for all is still widely believed to have been akin to vaccination. It 'did away' with illiteracy just as vaccination 'did away' with smallpox.

In fact a great number of people other than those who had received the privilege of formal education was able to read in the eighteenth, let alone the nineteenth century. By the 1830s, a popular political pamphlet could achieve a sale of 200,000 and a broadsheet one of more than a million, or about a fifteenth part of the whole population. A publication reaching a similar proportion today would be judged to have done very well. It is probable that at least three quarters of all adults were able to read without much difficulty a hundred years ago and that by the end of the century the proportion was about ninety-five per cent.

As literacy became more nearly universal, the question of *what* was being read, and by whom, is of increasingly greater importance than a simple ability percentage. By 1920, virtually everybody could read. There existed, in great variety and at prices as low as mechanical processes could make them, a prodigious amount of reading matter. Whatever proved to be in demand could easily be produced and reproduced. Channels of distribution were wide, numerous and efficiently organized. Paper was cheap. The last of the State taxes on the printed word had long since been removed. Government's recovery from its ancient phobia in respect of the political danger of over-informed masses had been further evidenced by the 1919 Public Libraries Act. Northcliffe was consolidating his newspaper revolution in preparation for the imminent wars of circulation. The commercial lending library was as commonly to be found as a post office.

Reading, clearly, was no longer the privilege of a few but an established habit of the majority of the population.

Newspapers were for the greatest number the main source of reading, sometimes the only source. The million and a half who took a daily paper in 1900 had swelled to more than two millions by 1914. Four years of war, during which even such evasive and doctored accounts of events as censorship allowed were avidly received, gave stimulus that proved permanent in effect. In 1920, there were five million daily readers and thirteen million readers of the Sunday press. The former were chiefly middle class people living in urban areas, while working class allegiance lay substantially with Sunday papers, in particular the *News of the World*.

Periodicals had been expanding in number, scope, and circulation at a rate no less impressive than that of the growth of newspaper sales. Northcliffe alone owned more than a hundred when he died in 1922. Discounting the technical and specialist journals, the children's comics and the juvenile weeklies, there was still a great mass of periodical reading matter in the 1920s and 1930s designed to entertain rather than inform. That this implies a recipe common also to the bulk of newspaper publication is not surprising: the same people owned both.

Book publishing had kept pace with the expansion of newspapers and periodicals since the mid-nineteenth century. Some two and a half thousand titles were issued each year in the 1850s and this number increased to just over six thousand in 1901. The next twelve years saw the doubling of the annual book issue. There was a recession during the 1914–18 war, but by the early 1920s the figure was back to more than twelve and a half thousand, only a quarter of which were reprints. Expansion was to continue until the second world war and to reach an annual total of more than seventeen thousand.

This meant that a buyer or borrower of books in the 1920s and 1930s could choose from between 180 and 210 brand new titles every week. A contemporary of Jane Austen would have been offered a selection from about ten.

Who were the customers for all these books, or rather for the fiction that formed a sizable proportion of them?

They were, in general, the same people who bought a daily newspaper and one or more of the sort of magazine that contained, in short story serial form, a 'good read'. They had an income high enough and of sufficient regularity for a shilling or two a week to be spared for subscription to a circulating library or to hire their reading from a 'chain' or lending library – apart from the occasional outright purchase of a novel to read on a journey or holiday. They were people who read with facility and by habit, whose hours of employment were not unduly long, and whose jobs did not leave them too tired physically to feel the need for combating boredom. They read for pleasure rather than for education, and to kill time, not ignorance (with which, in any case, they were not conscious of being burdened). There were many railway travellers among them, many passengers on buses and tubes, contributing to the 27% growth of London's outer ring of suburbs between 1921 and 1931. They doubtless included a fair number of the million-and-a-half wage and salary earners with entitlement in the 1920s to holidays with pay – a right which some ten million others were not to win until after 1938 and the Holidays with Pay Act. But the majority of these readers were not commuters or wage earners. They were women – the middle-class wives and mothers and daughters whose task it commonly was to select and bring home a fresh supply of the family's reading matter.

According to Mrs Q. D. Leavis, whose *Fiction and the Reading Public* was published in 1932, 'shops existing solely to sell books are rare outside the university towns of Oxford, Cambridge and

Edinburgh, certain parts of London and a few big cities. Serious book-buying has not increased in proportion to literacy; the bulk of the public does not buy many books but borrows or hires them.' Emphasizing that the subscription libraries – notably Mudie's, Boots and W. H. Smith's – stocked chiefly novels, she found it significant 'that the proportion of fiction to non-fiction borrowed is overwhelmingly great, that women rather than men change the books (that is, determine the family reading), and that many subscribers call daily to change their novels.' In suburban and even rural areas, added Mrs Leavis with characteristic asperity, 'it is common to find a stock of worn and greasy novels let out at 2d or 3d a volume'. 'Tuppenny dram-shops', she called these establishments, noting that a typical advertisement in one of them specified the following authors: 'Sapper', Sax Rohmer, Zane Grey, Edgar Wallace, William Le Queux, E. Phillips Oppenheim, Rider Haggard, and a group of seven women 'romantic' authors headed by Ethel M. Dell and Ruby M. Ayres.

The Boots Booklovers' Library was begun in 1899, at the instigation of the first wife of the manufacturing chemist, Jesse Boot. More than two hundred of the firm's branches were equipped with library facilities by 1909. In the mid-1930s, when circulating libraries were at the peak of their popularity, there were book sections in four hundred and fifty branch shops. From the beginning, the Boots Library was operated on a 'loss leader' principle. Shelves were always at the back of the shop and as subscribers passed through to change their books they became potential customers at the chemists' counters. The subscription was kept deliberately low. Originally half a guinea a year, it increased only slowly to thirty shillings. The service was being used by between a quarter and half a million people in the 1930s, despite competition from the new chain libraries, and it has been claimed that the library was buying for its 340 branches one and a quarter million books a year at one period. It was the last nationwide circulating library to succumb to the social and economic changes after the second world war: final closure came in February 1966.

Aiming as it did to attract maximum custom, Boots Library invariably placed emphasis on fiction, and this included a large proportion of crime novels. A similar policy was pursued – though not in their case purely as a device to encourage cash sales – by W. H. Smith and Son. Library facilities existed at most branches of Smith's by 1920. A review thirteen years later showed that more than three hundred shops and three hundred and seventy five bookstalls had a library service. The larger branches had over a thousand subscribers apiece; the majority of the others had between one and three hundred. No one seems to have kept a complete register of the numbers of borrowers, but the total must have been well in excess of a hundred thousand around that time.

After 1933, Smith's added what it called its 'Country and Small Branch Service'. This brought into the organization all the smaller or remote shops and stalls, and supplied them by post with books from a central library stock at the firm's London headquarters. In addition, a special subscription service was offered, on a group basis, to staff associations, clubs, certain banks, the Civil Service Clerical Association, teachers and local government officials. That this development was thought worth while underlines the essentially middle-class character of the circulating library public.

In the mid-1930s, a small branch of Smith's had between two and four hundred books on its shelves. The medium-sized shop offered from four to nine hundred volumes. There were a hundred and sixty branches in which the stock stood at a thousand volumes and over. The space needed was considerable, and it was this factor, more perhaps than any other, which figured in the decision to end the service in 1962, by which time the expanding and much more profitable business of selling gramophone records had taken precedence.

There was issued in the autumn of 1939 a list of popular fiction available through the W. H. Smith library service. Its hundred and fifty pages contained some thirteen thousand five hundred titles. About a half were romance, a quarter were adventure stories, and a quarter were crime novels. These figures lend weight to the contention that the subscription libraries were customers for

something like three-fifths of all copies of 'sensation' fiction that
were being produced. The multitude of suburban and provincial
lending libraries bought much of the remainder. It did not greatly
matter, from the point of view of publishers and writers of escapist
literature, that the rate-supported municipal and county libraries
remained comparatively unaccommodating in this field even after
the legislation that made them available – in theory, anyway – to
ninety-six per cent of the population by 1926. A big ready-made
market existed and, provided that an author's work matched this
or that approved formula, it was bound to sell.

The novelist Howard Spring declared in his introduction to a
collection of detective stories, for instance, that 'the present intense
outpouring is something unique in letters. There never has been in
the whole history of writing anything approaching a similar
output of invention on one subject; and whereas most writing is a
supply which humbly hopes to create demand, all this detective
writing is a clear case of a demand creating a supply.'

Indicative of just how heavy that demand was, and how widespread, is a report dating from 1933 by a West Country representative of one of the chain libraries. According to this, the firm's
branch at Poole, whose population was then 43,000, issued six
thousand books a week. The readers were predominantly from the
lower middle class and seventy-five per cent of them were women.
One woman was noted as taking out six books every two days.
Favourite authors among women were Denise Robins, Louise
Gerard, Ethel M. Dell, Elinor Glyn and P. G. Wodehouse; men's
preferences were headed by Edgar Wallace, 'Sapper', Sydney
Horler and Zane Grey. The proprietors must have been much
gratified by their representative's further information that each
book at Poole was made to last at least a hundred and eighty issues
and that stolen novels, or 'non-returns', represented a loss of no
more than one in eight thousand.

A question of special relevance to the type and quality of reading matter available to the public in the two decades before the
1939 war is how far the commercial libraries were able to
influence the publishing trade. One publisher, Stanley Unwin,

declared categorically that their effect was 'to assist the circulation of indifferent and bad books, and to retard the circulation of really good books, especially those by writers who have not yet established reputations'. He added: 'There is one circulating library that makes a boast of the extent to which it can force its subscribers to take what is given them, which means, in that particular case, what the library can buy cheapest.'

This doubtless was the case, but it always is arguable whether taste dictates catering or catering taste; that they interact is the only safe contention. The preoccupation of the circulating and chain libraries was that of all commercial organizations – to make money. It was natural, therefore, that apart from an occasional gamble on an unknown but potentially popular author they should play safe and stock their shelves with work of proved appeal. This policy was bound to exclude the innovator, the novelist of ideas, the 'disturbing' or 'depressing' writer.

Publishers, in so far as they were business men, could not escape the implications of the policy of their biggest customer. It is to the credit of many of them that they continued to accept and to champion works which had no hope whatever of scraping beneath the low-slung boom of the libraries' literary standards. A good deal of courage, not to say quixoticism, was needed to back a Lawrence, a Forster or a Virginia Woolf in an era when the lion's share of the rewards of publishing went to the managers of dream-factories and cliché-mills.

Apart from exerting pressure in obedience to 'lowest common denominator' economics, the commercial libraries occasionally applied their influence on a moral plane. Their propensity to do this varied according to the sensibilities of the directors of individual firms, just as public library censorship varied with the notions of committees from town to town. In general, discrimination against a supposedly 'naughty' book was quietly exercised by a simple failure to order it. Only when fuss was made by a disappointed subscriber or a slighted publisher was attention called to this aspect of control of public reading. Now and again a *cause célèbre* arose when an author of reputation offended against the arbitrary code whereby library stocks were supposed to be kept free of salacious and corrupting material. Just how ridiculous the code was may be judged by the names of some of the writers who managed to get involved in controversies of this kind. They included Thomas Hardy, H. G. Wells, Arnold Bennett and Compton Mackenzie.

Unfortunately for the high moral intention of the library arbiters, private and public, a common result of the publicity attendant upon their 'banning' of a book was a boost to its sales through other channels. Proscription actually became a cachet much sought by authors; it was worth a good many columns of advertising. The suggestion that in some cases condemnation was engineered by mutual agreement has a certain perverse attraction.

Censorship of an overt kind decreased towards the end of the inter-war period: probably because its practitioners had tired of being made to look foolish. Control continued to be exercised, but more tactfully. A notable example of this change in strategy concerned Compton Mackenzie's book about the abdication of Edward VIII, *Windsor Tapestry*, published in 1938. The occasion inspired a directive from the head office of W. H. Smith and Son:

> All 'A' shop, 'B' shop and stall managers will note carefully the following important instructions in connection with the above book which are to be adhered to rigidly. No objection will be placed in the way of the manager carrying such stock as is necessary to meet reasonable public demand, but special displays of the book, inside a shop, in a shop window or on a bookstall front are definitely forbidden. No advertising matter of any sort will be issued by head office for the book and no advertising matter is to be accepted from the publishers; neither will managers write 'home-made' tickets for the book. We repeat that these instructions are to be rigidly observed.

The significance of moral and political strictures by those who had acquired a near-monopolistic control of the distribution of popular reading matter is clearly considerable in principle. It would be a mistake, however, to conclude that the literary diet of library and bookstall customers was determined and imposed by management without reference to those customers' wishes. Supposing that D. H. Lawrence, George Moore, James Joyce and Havelock Ellis had been given equal shelf freedom with Edgar Wallace and Ethel M. Dell, the odds are that on the shelf they would have stayed, except for an occasional furtive airing by the prurient. They would, in fact, almost certainly have been bad business.

Charging commercial institutions with failure to educate public taste is an indulgence from which intellectuals will only be deterred when they grasp that a non-existent contract can be neither breached nor enforced. If commerce is to be indicted for anything, it can only be for commercialism, and whether that is a crime or not is a political question. Very few people who walked into the High Street from a library forty years ago with three or four thrillers and romances under their arm had the slightest misgivings about the freedom of choice they had just exercised. Even fewer would have been prepared for a moment to credit that the 'good read' to which they were looking forward was part of a process that debilitated taste, shrank discrimination and impoverished thought.

Despite the economic crises, chronic unemployment and widespread misery in the industrial areas, the mood of people not immediately affected by these things was predominantly one of satisfaction. Gilt-edged Victorian and Edwardian optimism had taken far less severe a knock from the murderous futility of the 1914–18 war than one might suppose. The middle class had suffered its share of casualties, of course, but it mourned them as it would have mourned bereavement by pneumonia or motor accident. Anger was felt hardly at all, and if there was little of the kind of pride which a nation-wide clutter of memorial masonry made pretence of witnessing, the 'sacrifice' by so many fathers and sons and brothers and uncles was accepted by most as having been a dutiful and responsible act. The Great Bore was over, the threat from foreigners had been removed for the moment, and the prospect visible from city suburb, commuters' village and provincial township was one of secure continuance of the old order and its gradual enrichment by the innovations of progress.

It might be asked how so complacent an attitude could have co-existed with conditions that gave rise to the use of troops against strikers and unemployed, to lockouts and riots, naval mutiny, the national paralysis of 1926 and the hunger marches of the 1930s. The reason is that the population of Britain was living then, to an even greater extent than it is now, in compartments. These were defined not only by class barriers but by physical, geographical divisions.

Thus it was quite possible to be leading a comfortable existence in a pleasant residential area of Gloucester or Hereford and be genuinely unaware that less than fifty miles away in the Welsh valleys whole communities were living on a bare survival level. Kindly Londoners who would have been shocked by the spectacle of a child shivering with cold simply refused to believe stories of schools on Tyneside in which, summer and winter, nearly half the pupils sat barefoot in class. The stories were true, as were those of Durham shipyard towns where only one man in three had a job, and of areas in Lancashire and Cumberland where malnutrition had hoisted the tuberculosis rate to between ten and twenty times that of the Home Counties. But distance – even a short distance – was a great insulator of conscience. So was the notion, inherited from the Victorian self-help school, that misfortune was somehow the consequence of fecklessness and therefore the unalterable lot of those who had allowed themselves to slip to the bottom of the pile. Yet another aid to the equanimity of the comfortably placed was the preoccupation of the Press with cheerful and trivial themes. With very few exceptions indeed newspapers were dedicated to the profitable Northcliffe slogan 'Give the public what it wants'.

What the public – the middle-class, reading public – clearly did not want was disquieting dispatches from beyond the frontiers of its own experience. Circulation managers noted that too frequent reference to menacing political situations abroad depressed sales, as did 'sordid' stories of industrial depression at home. News selection and treatment were adjusted accordingly. The *News Chronicle* (formerly Dickens's *Daily News*) was practically alone among national daily newspapers in consistently presenting foreign and home events with due regard to the realities of the situation. The readers of the rest were shown an Italy and Germany whose rulers, while not quite gentlemen, perhaps, were too busy building autobahns and getting trains to run to time for the entertainment of any aggressive intentions; a Russia of measureless malignance and cardboard tanks; a France consisting of the Promenade des Anglais, rude night clubs and the Maginot Line; and a motherland to which prosperity was slowly and surely returning while Mr Baldwin tamped his pipe, Mr MacDonald mixed his metaphors, and Gracie Fields led a crowd of happy, be-shawled mill girls in the chorus of 'Sing As We Go'.

The euphoric conspiracy was not completely solid. Apart from the predictable fusillade from left-wing polemicists, there came protests from relatively respectable quarters. Wells warned and Shaw taunted. George Orwell's dark prophesies frightened a few people. Hilaire Belloc declared England to be 'done' before he lapsed into silence in order to contemplate the enormity of the demolition of Hanacker Mill. The intellectual poets, Auden and Isherwood, blistered the smug compatriots whose salvation they were to leave others to complete when they opted for America in 1939. A particularly unkind cut, coming as it did from the author of *The Good Companions*, 1929's top favourite among solid citizens, was delivered by J. B. Priestley in 1934. His *English Journey* confirmed by personal testimony that there existed on a large scale places and conditions of unimaginable awfulness. Some library committees in the areas he described, persuaded that Mr Priestley had been less than fair, declined to stock the book.

Outside the rotting industrial areas, developments favourable to the expansion of a 'leisure' literature continued steadily during the 1920s and 1930s. The national income – the 'real' income, that is, in terms of purchasing power – rose in spite of political and economic uncertainty by 40%, thanks largely to a fall in prices of materials from abroad. The proportion of people in non-manual employment increased. Thus, between 1921 and 1938, the per-centage earning a living from insurance, banking and finance went up by nearly a fifth; while a similar rise was registered in the number of jobs in local government. Wage and salary earners in these kinds of work were more likely to have the means, oppor-tunity and inclination to read than were industrial and agricul-tural workers and an army of unemployed that fluctuated between one and a half and three millions. The provision of homes, which were, among other things, places to keep and read books, had become accepted as an important matter of public policy. Between 1919 and 1939, more than a million houses were built by local authorities in England and Wales and two and a half times that number by private enterprise.

A great number of the latter were in dormitory areas and strung out by 'ribbon development' through what previously had been attractive countryside. Railway and bus services were developed to link them with business centres. In less than ten years after 1920, the forty-eight local authorities then operating buses were joined by fifty-two more, and the number of passengers carried increased elevenfold. For millions, journeys by road and rail became a daily routine that a newspaper, magazine or novel helped to render less tedious.

And while they travelled, their wives – or at least the wives of the more prosperous among them – became increasingly engaged by another aspect of the problem of time-killing. There existed a reservoir of domestic help – maids, handymen, charwomen, gar-deners and laundresses – fed constantly by the wives and daugh-ters of the poorly paid, by war widows, disabled ex-Servicemen, pensioners and men out of work – that could be tapped for a few coppers an hour. Then, as the home use of electricity spread, the American example of domestic mechanization began to gain fol-lowers, as was instanced by the increase of annual vacuum-cleaner production in Britain from 37,550 to 409,345 between 1930 and 1935. Home leisure was ceasing to be the prerogative of the rich and the upper middle-class; it was well within the means of the wife of the £300 or £400 a year man, provided that the fashionable limit of two children had been observed. As often as not, she used some of her spare time in the same way as her husband used his travelling intervals between home and office. She read.

"THIS TOO, TOO SOLID FLESH."

CHAPTER 3

A very decent sort of burglar

The division of crime fiction into its twin limbs, the tale of detection and the felony-based adventure story, or thriller, was fairly clear by the beginning of this century. There have been sports and offshoots – Gothic shockers in the tradition of Sheridan le Fanu; documentary and psychological studies that Raymond Postgate, Gerald Bullett, Julian Symons and others were to give lasting literary authority; steady production by Bram Stoker's successors in the pernicious anaemia business; certain sorts of spy story – but each of the two main branches has preserved its own characteristics, modified only by changes in technology and fashion.

Both kinds have commanded popularity and do so still. Each, therefore, must supply in some degree and in its own special way those standard needs of the fiction-reading public: stimulus, diversion, relaxation, reassurance.

The detective story stimulates, or is supposed to stimulate, the intellect because it contains a puzzle. People who cannot be bothered with puzzles do not read it. It diverts because it presents a situation altogether outside the normal experience of the reader. It relaxes by the well-established therapeutic process of summoning effort for no other purpose than its subsequent discharge without effect in terms of work done. The element of reassurance subsists in the inevitability of the puzzle's being solved, with or without the reader's self-gratifying guesswork, by the end of the book. We do not like the outcome of a detective novel to be easily predictable (although it is surprising how many people turn first to the final page and then patiently wade through from the beginning) but confidence that there *will* be an outcome, and one of a morally acceptable kind, is all-important.

A much wider range of possibilities can be drawn upon to satisfy the demands of the reader of the thriller, without altering the definition of those demands. Stimulus need not involve a problem, or not, at any rate, a problem requiring applied thought. Mystery – always a useful ingredient of the thriller – is something else: it induces unease of that pleasant kind that may be dispelled at the author's convenience at any time without putting the reader to the bother of ratiocination. Then there is available a host of emotional stimuli capable of rousing, in greater or lesser degree according to the writer's skill and the reader's susceptibility, such enjoyable responses as patriotic zeal, indignation at breaches of fair play, feelings of cupidity, sexual desire, hatred (in a thriller the identity of the villain may legitimately be known from the beginning) or of rectitude, religious partisanship, and personal superiority.

The thriller also has greater scope than the detective story for offering diversion. Whether or not the apparatus of law enforcement be invoked, it does not have to be a pace-setter as in the *roman policier*. Investigation tends to be a static business, particularly when detailed evidence is being assembled and assessed. In the thriller, the scene is where the action is, not where a witness is answering a detective's questions about action that has taken place already.

This emphasis on action might appear to be incompatible with the relaxative purpose of light reading which, in the case of the detective novel, is fulfilled by allowing the mind to uncoil after exercise on some artificial and external problem. But the thriller achieves the same end by a more widely acceptable means, that of emotional catharsis. Just as there is no reason to doubt the assertion by some women that they like to go to the cinema to have 'a good cry', one recognizes the fact that very many people feel better for a good chase or a few good murders.

The fourth need, for reassurance, has always been met by successful thriller writers, and probably with less strain on their inventiveness than might be supposed. The record suggests that they often are people who themselves have an especially strong yearning for reassurance. Edgar Wallace, their king, was so hopelessly inept in the management of his own affairs that an income the size of a small national budget did not prevent his slide into debt. Yet on paper he spawned financial wizards and organizational masterminds. Mrs Q. D. Leavis and other stern critics of the 1930 literary scene were fond of ascribing the popularity of thrillers to the public's desire for 'wish-fulfilment', a fashionably pejorative concept at that time. None seems to have thought to blame the authors on the same count. Yet there was poor old 'Sapper', for one, sending forth his fantasy *alter ego* to smash that conspiracy of foreigners and Jews that so obviously haunted his imagination; while John Buchan, afflicted by the notion that the world's secret rulers were epitomized by 'a little white-faced Jew in a bathchair with an eye like a rattlesnake' (*The Thirty-nine Steps*) kept mobilized for five novels the British agent Richard Hannay whom he had created back in 1915.

It is interesting that one of the busiest leg-pullers ever to emerge from the fun-house of the Secret Service, Colonel T. E. Lawrence, was a great admirer of Buchan. His books, he said, were 'like athletes racing: so clean-lined, speedy, breathless. For our age they mean nothing; they are sport only; but will a century hence disinter them and proclaim him the great romancer of our blind and undeserving generation?' Even from another romancer, this was pitched a bit strong; the explanation could be that Lawrence had sensed behind the derring-do of books such as *Greenmantle* and *Huntingtower* a fellow-sufferer from that uncertainty and desire for self-proof that had motivated his own seeking after adventure.

Long after E. Phillips Oppenheim had made a fortune writing about mansions in Mayfair where seven hundred pounds in cash would be left around on furniture to meet day-to-day expenses, and about gentlemen stopping their limousines on impulse to buy gold and platinum wrist-watches for supper companions, he continued to enter every shilling and every cent of his earnings in a meticulously accurate account book. Sydney Horler's chronic self-doubts were evidenced by an altogether remarkable mendacity: Compton Mackenzie awarded him third place in his selection of the world's champion liars, after Ford Madox Ford and his close runner-up, Axel Münthe, Swedish author of *The Story of San Michele*, the famous but substantially spurious bestseller of 1929. So vehement and repetitive were Sax Rohmer's references to Asiatic plotting against 'white' civilization that they cannot be explained simply as the frills of melodramatic narration. The man clearly was possessed by some sort of private dread. Peter Cheyney, prolific author of 'tough' thrillers in an embarrassingly pseudo-American style, was himself a notably diffident personality. And A. E. W. Mason's boyishness embraced not only secret service work and a propensity to appear for morning dictation in bath towel and monocle, but close friendship with J. M. Barrie.

Mason, the boy-at-heart, produced heroes of a rugged, mannish kind. His detective, Hanaud, is a big middle-aged man who is dedicatedly professional and whose very clowning intimidates. By paradox of an opposite order, E. W. Hornung created a character who was the antithesis of the 'formidable Edwardian gentleman who didn't like teenagers very much' remembered by Nigel Morland. This is how Hornung, brother-in-law of Conan Doyle, conceived the exciting life:

His own hands were firm and cool as he adjusted my mask for me, and then his own. 'By jove, old boy,' he whispered cheerily, 'you look about the greatest ruffian I ever saw! These masks alone will down a nigger, if we meet one. But I'm glad I remembered to tell you not to shave. You'll pass for White- chapel if the worst comes to the worst and you don't forget to talk the lingo. Better sulk like a mule if you're not sure of it, and leave the dialogue to me; but please our stars, there will be no need. Now, are you ready?'

'Quite.'

'Got your gag?'

'Yes.'

'Shooter?'

'Yes.'

'Then follow me.'

(A Costume Piece)

Although Ernest William Hornung died in 1921, the popularity of the books featuring his hero, A. J. Raffles, the 'gentleman burg- lar', long outlasted him. The name of Raffles is still familiar to most people, if only vaguely. Forty years ago it was being used as part of the language. Any especially ingenious or lucky thief was likely to earn the epithet 'a real-life Raffles'. It was by no means a derogatory expression: the character was generally conceived to be admirable. The few lines of typical Hornung dialogue above are enough to indicate why this was so.

The instructions and advice that Raffles is giving his friend and confederate, Bunny, refer to a robbery on which the pair are about to embark. But they are delivered in a spirit which would be equally appropriate on the eve of a critical school sporting event. Raffles's coolness as he fits the masks is the coolness of a cricketer adjusting his pads. His 'By jove!' is not the expletive one would expect from a criminal. Rather does it betoken a decent up- bringing and a sportsmanlike disposition. Adventurous he obvi- ously is, but excitement evokes from him a cheery whisper, not the snarl that unquestionably would have escaped the lips of a crimi- nal under similar stress. The reference to Bunny as 'the greatest ruffian I ever saw' is good-humoured chaff and therefore an indi- cation that ruffianism is something alien to them both. The masks they wear would normally strike us as sinister equipment, but their purpose in this case is legitimate – to 'down a nigger' should so undesirable a creature be encountered in the course of their enterprise. The injunction to Bunny to remain unshaven tells us that good grooming is habitual to them, while the standard impeccability of their accent is implied by the necessity of the reminder by Raffles that they should adopt, in extremis, the 'lingo' of Whitechapel. The expression 'please our stars' also is significant. Although falling short of being a declaration of Christian orthodoxy, it does suggest an element of spirituality. This is no less reassuring to the reader than Raffles's application to a gun of the jocularly sporting term 'shooter'.

In 1928, there was published a collection of what the editor of the series, Dorothy L. Sayers, considered the finest examples to date of crime and mystery stories in the English language. She chose Hornung's *The Wrong House* to represent the work of the creator of Raffles.

Raffles and Bunny (Bunny is always the narrator of these tales) set out on bicycles to burgle the house of a rich stockbroker at Teddington. Raffles cuts a hole in the kitchen door and thrusts his hand through. His hand is seized on the other side by boys: the burglars have broken into the wrong house, one occupied by a 'crammer' and his pupils. Bunny urges the trapped Raffles to 'blaze through the door' with his gun, but Raffles refuses. 'You get out, Bunny, while you can; never mind me; it's my turn, old chap.' His free hand tightens in affectionate farewell.

Bunny breaks in through a window and succeeds in setting most of the boys off on a false chase. Only 'Beefy' – a 'red-faced barrel of a boy' – remains, still hanging on to Raffles's hand. Bunny seizes this boy round the neck 'with such a will that not a gurgle passed my fingers, for they were almost buried in his hot smooth flesh'. Raffles, freed at last, gives 'Beefy' the *coup de grâce* with a bottle of chloroform.

The master appears. Raffles and Bunny pretend to be innocent passers-by until they get a chance to make off on their bicycles (that ridden by Raffles is a Beeston Humber, smeared with vas-cline against the night air). The escape route is steeply up-hill and the boys give chase. 'All my fault!' wails Bunny, but Raffles protests that he would not have missed it for the world. 'Nor would he forge ahead of me, though he could have done so in a moment, he who from his boyhood had done everything of the kind so much better than anybody else.'

Raffles finally manages to beat back the pursuit by smashing the glass of his heavy electric torch in the face of the nearest boy.

Back safely at home, Raffles declares that he thinks it is an occasion for Sullivans (his own special brand of cigarettes). 'By all my gods, Bunny, it's been the most sporting night we ever had in our lives!'

'And he held out his dear old hand.'

While that dear old hand reaches forth from 1928, we have to remind ourselves firmly that stories at this level excited not ribaldry but wrapt devotion. They were written for adults – and for educated and relatively discriminating adults, at that. Their popularity was enormous and even those readers who smiled at their unlikeliest excesses were far from being persuaded of their general worthlessness. We may mock the archaisms of style, be repelled by the sickly sentimentality of Bunny's hero-worship and the sadistic overtones of the narrative, and wonder at the author's betrayal of a way of thinking at once ingenuous and vicious, but the fact will remain that these books were bestsellers for years. They must have reflected or confirmed some pattern of thought common to a great number of people. What were the 'notions . . . most acceptable to the present taste' (to employ again Lady Mary Wortley Montagu's useful phrase) that were to be found in the writings of E. W. Hornung?

There are certain elements of attraction that the Raffles books have in common with most other successful works of fiction. Flamboyant character and preposterous situation have in themselves an appeal that persists against the grain of logic and even of taste, if that is the best word for what might be otherwise described as literary conscience. Heroes do best for themselves when they are cheeky and daring. The memorable ones nearly always have an imbecilic streak that in the real world would render them liable to be shunned and perhaps locked up. Exaggeration is an expected feature of escapist literature – the 'larger than life' requirement. That it reads sometimes like parody means only that time has shifted our sympathies away from those of the readers for whom a book was originally written. Much of our own fiction will seem to be burlesque in twenty or thirty years.

Hornung's writing has pace. The stories, however ridiculous, carry the readers along briskly. Superfluous description has been avoided and account of action is to the point.

There remain certain peculiar characteristics to be considered.

The atmosphere, the dialogue and many of the events described in the Raffles books are schoolboyish. The excitement is at the level of a dormitory rag or a midnight feast. Even the mutual loyalty of the confederates is expressed in terms more appropriate to the Lower Sixth than to an association of armed criminals. 'Old chaps' in the sense of men mature enough to shave and sufficiently worldly-wise to have a smattering of thieves' argot, if that is what is implied by 'Whitechapel lingo', are not normally in the habit of clasping one another's hands. Nor do we expect a pair of foiled burglars to celebrate their escape from arrest by treating themselves to a cigarette apiece, however choice the brand. But Raffles and Bunny are not subject to the likelihoods of human development. Eternally callow, they mirror from the pages of fiction the reader's inmost desire for happy immutability.

'Sport' is a key word in the Hornung vocabulary, as it is in that of a whole group of popular authors at the time. Its emotive significance cannot be overestimated. Epitomizing a philosophy that over the years had been built into every stratum of rulership, instruction and administration by the public school system, this one little word served for a great number of people the combined purposes of civic code and religious regulator. It does still, to some extent, despite the educational reforms and social realignments of the intervening years and the discrediting by events of so many of the narrow and specious ethical concepts that held sway in the first third of the century. Then, the difference between a 'good sport' and a 'bad sport' was a clear distinction between the acceptable and the intolerable. When the novelist Sydney Horler wanted to pay a compliment to the Prince of Wales that would not seem impertinent in so awesome a context, he simply called him 'the world's greatest sportsman'.

The ascribing of 'unsportsmanlike' motives to enemies of all kinds and in all circumstances – particularly those in which they achieve success – is too familiar a propensity of the English to need stressing, but the converse attitude, as evidenced in Hornung, is worth examination. Raffles describes as 'sporting' an expedition which has involved the carrying of firearms, attempted robbery, the near-strangulation and chloroforming of one perfectly innocent boy and the felling of another with a vicious blow to the face. The readers, it may seem, thus are being invited to enjoy vicarious sadism on the assurance that such things are quite acceptable in circles of society able to appreciate the licence of 'sportsmanship'. Raffles, of course, belongs to those circles. He went to a decent school and moves, when he is not a-burgling somewhere, among people whose knowledge of what is 'done' and 'not done' he shares. The attractive implication is that the reader who admires, or even condones, the behaviour of A. J. Raffles, thereby shows himself qualified for membership of that same privileged group.

The supra-legal status of Raffles is possibly a further contribution to the character's popularity. He does not just break the law; he commits crime so frequently and successfully that the impression is created of his being above the law. Now the English, who so seldom do it themselves, love a man who cocks a snook at authority. No myth has been more cherished and expanded than that of Robin Hood. Our national heroes include only one saint (and him dubiously) but a score of pirates and highwaymen. Is Raffles in this company? Certainly he is a lone wolf, or one of a pair anyway. He spends part of his time fleeing from the police. He robs the rich (whom else could he rob?). Perhaps Hornung calculated that these attributes would be enough to make Raffles a satisfactory embodiment of the Robin Hood tradition. Undiscerning readers certainly have accepted him as such. But what he really personifies is something quite different, something inimical to the principles of justice, of the righting of wrongs, with which the rebel heroes of England have always been associated. Raffles is himself a product of privilege; he is unconcerned with justice; his crimes are mean, his commission of them purely selfish and arrogant. There can scarcely be excluded from any theory of why narration of his exploits sold so well the presumption that it reached some part of the reader's mind that was ready to applaud the success of even a bully and a thug, provided he had estimable credentials.

In 1944, George Orwell analysed in an essay in *Horizon* what he conceived to be the moral differences between the Raffles books and a work of fiction that had won comparable fame twenty years later. This was *No Orchids for Miss Blandish* by the Englishman James Hadley Chase, a semi-pornographic novel written in imitation of the American 'tough' school of William Faulkner and Dashiell Hammett and purporting to depict the crimes and rivalries of a gang of kidnappers. Orwell decided that although Hornung's hero lacked any real ethical code, he was sensitive to the distinction between 'done' and 'not done' and therefore a 'gentleman'. He baulked at murder, regarded friendship as sacred and, above all, was intensely patriotic. 'The Raffles stories,' wrote Orwell, 'belong to a time when people had standards, though they happened to be foolish standards.' *No Orchids*, on the other hand, took for granted complete corruption and self-seeking as the norm of human behaviour. Placid acceptance by the public of the book's multiple murders, floggings, violations, tortures and so on demonstrated to Orwell's satisfaction that by 1939 there existed 'great numbers of English people who are partly Americanized in language and, one ought to add, in moral outlook'.

Orwell, his prophet's eye fixed steadfastly upon political and cultural Armageddons, was eager to interpret the face-bursting, belly-plugging literature of Chase and his fellows as a sign of general decadence. He was therefore the more inclined to be tol-

erant of the relatively naïve and inhibited criminality described
by the earlier author. 'Comparing the schoolboy atmosphere of
the one book,' he concluded, 'with the cruelty and corruption of
the other, one is driven to feel that snobbishness, like hypocrisy, is
a check upon behaviour whose value from a social point of view
has been underrated.'

This is a curious suggestion indeed to have come from a man
who once considered himself an uncompromising revolutionary.
What Orwell perhaps insufficiently appreciated was that although
readers may be fascinated by accounts of extreme human perversion their consequent emulation of it is a very doubtful possibility. During long and lively discussion of the influence of
'undesirable' literature upon behaviour, there has come to light
not a single case in which a formerly normal person has been
induced by his reading to commit a violent crime. Whether
abnormal tendencies can be exacerbated by fictional example is
another question; there is plenty of evidence – including that
provided by the trial in 1965 of Ian Brady and Myra Hindley for
the 'Moors Murders' – that psychopaths tend to read about perversion, just as gardeners tend to read about horticulture. But no
one can justifiably assert that Brady would never have murdered
if he had not read the Marquis de Sade.

The influence of books is of a more subtle and involved nature.
The most lasting, and therefore the most serious, harm they can do
is to confirm – to lend authority to, as it were – an existing prejudice or misconception. Lies fully grown have been sent as strangers
into the world of books, but these have seldom survived for long.
The prospect is much better for the lies already present in embryo
in the mind – the 'feeling' that this or that is so – the 'fact' that
'everybody knows to be right' – the mistrust or dislike that cannot
quite be explained, 'but *you* know . . .' Any book performing a
placenta function for the nourishment of such ideas is likely to
prove more effective than one of blatantly corruptive intention.

One of the gangster characters in *No Orchids* is of so pronounced a masochistic disposition that when he is knifed he has an

orgasm. We may be confident that Raffles and Bunny would have considered both the knifing and the orgasm 'not done'. They would have described the one as 'foreign', the other as 'unspeakably filthy'. Bestselling authors have to be adept at finding such brief, emotive epithets that awaken response immediately. 'Foreign', for instance, makes quick appeal to nationalistic snobbery; 'filthy' short-circuits thought and gives prudes and hypocrites a pleasurable shock of virtuous indignation. Neither has anything to do with reason; neither is relevant to the real issues of violence and sexual deviation.

Yet Orwell suggested that the snobbishness and hypocrisy to which popular literature of the Raffles type pandered might have value as a check upon social behaviour.

If he was right, it is odd that one of the ugliest interludes of the early 1920s, the punitive activity of the 'Black-and-Tans' in Ireland, largely involved men of a type that could have come straight from the pages of a Raffles or Bulldog Drummond novel. Even more odd that American Prohibition – as fully-blown an instance of hypocrisy as anyone could have desired – engendered between 1919 and 1933 the crimes of which *No Orchids for Miss Blandish* was a pale reflection.

De rigueur at Monte

My name is Carmela Rosselli. I am English, of Italian extrac-
tion, five and twenty years of age, and for many years – yes, I
confess it freely – I have been utterly world-weary. I am an only
child. My mother, one of the Yorkshire Burnetts, married
Romolo Annibale, Marchese Rosselli, an impecunious member
of the Florentine aristocracy . . .

Such an introduction was enough to tell the reader that he – or,
more probably, she – had entered the world of William Le Queux.
An impression of what that world was like may be gained from a
paraphrase of *The Gamblers*, the typical Le Queux novel of
which the above is the opening.

Carmela lives 'in Kensington society' with her guardian, Ulrica
Yorke, a woman a few years older than herself. One autumn
afternoon, Ulrica suddenly declares: 'Carmela, I am ruined
morally and physically; I feel that I want a complete change', and
proposes that they go to Monte Carlo. They stop off in Paris on
the way and see the sights of the City. 'Need I describe them? I
think not. Those who read these lines probably know them all.'
Although both women are wealthy, they stay in a cheap pension
long enough to save money for the Casino tables and to amuse

themselves with the spectacle of 'the most extraordinary collection of tabbies, some I regret to say, are actually our own compatriots'.

At the gaming tables, Carmela and her guardian meet two men of London acquaintance. One of these men, Reginald Thorne, wins heavily at roulette; later, the two women find his murdered body in their hotel room. The second man, Gerald Keppel, is the son of a South African millionaire, whose splendid steam yacht has just arrived on the Riviera. Carmela, incidentally, has seen in Monte Carlo her former love, Ernest ('I loved Ernest with a wild, passionate love, and all others were now, and would ever be, as naught to me.').

As soon as their yachting gowns arrive from the dressmaker's, Carmela and Ulrica join the party which is to accompany Gerald Keppel and his father on a cruise. The ship sails out of Villefranche harbour. At sea, Carmela, unable to sleep one night, overhears a plot to blow up the yacht in order to conceal the death of a woman. Old Keppel seems implicated. All go ashore at Leghorn, where Carmela is accosted by a mysterious stranger, a dwarfish old man named Branca. She is persuaded to tell him what she has heard on her host's yacht; then, convinced that the ship is doomed, she takes a train for Paris. In the same compartment as Carmela is the woman supposedly intended for death at sea. She is later to prove to be the mother of Reginald Thorne. Old Keppel also is on the train. And – yes – Ernest Cameron, the man Carmela loves.

In Paris, there is much further eavesdropping, spying and following. Ernest is now bearded. He writes a code message on a café table top. Along comes a tow-headed woman whom Carmela believes to be her supplanter in Ernest's affections. The woman reads the message and then makes a rendezvous with the mysterious stranger from Leghorn, Branca. The scene changes to a secret gaming house in Paris. Carmela confronts Ernest. Ernest confronts the tow-headed woman, Julie by name, and accuses her of having killed Reginald Thorne. Julie demands to be allowed to pass, but Ernest raises a small whistle to his lips. Agents de police close in. Julie blames her Corsican accomplice – none other than Branca – for Reginald's murder. She shows them a thimble fitted with a hollow spike and explains: 'Within . . . is a small chamber filled with a most subtle and deadly poison, extracted from a small lizard peculiar to the Bambara country on the banks of the Upper Niger.'

The Corsican springs at her 'with all the fury of a wild beast' but then draws back 'uttering terrible imprecations'. Five minutes later, he has 'breathed his last in frightful agony, his ignominious career ended by his own diabolical invention'.

Need I relate how, on the following morning, Ernest sought me and begged me to forgive? Or how, with tears of joy, I allowed him to hold me once more in his manly arms, as of old, and shower fervent kisses upon my face? No . . . At Kensington Church, amid great éclat, within a month of our arrival back in town, my happiness broke into full flower . . . We have not visited Nice since. We prefer Cairo for the winter, with a trip up to Luxor and Assouan.

The sort of fulfilment presented in *The Gamblers*, as in so many other books by William Le Queux, was calculated to satisfy a much more modest appetite than his air of familiarity with riches might suggest. It was not, of course, for the Carmelas and Keppels that he was writing, but for those left behind in Kensington and places like it. A shrewd touch was the completion of the heroine's full circle. By bringing her back home after her adventures the author accomplished several useful things. He confirmed the simple parochial patriotism of the great majority of his readers. He made easier their feeling of being involved in a romantic climax, of sharing that 'great éclat'. And, thanks to the choice of a London district that happened to be a department store Mecca, he flattered not only its own considerable middle-class population but a host of suburban and provincial shoppers.

Flattery is distributed as generously throughout the pages of Le Queux as jewels in one of his gaming salons. 'Reader, you probably know the panorama of the Riviera . . .' Actually not; but the gracious implication is appreciated. 'White serge is, as you know, always de rigueur at Monte in winter . . .' But of course. And then, those sights of Paris. 'Need I describe them?' asks Le Queux, in airy tribute to the lady in the lending library who once almost went on a day trip to Boulogne. 'I think not.'

The technique, selectively examined, looks much more crude now than it would have appeared to even a fairly sophisticated reader in the years after the Armistice. There was about the escapist literature of that time an air of brash confidence in the reader's capacity to be impressed. The rigidity of class and economic barriers, the undeveloped state of cinema and wireless, the paucity and narrowness of curriculum in most schools, the lack of opportunity to travel – these were but some of the factors that made for naïve receptiveness. The gossip-writing Marquess of Donegal estimated in 1933 that those he termed 'the wandering élite' who could afford regular holidays abroad numbered only some ten thousand people. Whether or not his figure was accurate, there certainly was reserved for anyone who crossed the English Channel on pleasure special envy and respect. The Riviera was the supreme symbol of exotic self-indulgence. It was invariably 'the playground of the rich' in the obedient minds of newspaper sub-editors, and the public came to associate that short stretch of Mediterranean shore with all the romantic – and sinful – possibilities of wealth.

Opportunist novelists were not slow in appointing themselves guides to the flesh-pots of Cannes and Nice and to Monte Carlo's gaming rooms. That most of them belonged to the 'picture if you will, dear reader' school of authorship was due to a grounding in Victorian literary convention (Le Queux had been born as early as 1864, Phillips Oppenheim in 1866) but it must not be supposed that gush and pomposity were yet unacceptable. They in fact were peculiarly well suited to the telling of the sort of stories that created and elaborated the great Riviera fantasy.

Here is Le Queux, showing his English housewives the company that awaits their taking wing from Balham and from Bolton:

Publisher. "I LIKE YOUR STORY, BUT I WISH YOU'D GIVE IT A DIFFERENT SETTING; YOU KNOW—SOCIETY, THE RITZ, DEAUVILLE, ASCOT AND ALL THAT SORT OF THING."

Conscientious Literary Aspirant. "BUT I'M AFRAID I HAVEN'T ANY ACTUAL EXPERIENCE OF THESE THINGS."

Publisher. "OH, NEVER MIND ABOUT THAT. THE PEOPLE WHO'LL READ YOUR STORY HAVEN'T EITHER."

The two bejewelled worlds, the monde and the demimonde, ate, drank and chattered in that restaurant of wide renown. The company was cosmopolitan, the conversation polyglot, the dishes marvellous. At the table next us there sat the Grand-Duke Michael of Russia, with the Countess Torbay, and beyond a British earl with a couple of smart military men . . .

A precisely similar picture was being painted by a dozen writers of the period. A few were detective novelists, but in their case the choice of a Riviera setting was made only occasionally as a change from Mayfair and country manors. One feels in reading these particular whodunnits that uncertainty about French police procedure tended to detract from an author's enjoyment of murder among the best people. More often, the crimes depicted were robbery, fraud or blackmail. Jewels figured in preference to cash, with emeralds top favourites. When mere money was involved, the victim was generally an American. This would seem to reflect current English antipathy towards a nation that was suspected of having made late entry into the war for motives disgracefully unrelated to the welfare of the British Empire. Americans also were concerned in a good many stories with fraud as their theme. They nearly always lost their dollars to impeccably attired tricksters of high pedigree, and again the reader often was left to draw the inference that breeding, even when evinced by criminals, will prevail against upstart prosperity.

As for the third story-line, blackmail, a curious feature of its employment in the Riviera literature is the coy imprecision with which authors referred to whatever the victims were supposed to have done. Sometimes the mention of nothing more specific than 'a bundle of letters' was deemed sufficient. 'The affairs of a certain company', 'a moment of indiscretion', 'a regrettable association, long forgotten' – in such terms were defined the lapses whose discovery had thrust men and women of wealth and distinction into the power of extortionists. There is a reminder here, incidentally, of the obliqueness of reference in many of Conan Doyle's stories to aristocratic transgression, which Sherlock Holmes was almost invariably ready to conceal in the interest of avoiding scandal.

Why were the sensation novelists of that time so neglectful of what would commend itself to their successors as good copy? The answer is that they did not neglect their opportunity: they scorned it, and not entirely for altruistic reasons, either. It is true that these writers – or the successful ones, anyway – had profound respect for the socially eminent and took care to be on as good terms with them as they could afford. A. E. W. Mason, for example, had a yacht of his own and used to go shooting with no less illustrious a marksman than King George V. But they also recognized that their public, the loyalist and substantially puritan-minded dreamers of the lending libraries, would not be amused by revelations of the true nature of Le Queux's 'bejewelled worlds'. If the Scott Fitzgeralds, Cyril Connollys and Michael Arlens wished to be clever about Riviera society, that was their business. The rich and consistent rewards awaited the pedlars of illusion: theirs not to soil the image of a lotus land where wealthy men and exquisite women enjoyed eternally the ministrations of omniscient maîtres d'hôtel and suave croupiers.

No one learned this lesson to greater advantage than did Edward Phillips Oppenheim, the son of a Leicester leather merchant, who first tasted the delights of the Côte d'Azur when he was travelling in France on behalf of his father's firm. Oppenheim was what is sometimes called a 'born' writer, although 'compulsive' would describe him more accurately. His output in the long life that ended in 1946 was enormous. By the time he was forty he had written thirty novels and was already earning more than two thousand pounds a year in royalties when he decided to dispose of his inherited leather business and become a full-time author on the coast that had always attracted him. In the second half of his life, he produced four times as many books as in the first, making a total of 150 novels. Into these and countless short stories and articles he poured some thirteen million words.

Crime was an important but not the dominating ingredient of an Oppenheim story. His preoccupation always was the elegance and luxury of high life. Nothing but the best, the formula that won him the devotion of a huge public on both sides of the Atlantic, dictated that even a criminal had to be of Almanach de Gotha standard. Thus it was to the International Arch-criminal mythology that Oppenheim tended to contribute. His biographer, Robert Standish, in *The Prince of Storytellers* (1957), has suggested that Oppenheim consciously reinforced the average man's idea that 'the smooth-looking parties wafted to and from the best restaurants by limousine were not, as generally believed, members of the House of Lords, but the aristocrats of crime observed during their leisure hours. There they were, diamonds in their shirt-fronts, puffing away at big cigars, the women draped in sables, the living proof that despite all the moralists said, crime did pay.'

Edgar Wallace and others also echoed this impression and profited from the public's eagerness to read about the exploits of super-crooks who were scarcely ever out of evening dress as they rubbed shoulders with royalty and planned multi-million-franc coups. But Oppenheim had a special genius for understanding the fascination money exerted upon people who had just enough of it to be able to visualize (as the really poor could not) the possibilities which unlimited supplies could achieve. As Robert Standish pointed out, Oppenheim evolved a fiction in which money was 'as potent as deathrays, guns that shoot round corners, clairvoyance and coincidences'. Money, as employed for Oppenheim's literary purposes, created its own unique climate and a new set of standards. 'To people who suffered rudeness and tyranny from shabby little shopkeepers, it was a glimpse into a promised land to read of a tycoon who, because he did not like the way the chef at the Magnifico prepared his *sole Walewska*, bought the hotel and fired the chef.'

Selling glimpses of promised lands to others was such a remunerative business that Phillips Oppenheim never had any difficulty in paying for the upkeep of the material paradise he had gained for himself. He lived in a villa big enough for the entertainment of more than 250 guests at a time; his mammoth parties were famous throughout the region. Wherever he travelled, he

insisted upon the most splendid accommodation and the sort of
service normally reserved for potentates. No less Pasha-like was
the status he enjoyed at home. He was attended every morning by
a valet, a masseur, a secretary ready to pour out his coffee and slice
his toast into convenient fingers, a manicurist and a chauffeur. His
American wife, with whom he remained on more or less amiable
terms for more than fifty years despite his countless infidelities,
seems to have tempered the absolutism of her husband's domestic
monarchy with tolerance and good sense. Her presence, at board,
if not in bed, also must have given his reputation some protection
from scandal – a service no less necessary to a bestselling author
than that of his accountant. In gratitude, perhaps, for Mrs Oppenheim's patience he kept most of his sexual adventuring off-
shore. Not for nothing was the Oppenheim yacht known on the
Côte d'Azur as 'the floating double-bed'. He even took the
trouble of going all the way to a chemist in London whenever his
stock of contraceptives needed to be renewed. Whether he was
prompted to do so by tact or by residual patriotism one does not
know, but there always exists the intriguing possibility that his
prophylactics, like the hand-made cigarettes favoured by the
characters in his novels, were personally monogrammed.

There was, inevitably, a difference between the author pictured
by the readers of his diamond-studded fantasies and the real self-
disciplined businessman whose industry was such that it could
earn him £5,800 in just over six weeks in 1925. Ethel Mannin,
coming across him some years later in Ciro's Restaurant, found
that he was completely unlike her own conception of a thriller
writer. 'Fat and jolly, he looks more as though he would write nice
clean fun for *The Boy's Own Paper*'.

Other views of the Riviera existed, too, than that which the
Oppenheim novels presented year after year. Sydney Horler,
tempted by legend to go and see it for himself in 1934, reported
back in disgust that it resembled 'a cocotte awakening each winter
with a stifled yawn to dab some more powder on her face because
she expected a rich admirer'. He declared the area to be plagued
with lung and throat diseases and susceptible to typhoid outbreaks

occasioned by contamination of the public water supply. Its sunshine was frequently countered by treacherous icy winds blowing down from the Maritime Alps. Sanitation was bad and most of the streets neglected. Bathing was ruled out by reason of 'Gallic lack of hygienic sense'. After such unfortunate if brief experience of what he dubbed henceforth 'the most overrated locality in the world' Horler watched from his London-bound train the rising of mist from English meadows. 'I could have cried with joy.'

To say it was lucky for Phillips Oppenheim and his fellow miners in the rich seam of High Life fiction that very few indeed among the reading public could afford fact-finding trips to the Mediterranean is to misunderstand the issue. Certainly, the great majority had to be content with luxury by proxy and romance at one remove. But were not these, rather than the real articles, what they truly desired? To identify oneself with a character who rounds off the winning of a few thousand at baccarat with an exquisite supper and still has time to unmask a murderer or penetrate the disguise of a countess – that is one thing. It is quite another to see hard-earned money whisked away by dispassionate foreigners wearing intimidatingly smart suits; then to grapple with an incomprehensible menu, odd food and a terrifying bill; and to wind up by being discovered by a chambermaid in the act of mistaking the bidet for a drinking fountain.

It did not matter that travellers as jaundiced as Horler despised, or affected to despise, the pretensions of the Côte d'Azur (or Zone Septique, as some dubbed it); nor that intelligent and perceptive observers were aware that nowhere else on earth was there to be found a comparable community of spongers, frauds and phonies. The myth existed in splendid isolation from the facts, and it was sustained throughout the 1920s and 1930s by the determination of the readers of Oppenheim and his like to have a place in their imagination where they could dress up as millionaires and play at being respected, knowledgeable and powerful.

CHAPTER 5

The Bulldog Breed

There emerged from the British Army in 1919, with the rank of Lieutenant-Colonel, a man named Herman Cyril McNeile. In 1920, he published a book under the pseudonym 'Sapper', which had been bestowed upon him some years earlier by Northcliffe on his acceptance of a story for the *Daily Mail*. The book was entitled *Bulldog Drummond*. It was the prototype of a series that made McNeile one of the most avidly read authors in Britain.

McNeile himself seems to have had a personality closely akin to that of his hero. It was of the sort that can most kindly be described as ebullient. He had a loud voice and employed it unstintingly in company. His laugh was very loud indeed. He liked to enliven clubs and restaurants with the sight and sound of military good fellowship. The meals that he was able to order with part of his dividends from literary success always included immense quantities of caviare and were followed by equally generous intakes of vintage port. Lieutenant-Colonel 'Sapper' McNeile, as his friend and biographer, Gerard Fairlie, would later concede, was 'not everybody's cup of tea'.

And yet Bulldog Drummond – the fictional extension of the man himself – proved as nearly universally popular as any creator of characters could desire. The books sold in huge numbers in their author's lifetime and even after his death in 1937, when the 'ghosting' of additions to the series was undertaken by Fairlie. This success confirmed the truth of Fairlie's declaration: 'Once a fan, always a fan.' One story, *The Final Count*, which was first published in 1926, went into no fewer than forty editions in the next twenty-five years. Drummond was put upon the stage and featured in films, receiving the accolade of the cinema industry in the form of portrayal by Ronald Colman. (It was Colman, incidentally, to whom the not dissimilar roles of 'Raffles' and 'Beau Geste' were assigned.)

Drummond is worth careful examination, for his popularity could only have been won by a character whose qualities made immediate and strong rapport with the ideas of the reading and, subsequently, the cinema-going public.

In the first place, he satisfied conventional British ideals of physique. He 'stood just six feet in his socks, and turned the scale at over fourteen stone'. He was 'hard muscle and bone clean through . . . a magnificent boxer, a lightning and deadly shot with a revolver, and utterly lovable'. His friends were happily aware of his propensity to 'burble at them genially, knock them senseless with a blow of greeting on the back, and then resuscitate them with a large tankard of ale'. They also recognized his deservedly good fortune in being 'married to an adorable wife'.

Such was Drummond's strength of personality that those he led into adventure 'never questioned, never hesitated'. He was invariably contemptuous of odds, which he countered with enormous personal strength and an armoury of assorted weapons that today would be considered distinctly anti-social in character. With the police he had very little patience and he would not hesitate to incapacitate any whose bumbling regard for the proprieties threatened to interfere with his fight for right.

His flamboyantly aggressive patriotism was matched by his loyalty to his friends. In moments of excitement, he found expression in the vocabulary of the public school First Fifteen changing room, using the word 'show' a great deal and occasionally crediting an enemy with taking 'a darned sporting chance'. Drummond's warning of the gravity of a situation was likely to be delivered as: 'You're up against something pretty warm, old lad ... I take off my hat to 'em for their nerve.' The few occasions on which his loquacity failed included those when death seemed imminent and thoughts flew to loved ones – 'You might – er – just tell – er – you know, Phyllis and all that . . .'

Drummond's reticence also applied to religion. It was, as doubtless his readers would have agreed, one of those things that one just didn't talk about. One rather curious feature of his speech, though, was the frequency of his use of the word 'devil' and its derivatives. It is true that this was a literary device of the time to signal conflict between tough heroes and unprincipled adversaries, but 'Sapper's' devotion to it was extreme, and perhaps psychologically significant. Another sphere in which Drummond preferred action to words was politics. His rare references to the subject were characteristically forthright. 'Years ago we had an amusing little show rounding up Communists and other unwashed people of that type. We called ourselves the Black Gang, and it was a great sport while it lasted.'

Such were the chief idiosyncracies built by Lieutenant-Colonel McNeile into a hero to whom millions responded sympathetically from 1920 onwards. Bulldog Drummond was a melodramatic creation, workable only within a setting of melodrama. The stories provided for that purpose were models of unselfconscious absurdity. They had been vigorously purged of likelihood and were uncontaminated by the slightest suggestion of subtlety of style. Perhaps the most splendidly ridiculous of the entire canon was *The Final Count.*

Robin Gaunt, a scientist, has perfected a poison capable of dealing 'universal, instantaneous death'. He believes that Britain should be prepared to use it in order to stop other nations going to war. The day before he is due to give a secret demonstration before the Army Council, he disappears. Two of his friends, John Stockton and Toby Sinclair, discover Gaunt's terrier, 'a topping little beast', dead in the scientist's rooms. A policeman who touches the dog dies at once in a paroxysm and his colleague exclaims: 'But it's devil's work. It ain't human.' Sir John Dallas, celebrated toxicologist, suggests the deaths have been caused by a poison known previously to the Borgias and to the Aztecs. Such a substance could be of great military importance.

At Toby Sinclair's rooms, Stockton meets Bulldog Drummond. The three friends proceed to lunch at Hatchett's, in Piccadilly, Drummond giving 'a grin of pure joy' and exclaiming: 'Is it possible, my jovial bucks, that once again we are on the war-path?' They reassemble in a low pub in the sinister London suburb of Peckham. Stockton is disguised as 'a mechanic with Communistic tendencies' and Sinclair as a 'nasty-looking little Jew'. They overhear an address, go to it, and notice strange noises. Drummond declares: 'I'm going in, trap or no trap; there's foul play inside that room.' They find a rat-faced man hanging, shoot a man who is about to syringe them with Gaunt's poison, and tangle with a dozen police led by Inspector MacIver, of Scotland Yard. Friendly relations are restored by Drummond's remark: 'The fact of the matter, MacIver, is that we're up against some unscrupulous swine.'

The rest of the evening is taken up by Drummond's disposal of two outsize tarantulas, delivered to his Mayfair home in separate boxes addressed to him and his wife, and accompanied by sarcastic notes. He drowns one spider and hits the other between the eyes with a poker while it is scuttling about, 'hissing loudly'.

Drummond recruits several more friends. After further violent encounters with Gaunt's kidnappers, the scene changes to Land's End, whither the gang has been traced thanks to a chance remark. Drummond and his forces arrive at Penzance in his Hispano-Suiza. Stockton notices odd comings and goings at a deserted tin mine. Drummond distributes ropes, gags, heavily loaded sticks and bottles of chloroform. They converge on the mine, disposing of sentries as they advance. One is 'put to sleep', another given 'a good biff' and a third 'dotted one'.

Confronting the rest of the gang at gun point in their hideout, Drummond says to the man he habitually addresses as 'fungus face': 'Only a keen sense of public duty restrains me from plugging you where you sit, you ineffable swine.' Less scrupulous, 'fungus face' floods the room with the 'universal death' liquid. Robin Gaunt, now insane, appears just in time to drain off the poison, before it rises to the level of Drummond's table-top refuge. An airship has arrived overhead and it is into its tanks that the poison is pumped by Gaunt.

Search reveals papers written by Gaunt before he lost his reason. They express his fear that his secret would fall into the hands of 'Russia, ruled by its clique of homicidal, alien Jews'. Also described is an attack by airship upon a yacht crowded with Society people wearing jewels, their deaths by poison, and the robbery of their corpses by Bolsheviks – 'the most frightful gang of murderous-looking cut-throats I've ever seen (officers seem to have no control)'.

Drummond realizes that behind the whole affair is Carl Peterson, arch-criminal. It also dawns upon him that the airship is the same as that supposedly owned by a mysterious American millionaire calling himself 'Wilmot'. He remembers that he has been sent two complimentary tickets for a trip on 'Wilmot's' airship that very night. He drives his friends back to London. Gaunt is disposed of with the remark: 'Well, since the poor bloke is bug house, I suppose we'll have to stuff him in a home or something.'

The airship of 'Wilmot', who is really Peterson, is crowded with fashionably dressed guests, including at least one duchess. At dinner, Peterson asks 'the distinguished officer on my right' to propose the Loyal Toast in 'an old Chinese wine the secret of which is known only to a certain sect of monks'. Captain Drummond (for it is he) calls: 'The King!' Then he smells his glass. 'For God's sake don't drink! It's death!'

To Peterson, he cries: 'Drink, you foul brute: drink!' Peterson knocks the glass from his hand, spilling its contents upon his own wrist. Before he dies, the expression on his face reveals him for what he is. 'And of that revelation no man can write . . .'

Questioned by an earnest investigator of popular reading habits, such as Mrs Q. D. Leavis, the average Bulldog Drummond enthusiast would probably have asserted that he enjoyed the stories simply 'as good yarns' without for a moment giving them credence. They were, after all, in the tradition of all wildly extravagant tales designed to pass an idle hour and 'take people out of themselves'. The impossible was more fun than the all-too-probable.

This would have been true as far as it went. 'Sapper' was fulfilling a function defined by that writer in the *Quarterly* sixty years before who had declared that 'keepers of bookstalls, as well as of refreshment rooms, find an advantage in offering their customers something hot and strong, something that may catch the eye of the hurried passenger, and promise temporary excitement to relieve the dullness of a journey'. But not everything 'hot and strong' becomes an addictive taste. Reams of picaresque nonsense, more or less similar to the 'Raffles' and Drummond novels, were produced every month without promoting enough response to justify a second printing. What did they lack that gave something else, no better and no worse in terms of plot, subject and style, a runaway success?

Robert Standish wrote of E. Phillips Oppenheim: 'If he had his finger on the common pulse, it was because he had his finger on his own.' Again, 'There was in him, as there has been in almost every man or woman who has found a place in tens of millions of human hearts, a wide streak of mediocrity.' Those two statements could well be amalgamated to form a general First Law of bestsellers. 'Sapper' confirmed it to the letter.

Throughout his work there is discernible an inborn appreciation of what would excite his readers without disturbing them; what they were likely to admire or despise (as distinct from loving and hating, with which popular fiction has nothing to do); and what would make them feel flattered, but not patronized. There can be little doubt that such understanding was instinctive and not the product of a calculating intelligence. The public is remarkably sensitive to 'tongue in cheek' attitudes; it recognizes and rejects every attempt to write down by an author who does not himself share the popular ideas he pretends to approve.

If 'Sapper' had set about investing the character of Bulldog Drummond with qualities other than those he genuinely considered admirable, the books would never have succeeded. Whether his notions were sensible or silly, beneficent or vicious, has much less to do with the success that did come his way than the fact that they were sincerely held. C. Day Lewis called 'Sapper's' hero 'that unspeakable public school bully'. He was expressing the aversion that the arrogant, small-minded and aggressive Drummond was bound to arouse in anyone of a thoughtful and tolerant disposition and egalitarian leanings. But fantasy heroes usually *are* bullies. They must win, and since their opponents seem to enjoy a monopoly of cunning, sheer physical advantage has to be invoked.

Much play of this is made in the Bulldog Drummond saga. Some of the scenes are strongly reminiscent of rugby football scrums and the author's enjoyment of the portrayal of zestful mayhem communicates itself strongly. Drummond himself is the embodiment of 'hard muscle and bone' superiority. His consistently successful encounters clearly imply that the simple answer to evil is 'a good biff'.

Violence was not, in the 1920s, the psychological abstraction that has so deeply concerned social diagnosticians since the end of the second world war. Although millions had been slaughtered and more millions maimed, the survivors of the 1914–18 war saw no relationship between the ferocity on the battlefield and cruel behaviour elsewhere. Perhaps because the conflict had been mainly one of attrition, a static killing match geographically confined, civilians regarded its horrors as a special case – deplorable, certainly, but quite separate from domestic ills. Thus, the upsurge of pacifism that reached its peak in the Peace Pledge of the 1930s was essentially an anti-militarist reaction which had much narrower implication than the attempts by young people thirty years later to repudiate force as such and even to contract out of a society committed to the use of force.

Drummond's preference for the upper-cut as an effective and proper argument was by no means inconsistent with contemporary relief at the return of peace. The 'Hun' had been fairly beaten, if not by precisely the same mode of assault, at least in the same spirit. The feeling of a great number of ordinary people was that subsequent tiresome complications at home and abroad could have been avoided by the delivery of a few extra 'biffs' for good measure. Could the odious Peterson, archetypal scheming foreigner, have been given his quittance by the deliberations of the old men of Versailles? Of course not. Disposal of Peterson and like afflictions called for a strong arm propelled by simple resolution.

'Sapper' reminds his readers from time to time of Drummond's military antecedents by having other characters address him as 'Captain'. The choice of rank is interesting. It is high enough to suggest experience and prowess, without implying advanced years or too marked a social eminence. 'Captain' connotes good fellowship; it has something of dash about it. Generals scarcely ever appear in popular fiction: they sound old and forbidding. Colonels crop up frequently but they seem reserved for chief constableships or country character roles in detective novels. A major is only recruited when a dipsomaniac of private means is required by the plot. In Captain Drummond, however, we have a man with exactly the right status to appeal to a generation with a constitutional respect for titles and with minds in which the word 'ex-Service' had attained special emotional lustre to compensate for the drab realities of demobilization.

Emphasis is laid upon the fact that none of Drummond's companions ever questions the rightness of his decisions or fails to carry out his orders. There is no argument, no 'argy-bargy' of the kind that so unhappily complicates the business of getting things done in real life. Action throughout the novels flows straight from situation to situation and it gets all the right results in the end, despite the evasions and counter-attacks of the enemy. Not only is this satisfying in terms of the story, but it is pleasingly suggestive of the possibility of events in the actual world being amenable to a strong man's dealing. One of Britain's special misfortunes in the inter-war years was to suffer a series of governments uniformly dim of intellect, unsure of purpose and inept in action. It was tempting in the atmosphere of frustration thus created to wonder whether

dictatorial methods might not be preferable to the long-wind-
edness and muddle of democratic administration. On the face of
it, Bulldog cut a better figure than a MacDonald or a Baldwin,
while Tiger Standish, Nayland Smith, Sanders (on home leave
from The River) and the rest of popular fiction's go-getters each
served in his way to underline the ineffectualness of Government
as it actually existed.

Relevant, perhaps, to this aspect of leisure reading is the currency in the mid-1930s of the highly romantic notion that
T. E. Lawrence of 'Lawrence of Arabia' fame, ought to be sent as
plenipotentiary envoy to Hitler's Reich. There was considerable
confidence in his ability (at a single bound, no doubt) to settle the
hash of the troublesome little German so far as Britain's interests
were concerned. Before the theory could be put to the test, Lawrence's fatal motor-cycle accident supervened. An earlier and
more mundane example of myth being harnessed to politics was
the adoption of Edgar Wallace as one of the candidates for a
parliamentary election. If his subsequent appearance at the
bottom of the poll proved anything, it was that public readiness to
identify an author with his creations is not to be relied upon.

The only national political development that could be suspected of indebtedness to Bulldog Drummond was the rise, after
1931, of the British Union of Fascists. The connection, though,
was not one of cause and effect. Popular fiction is not evangelistic;
it implants no new ideas. Fascism sprang, in Britain as elsewhere,
from frustration caused by economic chaos and political in-
eptitude. That same frustration had made readers' minds recep-
tive to tales of improbable heroics, but acknowledgement of a
common source is not the same thing as saying Mosley's fascism
derived from McNeile's fiction. They simply possessed a certain
family resemblance.

CHAPTER 6

King Edgar, and how he got his crown

A familiar source of argument is the question of whether a man can become a bestselling author entirely by his own volition or whether he must have the aid of massive publicity. The opinion that predominates today is in favour of the promotion theory. It certainly is true that very large sums of money have been and continue to be spent in support of particular books considered to have high potential value, notably as film 'properties'. Authors, as authors, are more rarely the subject of this kind of speculation, although one or two have been persuaded to make over their future output to firms that give them in return a regular income and the sort of paternal solicitude that might be lavished on an oil well or a stud mare.

Raymond Chandler's view of bestsellers, expressed in his essay *The Simple Art of Murder*, was characteristically sardonic. He saw them as 'promotional jobs based on a sort of indirect snob-appeal, carefully escorted by the trained seals of the critical fraternity, and lovingly tended and watered by certain much too powerful pressure groups whose business is selling books, although they would like you to think they are fostering culture'. The difficulty of deciding what effect is really achieved by systematic campaigning on behalf of books is the same as that of assessing the value of any major advertising process – the sound and fury of the operation itself are apt to drown doubts. If there is one thing that the promotion industry does superlatively well, it is to promote itself.

The facts of the matter are probably these. A writer whose work, irrespective of literary merit, fails to press all or most of the buttons that provoke stock responses, and consequent satisfaction, in the mind of the average reader, can be publicized as diligently as a detergent or a breakfast food, but he will never achieve commensurate sales. On the other hand, an author with instinctive button mastery, allied with inventiveness and staying power, could enter the bestseller lists with his eighth, tenth, or fifteenth book and remain there without the help of promotion. With it, success might be reached from six to a dozen books earlier, and maintained at a slightly higher level.

In the 1920s, the accepted principle was that the public could safely be left to choose, with a minimum of prompting, its own favourites. Advertisements of books were issued, the bulk of them for insertion in the literary sections of newspapers and magazines, but they generally took the form of conventional announcements that made no attempt at systematic build-up of particular reputations. Most publishers in those days would have viewed very dubiously the modern advertising technique of presenting every other book as the ultimate apocalyptic fulfilment. One there was, however, who believed that if the right man came along – a writer of prolific capability and facile inventiveness – he could turn him into a money-making machine that would be the envy and the wonder of the publishing world.

This optimist was Sir Ernest Hodder-Williams, head of the firm of Hodder and Stoughton, and the right man who did come along was Edgar Wallace.

At first sight, Wallace in 1920 would seem to have been an extremely unlikely candidate for the role of king of thriller-writers. He was already middle-aged. His life so far, though colourful, had not been particularly successful. He was by nature a lazy man and an unbusinesslike one. With such books as he had written he had parted easily, selling the copyrights for less than a hundred pounds apiece. Anyone less shrewdly intuitive than Sir Ernest might have supposed that Wallace had inherited from his illegitimacy, his street-arab childhood, and a succession of jobs that included a newspaper correspondentship in the Boer War, too feckless and self-doubting an attitude to warrant confidence in his future performance.

But these were not the factors that Hodder-Williams took into account. He noted instead that Wallace had one abiding ambition – to make a fortune. This he recognized as a driving force that needed only organization and discipline to prove mutually profitable. Wallace had other obvious qualifications for thriller kingship. His mind at forty-six was of extraordinary quickness. It could grasp ideas at once and build them unerringly into a fabric of drama. He was capable, when encouraged, of working at great speed and for long periods. His contempt for 'highbrow' authors went with a determination to make all his own writing objective and not subjective, to let nothing interfere with the action. He was not noticeably afflicted with that fatal disqualification from best-sellerdom, a sense of humour. Above all, Wallace's essential vulgarity of mind – in the non-pejorative sense in which a publisher of popular fiction would view it – guaranteed his ability to gauge and satisfy the appetite of the ordinary reader.

Wallace's first contract with Hodder and Stoughton called for six books, for which advance royalties of £1,500 were paid. This initial step by his new publisher was tactically sound. By putting Wallace on a piecework basis, it provided the stimulus to his industry that previously had been lacking. Hodder-Williams also probably calculated that to hand a comparatively big sum to a man eager to indulge expensive tastes was the surest way of setting him on a road that he would not be able to leave again. In the following ten years, during which he wrote forty-six books for Hodder and Stoughton, Wallace proved that £1,500 to have been the most profitable literary investment of the age.

Edgar Wallace was not a difficult man to publicize. He fitted exactly the popular conception of what an author ought to look like and how he ought to behave. He worked all day in a dressing-gown, chain-smoked through a flamboyantly long cigarette holder, and drank endless cups of tea. A hatred for draughts compelled him to have constructed a sort of inner office of glass, within which he sat at his desk like a live exhibit in a showcase. Outside his home, he indulged his physical laziness almost to a point of eccentricity. He never used stairs when a lift was available and would take a taxi rather than walk a few dozen yards.

Such idiosyncracies were very much to the taste of a public who believed that success ought to be worn as a visible garment to offset the drabness of the life of the majority. When Hodder-Williams decided to step up the promotion of his firm's biggest asset under the slogan 'Make this an Edgar Wallace Year', it was already obvious that the man was an ideal subject. The sheer volume of his production meant that every bookstall in the country was a billboard for the display of his name and the smoothly handsome profile beneath the down-turned hat brim. That bizarre holder which kept an eternally smouldering cigarette at least twelve inches clear of calm, worldly-wise eyes became a nationally familiar symbol.

Wallace's own experience as a newspaperman had given him the immense advantage of knowing what sort of performance commended itself to the Press. He took care always to be accessible, easy to interview, and unfailingly opinionated. He readily contributed articles on whatever matters happened at the moment to be uppermost in the bird-brains of Fleet Street. The *Evening Standard* actually featured Wallace for some time as its racing oracle. How any paper, even a Beaverbrook organ, could have been so splendidly self-deceptive as to employ as tipster a man who lost £100 a day on his own bets is a measure of the power of the Wallace legend.

Disastrous devotion to the turf was not the only means whereby Wallace unburdened himself of an income which by 1928 had reached £50,000 a year. He spent £25,000 on a country house outside London, but when it was more convenient to be in town he would take over a suite in the Carlton Hotel and live there with his family, having first had installed a private telephone line to his secretary's flat. The wages of the secretary and a score of household servants cost him nearly £50 a month. The travelling needs of his wife and himself were served not by one Rolls-Royce but by a pair; he also presented a car apiece to two of his children and another to his secretary. Guests at the supper parties for which he hired the entire Carlton Restaurant sometimes numbered two hundred. One of the biggest drains of his resources was occasioned by his hopelessly unbusinesslike handling of stage ventures. By keeping them running too long and 'milking' box office receipts he largely nullified the £100,000 profit which plays such as *The Squeaker* and *The Ringer* made between 1926 and 1931, the year of his death.

So sensational a display of high living increased rather than diminished the affectionate awe in which Edgar Wallace was held by the reading public. They loved this dogged sportsman whose horses (like theirs) always lost. They applauded his big spending as if some of the scattered coins had rolled their way. And they adored – no doubt about it – the stories that he still found time to turn out at a prodigious rate from that curious three-sided glass box.

From the analysis of the method and content of Wallace's work which Margaret Lane has offered in her book, *Edgar Wallace: biography of a phenomenon*, the picture emerges of a writer supremely adept in an 'off-the-cuff' technique but observant all the time of a set of strict conventions. The nature of these conventions cannot be unrelated to what must have been the mental and emotional climate of fifty years ago, for Wallace came nearer to being universally read by his generation than did any other author.

The first of the Wallace rules, as listed by Miss Lane, was subordination of everything to action. Nothing was to be what it seemed; confusion and suspense were to be maintained to the end, with none of the two-dimensional characters allowed a static moment. There was not a floor, not a wall, that might not

Bookstall Salesman: "Sorry, THE YARD Book ISN'T WRITTEN, SIR?"

suddenly go into motion. Even in the realm of crime fiction, there have been very few writers so constantly suggestive of restlessness.

All this, however, had to be resolved to satisfy the second convention: that the world be seen as an essentially safe place, a sunny garden at the end of the secret passage. No serious harm could be allowed to befall any of the 'good' characters, however horrifying the means of dispatch that the 'bad' ones might prepare for them. It was permissible for criminals temporarily to thwart the law, but never in a way that might shake the reader's confidence in it. (Wallace's policemen were sometimes baffled; they were never ridiculous).

The third convention was the banishment of anything that might produce genuine emotional reaction, anything capable of upsetting standard assumptions. Margaret Lane defined the objects of this rule as 'excitement without anxiety, suspense without fear, violence without pain and horror without disgust'. She could have added crime without sin and sentiment without sex.

Trying to assess Wallace's work in literary terms would be as pointless as applying sculptural evaluation to a load of gravel. He wrote as well as he needed to write in satisfaction of a voracious but uninstructed public appetite. At least he spared his readers the pages of portentous padding which less brisk operators saw fit to inflict upon theirs, while here and there, one even detects a spark of original and lively characterization. It is a pleasant surprise, for instance, to receive this piece of information about his detective, Mr J. G. Reeder:

> All his life he had had a suspicion of milk. He had calculated that a nimble homicide, working on systematic lines, could decimate London in a month.

For most of the time, though, Wallace's story-telling was fast, facile and careless. A man who habitually planned six and more novels simultaneously and who once completed a book of 80,000 words in a single week-end could not afford to linger over the fashioning of phrases. He had to snatch them out of stock. The following are but a few of those he used in one typical sequence of events in the story of *Terror Keep* (1927):

> She had hardly done so when she heard a sound which brought her heart to her mouth ... slipping off her shoes, she sped along in the darkness ... plucking up courage, after a few minutes she retraced her steps ... when, to her horror, she felt it moving away from her and had just time to shrink back when ... hoping and praying that she would find a niche into which she could shrink ... with a gasp of horror she realized that in the confusion of the moment she had taken the wrong direction ... as she stood motionless with fear ... for a second he stared at her as though she were some ghastly apparition of his mad dreams ... in a second she was flying up the awful staircase ... not for a fortune would she have looked behind ... her breath was coming in long sobs; her heart beat as though it would burst ... and then there came a sound which froze the marrow of his bones ... the scream of a human soul in agony ... suddenly Margaret saw something which made her breath come faster ... in terror she struggled madly, but the man held her in a grip of iron, and then her senses left her and she sank limply into his arms ... it seemed almost an eternity before she came to the surface. Fortunately, she was a good swimmer ...

The plots of the Wallace books were simply hastily contrived vessels into which could be poured a stream of cliché of the above order. Here, by way of general illustration, is that of the *Three Oak Mystery*.

Detective Socrates Smith, retired from Scotland Yard with the help of a legacy of £6,000 a year, is invited to stay with a former colleague, John Mandle, at his country house near London. Mandle has a pretty step-daughter, Molly Templeton, and two near neighbours. One is Bob Stone, yet another ex-Yard man; the other is a Mr Jetheroe, soon to be identified as a former convict. Smith's fellow guest at Mandle's house is his brother, Lexington Smith, who falls in love with Molly.

One morning the brothers find Mandle shot dead. Stone is

discovered trussed up at his home. The police are informed but they hand over the entire investigation to Smith. Smith hopes that a clue to the reason for the murder may be found in a secret drawer of the dead man's desk. Before he can search, somebody fires the house and it burns to the ground. Undeterred, Smith buys a hatchet in the nearest village and chops up the charred remnants of the desk. He finds two keys, labelled 'Pool-in-the . . .' and succeeds in connecting this partial address with a deserted house on Dartmoor. Meanwhile Jetheroe has been shot and his body has disappeared.

Smith travels with his brother to Devon, finds 'Pool-in-the-Moor' and cuts his way through the overgrown garden with another hatchet, this one bought at Exeter. Inside the house, which no one has entered for twenty years, Smith finds bloodstains and a spent bullet. A scorched fragment of a thousand-franc banknote lies in the fireplace. It looks to Smith as though he has discovered the scene of the murder of Deveroux, the Lyons Bank robber, who was supposed to have escaped abroad in 1902 after eluding Mandle and Stone, both at that time policemen officially on his trail.

The brothers return to the house of Bob Stone, where they had left Molly Templeton after the fire. She has disappeared. False messages send them to London in search of her. On their return, Socrates confronts Stone and accuses him of Mandle's murder and the abduction of Molly. Stone admits his guilt, produces a gun and locks Smith in a cupboard.

At the house of mystery, 'Pool-in-the-Moor', Molly is in the custody of a woman with a criminal record earned while she kept a private lunatic asylum. During the night, Molly descends to the cellar and with a pick that has been left lying about she demolishes a brick wall, disclosing the skeleton of Deveroux, the Lyons bank robber. This upsets her, as does the sight of the face of a mysterious stranger at an attic window.

The stranger proves to be a policeman, assigned on Smith's instructions to keep an eye on Molly. When Stone arrives and tries to extort from Molly a promise of marriage, the policeman appears in the doorway and announces: 'My name is Sub-Inspector Frank Weldon from Scotland Yard. I shall take you into custody on a charge ...' A shot rings out and Weldon pitches forward. Stone has fired from the hip. He bundles the body into a car and dumps it in a nearby lake. He then enters the cellar armed with two automatic pistols and awaits developments.

Socrates and his brother are not long in making an appearance. Another arrival is Mr Jetheroe, recovered from his wound so fully that he has been able to scale the fourteen-feet-high garden wall, set with broken glass. He proves to be none other than Molly's father, who has been awaiting a chance to clear his name. Sub-Inspector Weldon also has revived, thanks to the coldness of the water in the lake, and reports for further duty.

Stone dies in the shooting that ensues. Molly accepts Lexington Smith's offer of marriage. She says she cannot take a penny of Mandle's ill-gotten fortune (his share of the loot of Deveroux, the Lyons bank robber). Socrates says: 'Anyway, Lex has got quite a lot.' Jetheroe adds, fondly: 'And so has Lexington's future father-in-law.'

Lexington's eyes meet the girl's. 'Money!' he says, contemptuously.

It may readily be judged that the readers of the 150 or so novels which Edgar Wallace turned out on essentially similar lines to *The Three Oak Mystery* were in no great danger of philosophical, moral or political derangement. They were treated to nothing worse (provided they were not stylistically sensitive) than a vicarious dash from one unlikely situation to another. How exciting this was felt to be depended on the individual reader's degree of ignorance of real life; alternatively, on the extent to which he was ready and able to disregard the voice of experience and reason in the interest of his own entertainment. Practice, it seems, can make the suspension of intelligence a progressively easier matter. Wallace's books would never have achieved the astonishing sales that ultimately they did if they had been rejected by all sensible and educated people. The author Clemence Dane wrote in 1933: 'There is a joyous crowd of story-tellers which frankly accepts the fact that good stories and money-making go together. Edgar Wallace is their king ... And though he may sneer, the highbrow generally reads the low-brow's *Blood-stained Cabbage-stalk* avidly ...' She was right: in or around that year, it was estimated that of every four books being read in Britain one was an Edgar Wallace.

Such a situation indicated something more than casual, undiscriminating acceptance. Wallace was demanded. Censorious critics of the time used the word 'drug' repeatedly in connection with his work. The epithet was appropriate enough, no doubt, but it did not explain *why* this deluge of superficial, silly, slipshod fiction found addicts at every social level. Clemence Dane's reference was to 'good' stories but if by that she meant to connote convincing characterization, ingenuity of plot, credible conflict and logically satisfying resolution, Wallace was a non-starter. Orwell accused Wallace of intellectual sadism. It seems unlikely, though, that anything so subtle would have won readers by the million. Wallace never created a scene of cruelty comparable with those that were to be commonplaces of crime fiction twenty years after his death. Nor did any of his novels portray sexual behaviour beyond the stage of chaste enfoldment in arms. He himself declared more than once that there was 'too much nastiness in modern literature'.

From these facts emerges the strong possibility that Wallace's success was, in large measure if not completely, due to those very characteristics of his writing which a critic believing himself to be sophisticated would consider deficiencies.

Taking his last-mentioned attribute first – the disinclination to treat of sex save in the most perfunctory, unreal terms – might not this in fact have matched a widespread public attitude? Britain in the 1920s was not populated exclusively by Bright Young Things, nor had Suffragettism and the Black Bottom seduced a war-sickened generation to the delights of free love. The solid majority was still bound by Victorian inhibition, the result of sexual ignorance and fear. It was tolerant of titillation at the level of 'bathing belle' pictures in newspapers and the regimented leg waving of revue choruses, but regarded Marie Stopes as a filthy-minded eccentric and poor D. H. Lawrence as a menace to society. To these people's self-defensive puritanism, Edgar Wallace offered nothing offensive, nothing disquieting. Negative virtues commend themselves to negatory minds.

Perhaps it also holds true that there is a quality in the contrivances of a lazy mind that appeals to people whose mood is one of reluctance to think. A Wallace book, like any other piece of escapist literature, was bought or borrowed as a means of temporary withdrawal from the demanding, worrying, disappointing world in which the reader normally lived. In that world, there were as many three-dimensional characters as he could cope with; it was a welcome change to be among a two-dimensional variety that required no effort to understand. All the cardboard figures were labelled – hero, heroine, villain, comic manservant, policeman – and so sympathy could be simply and accurately apportioned until the time came at the book's end for it to be collected up again like so much play-money.

As for silliness of plot: its heavy reliance on coincidence, pseudo-scientific devices, unidentified foreign powers, miraculous survival, intuition, and all the other intelligence-defying tricks of the pot-boiling trade – here again, it may be that Wallace offered not an affront but solace of a kind. People were aware in their hearts that the 1914–18 war had solved nothing and that the public optimism of the politicians masked their impotence and perplexity. There was as yet no question of impending catastrophe, but something seemed to have gone sadly wrong with the process of perpetual improvement that had been assumed to be natural law not only by the Victorians but by many of their successors. To read of events reaching a happy conclusion by manifestly *un*natural and illogical means provided relief from the unpleasant feeling of having been let down.

CHAPTER 7

Excitable Sydney Horler

Edgar Wallace was killed quite suddenly by the diabetes which he had unknowingly exacerbated by drinking vast quantities of well-sugared tea throughout every working day. He died in America during a visit in 1931 to help with the film production of one of his stories. The return of his coffined body by sea to Britain was like the home-coming of a dead monarch. The crowds that gathered in tribute to the most popular writer of the century were not to know until later that the king was nominally a pauper. His liabilities, including £58,000 owed to the limited company into which he had turned himself in 1927 as a means of reducing income tax, amounted to £140,000. All these debts were to be either paid or wiped out by negotiation and legal argument by 1937, the year of the formation of a new company, Edgar Wallace Limited, with his copyrights as sole assets and his four children as shareholders.

Soon after Wallace's death, a sale of his furniture and personal belongings was held at the big house he had occupied at Bourne End, Buckinghamshire. Among the bargain hunters and sightseers was a plump, bespectacled, jolly-looking man who might have been taken to be a middle-aged family grocer on a day out. In two articles he displayed special interest and when the auctioneer reached them it was he who outbid everyone else. Sydney Horler, forty-three-year-old crime novelist, had gained possession of the Master's desk and Dictaphone. He was also to acquire, though by somewhat different means, the services of the late author's extraordinarily efficient and long-suffering secretary.

Horler at that time was probably less than half way towards matching Wallace's output, but he enjoyed already the reputation and rewards of a fast and steady producer of popular fiction. Library shelves were packed with brightly jacketed novels bearing the 'Horler for Excitement' slogan. Smith's bookstalls gave his work consistently prominent display. By being serialized in the *News of the World*, it reached the biggest newspaper readership in the country. Horler's own estimate of the number of books he had sold by the early 1930s was two million. Although self-reckoning was not an exercise he pursued with much restraint, even half this figure would have represented a notable achievement.

The buying of the Wallace desk and Dictaphone typified the amiable exhibitionism of a man who never neglected an opportunity of advertising himself. Not long afterwards he was ringing up a London paper with a story about a voice – 'unquestionably' that of the late Edgar – which had interposed itself between two passages of Horler's dictation on a new Dictaphone cylinder. He lent the cylinder to the newspaper as evidence and an account duly appeared on predictable 'back-from-the-dead' lines. This was only one instance of how Horler, himself a former newspaper man, availed himself of a Press as unfailingly accommodating in matters spurious and trivial as it was impervious to news of real significance. An untiring writer of letters to newspapers, he anticipated by many years the modern publicity technique of denying what has not been alleged. His favourite disclaimer concerned 'the mantle of Edgar Wallace', which he declared he had no ambition to assume.

In point of fact, Horler's work owed much more to 'Sapper' than to Wallace. It was breathless, trashy stuff, vitalized by the deeds and chatter of such super-heroes as his Tiger Standish. Standish (the Honourable Timothy Overbury Standish, son of the

Earl of Quorn) could have been Bulldog Drummond's twin brother. He was about thirty years of age, immaculately tailored, broad of shoulder and lean of hip, nearly six feet tall. His nose was slightly askew – 'a relic of a scrap somewhere or other' – and a wide mouth displayed strong, white teeth. 'I tried,' Horler once told a radio audience, 'to endow Standish with all the attributes of a thoroughly likable fellow ... he likes his glass of beer, he is a confirmed pipe-smoker, he is always ready to smile back into the bright eyes of danger ... Standish is not always the soul of courtesy. Just as he has a way with a girl, so he has a way with an enemy. He is speaking now to Aubrey Hamme, the unpleasant piece of work he strangles at the end of *Tiger Standish Comes Back*: "Didn't recognize you at first, but it's Ye Merrie Hammebone, surely? Sorry I didn't notice the frill round your neck. How's your pal Carlimero? Still in hell? And the bloke with the pickled face – let's see, what was his name? Rahusen or something like that?" "You ought to know how Rahusen is," retorts Hamme. "I? Why, I haven't set eyes on the thug since I croaked his junior partner, that stinking Italiano." A terror to his enemies, a hero to his valet and a male-angel to his wife: that's how I like to think of Standish.'

And that, no doubt, is how millions of readers also liked to think of the clean-limbed, virile, no-nonsense sportsman in whom his creator honestly believed he had enshrined the best qualities of his race and class. For Horler was far too serious-minded to have perpetrated Standish as a joke, and much too innocent of cynicism to have devised this or any other character simply to exploit the prejudices and credulity of a mass readership. It is true that he once declared that he had only two missions in life: 'one, to write books, and the other, to see that they bring me in as much money as possible.' But many another bestselling author has made this kind of claim. Candid avowals of love of money are believed to sound endearingly raffish; they must not be taken to indicate lack of sincerity in these writers' work. Horler's personal convictions were no different from those proclaimed in his books. That they happened also to be shared by his readers, his sales proved.

What makes Horler an especially rewarding subject of study in relation to the ideas that prevailed in large sections of British society between the wars is the fact that he was more voluble, more anxious to put his opinions on record, than any other non-intellectual writer of the period. Not content with allowing characters in well over a hundred novels to echo his notions, he was forever sending declamatory and argumentative letters to newspapers and to individuals. Those that editors declined to print – probably for fear of libel actions – Horler unashamedly worked into one or another of the collections of self-revealing snippets that he published from time to time in book form under such titles as *Strictly Personal* and *More Strictly Personal*.

Surveying his own field of authorship, Horler professed to see little of worth. He considered that far too many novels were being written by 'half-baked Oxford undergraduates, man-obsessed old maids, homosexuals with polished periods, and pin-heads of all descriptions'.

D. H. Lawrence he regarded as a 'pathological case, a consumptive who was driven by his disease to write about sex'. The experiment of reading *Lady Chatterley's Lover* in the unexpurgated edition, Horler said, had made him retch. 'If that was art, then every sanitary inspector should be able to turn out a literary classic.' Nothing could have surprised him less than the assertion by a friend returned from Monte Carlo that Lawrence was 'loathed by every decent-minded person on the French Riviera'.

Michael Arlen he dismissed as 'the only Armenian who never tried to sell me a carpet'.

Proust was 'the neurotic and probably decadent Frenchman who worked in a cork-lined room, and whose habits and views on life are naturally abhorrent to most healthy human beings'.

Three lines of a prose work by Aubrey Beardsley had been enough to give him the urge to be violently sick. 'Even for a genius smitten by tuberculosis, Aubrey had a mind like a sink: it was a mercy, I think, that he did not continue to live to perpetrate further ghastly obscenities.'

Horler's horror of explicit sexuality may appear from these comments to have been obsessive, but it must be remembered that when an exactly similar attitude was displayed by police, magistrates, and the Home Office in relation to books and works of art – as it frequently was during the 1920s and 1930s – the public as a whole was acquiescent.

Writers whom Horler admired included A. E. W. Mason, his favourite; 'Sapper' and Wallace, his models; John Buchan, J. B. Priestley and P. G. Wodehouse. Valentine Williams, a prolific producer of spy stories and thrillers, impressed him as a creator of masterpieces; but John Dickson Carr, specialist in sealed room mysteries, 'bewildered' him. Of Dorothy L. Sayers ('that industrious woman') his opinion was low until she wrote a derogatory notice of one of his own books, when it plunged to a depth at which expression was no longer possible. American writers who won his approbation were Harold MacGrath, S. S. van Dine and Earl Derr Biggers, but he thought the crime fiction of their compatriots – Dashiell Hammett in particular – 'crude to the point of mental disgust'.

Horler once declared that he would rather be read in Wapping than in Bloomsbury. The psychological novel, 'with its problems and soul-searching', made no appeal to him and he said that writing sensation fiction was a trick the highbrows were incapable of pulling off. 'Their stuff doesn't thrill, it merely twitters.' But . . . 'give me a pretty girl, a likable young man, a Bentley sports car and a spot of trouble round the corner – then I'm working at my trade'.

Two qualifications Horler would have insisted upon: that the pretty girl be adequately dressed, and that the young man possess an unquestionably heterosexual disposition. Modesty of women's clothing was a question on which Horler felt as strongly as any of those hundreds of people who seem to have had nothing to do after 1930 but write to newspapers about carnally provocative fashions. He was distressed when J. Jefferson Farjeon, author of historical romances, complained in a review of one of Horler's books that the heroine was 'too rapid'.

'I like my heroines to be peppy,' retorted Horler. 'If they could be induced to give one their confidence, they would all be found to wear what the Americans, with their marvellous slang, call "scanties" – winter and summer.' But when a man stopped him in the Strand in order to pursue the subject, he 'had to tell him that, whilst my heroines might be peppy, they were invariably pure'. And later that summer Horler was siding with those spectators at an Eastbourne tennis match who publicly showed their disapproval of a girl player's shorts.

One of his last recorded pronouncements on female exposure suggested some mellowing of attitude. He congratulated the *News Chronicle* on its 'Open-air Girls, 1934' competition and declared that some of the entrants were charming examples of the 'thoroughbred' Englishwoman, with whom there was no one in the world to compare.

Homosexuality, according to Horler, was rife in the London of 1932. He urged that it was high time for Scotland Yard to tackle 'the alarming increase of sex perversion' in the capital. Whilst on his way to call on Mr Matheson Lang, the actor, he had been accosted three times by male prostitutes in Wardour Street. 'At least ten youths with painted faces and peculiarly cut clothes' had been in evidence, to say nothing of a 'clergyman with rouged cheeks'. Two years later, the situation had not improved, apparently, but at least Horler had managed – during an exploratory tour of the underworld for the London *Star* – to discover a root cause. 'An authority' whom he consulted 'blamed in part the public schools and told me some amazing facts'.

The aggressive masculinity with which Horler and his fellow thriller writers endowed their heroes may well have been found reassuring by a generation that war had sadly depleted of young males. He himself was clearly anxious, for whatever reason, to be identified with his Tiger Standish. 'Yes,' he mused, 'a pipe, a dog and a golf club: if you want to win the heart of a man, give him one of these. And when I say a man, I mean a *man* – not one of these emasculated cigarette smokers.' He declared that the thought of Ivor Novello made him groan with despair.

All this may sound like parody, but so do many of the sincere protestations of an age not yet far enough removed in time for its ideas to cause us no embarrassment. Effeminacy was not only regarded as something absolutely reprehensible in itself; it was felt in some strange way to lurk within other things of which one disapproved. Eventually, advertising and the spread of habit removed the stigma from cigarettes, but minority tastes that failed to qualify for commercial promotion – from vegetarianism to classical music – continued to be linked in many minds with unmanliness. 'Sissy' was a useful, because nebulously emotive, word with which disparage anything not shared or not understood.

Even Bernard Shaw, whose beard at least was the antithesis of femininity, did not escape the dislike of the plain dealing, plain thinking Little Man. Was it, perhaps, because his high degree of articulacy was, like most intellectual attainments, considered 'sissy'? Horler knew only that the mere sight of Shaw's photograph in a newspaper was enough to rouse him to a state of fury. 'He ought to be severely suppressed,' he wrote of this man whose 'megalomania has induced him to cut grotesque capers at an age when he is much too old not to know better.' No one had asked Shaw to come to England, and yet, having been welcomed, all he did by way of gratitude was to scoff 'at our religion, our laws, the traditions which we admire and do our best to uphold'.

Shaw, of course, was a great irritant of complacent people – as he had set out to be. His cleverness puzzled and therefore infuriated; it was promptly labelled 'sarcasm' and as such could be discounted. A fondness for appearing in a state of near-nudity on beaches, where he invariably was photographed by journalistic pilot-fish, also offended a good many folk. The fact that he was a kindly, generous man, whose wit disguised the fallibility of his opinions, would not, even if it had been generally known, have much modified their view of him as an atheistic, meddlesome, unpatriotic old faddist. England had reached that stage of religious decline and imperial decay when people who no longer went to church or seriously believed in the efficacy of gunboats were fiercely resentful of being complimented on their loss of faith. The casting of slurs on religion was a highly risky business, as novelists and playwrights learned to their cost as soon as they were tactless enough to put clearly into words the widely, if guiltily sensed deficiencies of the established creed. Significant was the choice of a bishop, not a politician, to set off the chain of events designed to remove the awkwardly disposed Edward VIII from the throne in 1936.

Aware of their public's spiritual perplexity, the writers of leisure fiction took care to side with the angels. Just as the majority of crime novels had blatantly nationalistic overtones, such religious sentiments as their characters occasionally expressed were of an order that even the most sensitive of Britain's non-practising Christians would approve. Horler was one author who did not need to dissemble in this matter (unlike the writer he so much admired, A. E. W. Mason, who had to borrow a prayer book from his chauffeur's wife whenever he wished to play squire in the church near his country estate) for Horler had only to hear a broadcast of the wedding of the Duke of Kent to Princess Marina to be moved to eulogy:

'I have just listened to the finest utterance of the English language I think I have ever heard: the address of the Archbishop of Canterbury to the Royal couple ... His Grace must have been inspired to speak such truly noble and surpassingly beautiful words.'

In general, though, he and his fellows were too busy following up that 'spot of trouble round the corner' to act as guides to the restful plateau of high-mindedness. This was a job for a full-time professional and there was no shortage of those in Fleet Street, where proprietors collected James Douglases and Godfrey Winns like Belshazzar collecting soothsayers. Nor did crime writers bother their readers' heads with any political issue more complicated than the unspecified machinations of this or that 'foreign', and therefore malevolent, power. Horler considered pacifist novelists to be wasting their time and their talents. 'I don't think a hundred thousand Storm Jamesons are likely to change human nature, and as long as human nature is human nature there will always be the possibility of another war.'

Acceptance of the intractability of 'human nature' was one of the favourite refuges of the time. It provided simultaneously shelter from unpleasant facts, defence against troublesome argument and, not least, a philosophical screen to dignify poverty of thought.

Writer of innumerable Thrillers. "I'M NOT REALLY BOTHERED ABOUT ALL THE STUFF YOU'RE TAKING AWAY. WHAT GETS ME DOWN IS THAT

CHAPTER 8

The Golden Age of detective fiction

The years between 1920 and 1939 have been called the 'Golden Age of the Detective Story'. Quantitatively, the definition is just. Novels of detection flowed from the presses month after month, year after year, in an ever-increasing tide. The appetite for them seemed to be insatiable. Here was no passing fashion; the weekly ration of whodunnits came to be one of the staples of life for thousands of middle-class families. Housewives brought it home in the shopping basket as conscientiously as they remembered to renew the family supplies of bread and sugar.

A surprisingly high proportion of professional people and academics was similarly addicted. Mrs Q. D. Leavis discerned a 'highbrow cult' – as well she might, for by 1930 it had become respectable for literary critics and essayists to write about detective fiction, and even for a don or two to turn out thrillers on their own account. Father Ronald Knox was a notable contributor until he deferred to church superiors who were unhappy lest such activity be construed as trespass on diabolical prerogative. Other intellectuals whose liking for the construction of detective stories led to their becoming familiar library names included G. K. Chesterton, inventor of Father Brown; the economist

G. D. H. Cole and his wife, Margaret; Cecil Day Lewis, Poet Laureate-to-be; Dr Alington, the Dean of Durham; and an Oxford don, J. I. M. Stewart, alias Michael Innes.

By the end of the period, detective fiction was accounting for one quarter of all new novels published in the English language. It seemed that a literary formula had been perfected of which the public, both in Britain and in America, would never tire. Psychologists and social historians were puzzled then and have remained puzzled by a habit so peculiarly persistent as to appear almost immune from the influences of circumstance and fashion.

The style of the detective story was not greatly different in 1939 from what it had been twenty or thirty years before. The work of old hands such as R. Austin Freeman, J. S. Fletcher and Freeman Wills Crofts, some of which pre-dated the first world war, was still being read avidly on the eve of the second. The popularity of Conan Doyle, enormous by the time his last new story was published in 1927, never flagged thereafter. Nor were the classic originators, Edgar Allan Poe and Wilkie Collins, ever relegated to the status of venerable curiosities: people continued to read them for entertainment, despite their wordy portentousness. Indeed, the passing of time invested the older detective novels with a kind of nostalgic charm that compensated for their loss of capacity to thrill. No one today would marvel at the revelations afforded by Dr John Thorndyke's microscope, but many might be pleasurably intrigued by the peaceful and predictable world in which Freeman shows him preparing his slides.

Austin Freeman, Fletcher, Crofts, H. C. Bailey, John Rhode, E. C. R. Lorac – all these were typical members of the small army of industrious craftsmen on whom chiefly depended the satisfaction of the demand for detective fiction between the wars. It was a job for full-time writers in whom a capacity for steady output of variations on an accepted theme was more important than liveliness of style or wealth of characterization. Their plots tended to be mechanical, with much emphasis on time-tables and geographical layout. The practice of inserting meticulously drawn ground plans eventually became a joke and had to be abandoned, but some plots were so complicated and their authors so weak on description that pictorial aid was essential. Clues, too, played a considerably greater part in the standard form of detective novel of the period than later readers would have patience to bear with. Lives did literally hang by single hairs (identifiable, of course, as uniquely associated with a breed of rabbit in a part of Dorset lately visited by the murderer) and it was not uncommon for a book's solution to turn upon such nice points of knowledge as the construction date of Brooklyn Bridge or the size of mesh in a bee keeper's veil.

While the established professionals were milling out acceptable self-repetitions, the market continued to expand at such a rate that practically anyone capable of knocking together some sort of a plot based on homicide could get the result published. Almost as many people turned to crime-writing as to keeping poultry or starting mushroom farms. Authorship required smaller capital investment, and the public was less fastidious about the freshness of plots than of eggs. Also there was something tremendously attractive in the idea of the independent life that writing was popularly supposed to make possible. One might have to wait a year or two before anchoring one's yacht alongside those of Mason, Oppenheim and Arnold Bennett, or even equalling John Buchan's £9,000 a year, but in the meantime there was always that country cottage and the respectful glance of the postman as he handed over the envelope containing one's monthly (would it be monthly?) royalty cheque.

In no other field of literature was there a comparable influx of hopeful newcomers. Most of them dropped out again after a brief flare of inventiveness and the shock of learning that its reward was a once-and-for-all payment of between twenty and fifty pounds. Others followed and were eclipsed in turn. A small minority persevered and proved to have the productive capacity necessary for success.

While demand matched and even exceeded supply, it was not to be expected that the general standard of detective fiction should be high. Publishers had early adopted the practice of marketing these stories in a form easily recognizable by booksellers, library buyers, and members of the public. Jackets were of a more or less standard character, their common features being crude colour, ill-designed type, and the display, often in defiance of a book's actual contents, of a sprawled corpse in expensive-looking clothes. The inclusion of a weapon of some kind (not necessarily that mentioned in the story) was another pictorial convention, curiously wrought oriental daggers and great liquorice-coloured automatics being top favourites.

Insistence upon titles unmistakably suggestive of criminality was stock policy, one unsought consequence of which was the occasional suspicion in some readers' minds that they were being offered the same novel over and over again. And so, in a sense, they were. As time went on with no sign of a slackening in the boom, the trade conception of detective fiction became increasingly that of a mere commodity to be produced with as much haste and as little discrimination as possible.

Book reviewers settled into an attitude of good-natured, if slightly supercilious, tolerance. They, too, had fallen in with the notion of detective stories being in a class quite separate from 'legitimate' literature and therefore not subject to the ordinary rules of criticism. Editors provided a segregated hutch for mystery novels, where they could be dealt with, a whole litter of twenty or thirty at a time, by means of a sentence apiece. There was evolved for this purpose a special style of reviewmanship. It was (and is) slightly facetious in flavour, crisp and insubstantial, like lettuce. It revealed singularly little about the books and although in most cases this was a blessing for their authors, the rare novel of quality was likely to suffer the injustice of exactly similar treatment simply because it happened to treat of crime.

Librarians unwittingly performed a like disservice to the few writers in the field who believed that if a book of any kind was worth writing it was worth writing well. Assuming that addiction to thrillers, like addiction to drink, impaired its victims' selective faculties and sense of direction, they put the stuff all together on easily accessible shelves.

The result of the combination of forced production, ama-

Modern Publisher. "I LIKE YOUR BOOK ON WATER-BEETLES ; BUT COULDN'T
U CONTRIVE SOMEHOW TO INTRODUCE A DETECTIVE INTEREST ?"

teurism, segregation and suspended criticism during this 'Golden Age' was the literary equivalent of the jerry-building of the same period. Nine out of ten detective stories were as shoddy and derivative as the rows of semi-villas that ribboned out to accommodate their readers. Perhaps a dozen or so talented craftsmen – whom over-reverent jobbing critics were fond of terming 'masters of the genre' – contributed a steady supply of reasonably well-written and convincingly plotted stories. An even smaller number, novelists or poets in their own right, turned to detective fiction partly for their own amusement and partly to profit from a wider readership. The others – the great majority of detective story writers – were third-class passengers on a very capacious band-wagon. It was they whom Raymond Chandler had in mind when he wrote in *The Simple Art of Murder*: 'The average detective story is probably no worse than the average novel, but you never see the average novel. It doesn't get published.'

Chandler had a special entitlement to pronounce judgement on *The Golden Age*. Although an American, he had been educated in England and understood the temperament, humour and social peculiarities of its people. He had a sound knowledge of English literature and could be objective enough in his Californian remove to see that 'the English may not always be the best writers in the world, but they are incomparably the best dull writers'. Only an Englishman, or an American familiar with the wry self-deprecation of the English, could have written that. Chandler himself never produced a dull line, but America between the wars was heavily dependent upon the imported detective novel and when he began to write about crime and criminals with 'the authentic flavour of life as it is lived', he was flouting conventions that had equal force on both sides of the Atlantic. Indeed it was America that proved to be the more obdurately devoted to the old, unreal formula that had served almost every mystery writer from the days of Doyle, not excluding America's own S. S. Van Dine, Mary Roberts Rinehart and Earl Derr Biggers. Chandler's novels entailed the replacement of myth and assumption with fact and perception, of pasteboard figures with live characters, of tritely worked out artificial puzzles with human problems that violence might change but could never solve. Such a challenge to the law according to Doyle, Christie and Sayers might be supposed to have found readier approval in the United States, the location of Bay City, than among the compatriots of Lord Peter Wimsey, yet from the first, Chandler's books sold much more quickly to the British public than to the American. It would be interesting to know if twenty years' consumption of middle-class fantasy fiction on the theme 'God's in his heaven; all's well at the Yard' had left the British, who had had no Al Capone, in greater need of an astringent than the Americans.

Dorothy L. Sayers was, in the opinion of many earnest examiners of the detective story, the most accomplished practitioner in the field. She had a world-wide reputation based on fewer than a dozen carefully written, fairly long novels of considerable complexity. Throughout the 1930s, the Press treated her as the supreme oracle on crime fiction, to which she brought the academic approach of an honours graduate of Somerville College, Oxford.

Here is Chandler on Sayers: 'Her kind of detective story was an arid formula which could not even satisfy its own implications. It was second-grade literature because it was not about the things that could make first-grade literature. If it started out to be about real people ... they must very soon do unreal things in order to form the artificial pattern required by the plot. When they did unreal things, they ceased to be real themselves. They became puppets and cardboard lovers and papier-mâché villains and detectives of exquisite and impossible gentility.'

If Miss Sayers was guilty as charged, there would be no point in entering a plea on behalf of the hundreds of contemporary authors of lesser reputation who employed exactly the same methods. Chandler was not seriously exaggerating when he declared that 'the only reality the English detection writers knew was the conversational accent of Surbiton and Bognor Regis'. In book after book they appear – the diffident, decent young pipe-smokers; the plucky girls with flower-like complexions; the wooden policemen,

slow but reliable; the assorted house-party guests, forever dressing
for dinner or hunting missing daggers; the aristocrats concealing
their enormous intellects beneath a veneer of asininity; the ubiqui-
tous chauffeurs, butlers, housemaids and the rest of the lower
orders, all comic, surly or sinister, but none quite human. The
world they inhabit is self-contained and never changing. We are
shown the same flats in Half Moon Street, the same Tudor mansions half-an-hour's Bentley ride from town, with the same libraries and studies, the same french windows opening upon the
same lawns. There is no deviation from time-honoured behaviour.
All the characters are regular churchgoers, if only to reinforce
their alibis. Meal-times are scrupulously observed even when the
host lies transfixed or garrotted (no murder is ever committed in a
dining-room). The hours of darkness are strictly for sleep or crime,
never for sex. Even violence itself, the books' reason for being, is
somehow conformist, limited, unreal. A bullet-hole almost invariably is 'neat' (as a putt in golf, perhaps?) while scarcely a knife
is on record that has not been embedded tidily between shoulder-
blades. Blood is generally a 'spreading stain' or a 'pool', both
fastidious expressions that convey nothing of the terrible glistening
mess that is made by human butchery.

The air of tennis-club amateur dramatics which pervades the
work of this school of crime writing can only be appreciated by
direct sampling. The following extracts are from one of the multitudinous 'average' detective novels of the period, *The Moorcroft
Manor Mystery*, by Ralph Trevor.

'She is rather wonderful,' Sinclair owned. 'I have heard her
described as one of the most efficient women in the whole of
London. She possesses a perfect genius for marshalling the
requisite ingredients for a successful house-party.'

The subject is the hostess, a titled society woman. A genuine tribute is intended: hence the bombastic prose of the second sentence, which seems to the author to be proper to the description of
a knowledgeable upper class person. No one would really talk like

this, but how else would readers be persuaded that they are in the presence of elegance?

A trim maid entered with tea, deliciously fresh-brewed, with toasted scones heaped with half-molten butter.

Further evidence of the Good Life. Buttered scones, without a preliminary of bread, are symptomatic of privilege. The adjective 'trim' is significant; it effectively de-humanizes the servant while suggesting her mistress's selective good taste.

'Mr Merrivale? I seem to have heard the name before. Do you think I've met him in London? Lady Forrester didn't mention him particularly. I must have overlooked his name in the list of guests.'

'Merrivale' is a name exactly in the tradition of tennis-club literature, where no one ever is called Ramsbottom or Golightly or Snagg. The right note, too, is struck by 'Lady Forrester' – who, it will be noted, gives parties so often and to so many people that the guests actually have to be catalogued.

In the sudden resuscitation of conversation that followed Lady Forrester's remarks, the matter vanished from his cogitation.

This sort of statement reminds readers that they are in the company of distinguished people, whose extraordinary vocabulary they are flatteringly implied to understand.

It was a short-handled dagger, undoubtedly Spanish in origin and, judging by the perforated fetter-lock on the blade, probably belonged to the sixteenth century. The tapering hilt was exquisitely chased and surmounted by a monogram.

More reader flattery here. It is pleasant to be given credit for recondite knowledge of armoury, when in fact one could not tell a poniard from an ice-pick.

'Sir John Forrester has many friends at Scotland Yard.' 'Sir John Forrester, did you say, sir?' The sergeant's tone had undergone a curious change. 'I'd no idea he was so important, sir. Really, I hadn't. I hope I haven't given any offence, sir?'

The idea that people of substance could, and did, treat the police as their personal servants was widespread in England up to the second world war. That there was substance for it is not now denied; but what comes as something of a surprise is the approval of the situation which many crime-writers of the time seem to have assumed in their readers.

It was discovered that Merrivale had for some months previously been living considerably in excess of the allowance due to him under the terms of his father's will. After his daily legal duties at the Temple were over he sought distraction in a whirlwind of social gaiety. He was then a member of the Three Star Club, which as you know, has a reputation for its high stakes at bridge . . . Merrivale became involved in the toils of a moneylender.

Living beyond one's means was something that struck terror into the middle-class soul – as well it might, for at the bottom of that slippery slope was the awful pinch-and-save dwelling-place of Those in Reduced Circumstances, perhaps the most pathetic section of British society. Merrivale's fate had special implications of tragedy that would not be lost upon the reader. Not only had he been impoverished by the most respectable of card games, but he had then cast off his last shred of decency by having recourse to a usurer.

'He grasped my wrists and tried to draw me towards him in an attempt to kiss me, but I was strong and I freed myself just as his face was nearing my own. Oh! it was horrible . . . Then I ran from the room and locked myself in my bedroom until cook came back.' 'The cad! The mean, despicable cad!' exclaimed Sinclair, his hands clenched and his lips pressed into a thin, bloodless line.

The Victorian 'worse than death' fixation persisted despite the moral laxity that was characteristic of the decade after 1918, but it was now to be found mainly in the middle and lower-middle classes. Drug-taking, alcoholism, promiscuity and hooliganism were almost exclusively diversions of the well-born. The above passage may, therefore, appear anachronistic, for it is wealthy people who are being written about. The inconsistency is a small matter compared with the need to confirm and approve the *reader's* moral attitude by giving him characters who share it.

> Helen, her eyes suspiciously moist and a lump in her throat, arose from her chair and held out a small, slim white hand towards him. Sinclair took it in his own, and for a brief moment their eyes met. Then she hurried from the room . . .
> . . . That chair over there where she had sat: now it was invested with the gold of romance. A sense of spiritual sanctity pervaded it. For ever in Sinclair's eyes, it would be hallowed.

Hack sentimentality of this order was a common ingredient of detective novels. Purists objected. Somerset Maugham, in his definition of an ideal detective story, firmly ruled out love interest. But many authors, including Edgar Wallace, persistently admitted it. They possibly were well aware that family reading was generally chosen by women.

> Endsleigh Gardens, seldom the scene of any very great amount of activity, were more deserted than ever. Many of the well-built houses had their linen blinds drawn over every window, for few folk who can arrange otherwise ever remain in town over the Christmas holidays, and Endsleigh Gardens is peopled by those who have been well served by the Goddess of Fortune. Many of them preferred to pass the winter on the Riviera . . . others had 'little places' somewhere in Scotland, while those less fortunate had to be content to remain at home.

In the last category of course, were the readers of this kind of book. They seem never to have tired of living vicariously what they were led to believe was the life of those 'well served by the Goddess of Fortune'. British films and plays of the period, almost

without exception, also presented with tediously repetitious doggedness the supposed world of the 1.8% of the adult population
who in 1936 owned two-thirds of all private property in the
nation.

'Bless your 'eart, sir! Didn't I just say that the Missus 'ud do
anything for you? I'll go up and tell 'er now, sir, and I'd like to
bet that you'll be 'aving something in less than 'arf a jiffy.'

Typographical resources must have been severely strained by
the demands of detective story-writers anxious to give vocal reality
to their characters from the lower orders. It seems a pity that so
huge an outlay of apostrophes was wasted on the painful parodies
that were the best that Mr Trevor – or Miss Sayers and Mrs
Christie for that matter – could produce in imitation of working-
class speech. Once again, though, it was an attitude of mind rather
than regard for actuality that their writing displayed.

'Hands up,' rang out the stern order, and Helen, hearing the
familiar voice of Superintendent Nelson, felt herself slipping
away against her will into oblivion. The tension had been more
than her overwrought nerves could withstand, and Nature,
knowing best, had prescribed a natural sedative.

Slipping into oblivion used to be one of the hardest worked
devices in crime fiction. It was a convenient method of disposing
of unwanted time. Four ways of depriving a character of con-
sciousness were then common: a knock on the head, a doped
drink, a chloroformed pad and – for women – swooning with
terror or relief. Only the first two are now considered legitimate.
One of the biggest mysteries of mystery-writing between 1920 and
1940 was the amount of chloroform assumed to be available to the
general run of criminals. The prevalence of fainting among female
characters is more easily accounted for. It is clear from the advertising and the magazine correspondence columns of the time that
the establishment of electoral equality in 1928 had done singularly
little to dissuade men – or their wives, either – from clinging to the

notion that every woman lived in constant peril of flaking out, particularly at 'those worrying times of the month'.

'Go in and win her,' said Merrivale, huskily. 'She's yours, old man – always has been.'

Compare these clipped sentences with the earlier examples of conversational style. Emotion is here at work, reducing articulacy to a minimum. It is interesting to note that, from 'Sapper' onwards, crime novelists were liable to fall back on this curiously military mode of expression whenever deep feelings were supposed to have been aroused. Many, of course, had been through the 1914–18 war themselves. What seems to a later generation to be a slightly comic affectation might well have been a defensive mannerism born of an experience so appalling that it rendered millions emotionally emasculated.

CHAPTER 9

The Orientation of Villainy

Real life is disobliging. People like to think, or feel, in black and white. Having to assess the relative values of all those intermediate greys is tiresome and perplexing. So fiction, if it is to be easily understood and therefore popular, must offer the clearest delineation between 'good' and 'bad'. An extreme example of this uncompromising polarity was the stage melodrama of the Victorian Age. Audiences at presentations of *The Silver King, Maria Marten* and *Sweeney Todd* had not the slightest difficulty in deciding whom to cheer and whom to boo. Scarcely less specific directions were offered in the novels, novelettes and serials written primarily for money. Even so masterly a writer as Dickens, rich in vocabulary and visual imagination, used only primary colours in his portraiture of character.

Early crime fiction was simply melodrama in print. It embodied all the declamatory phraseology of the barn-stormers, with 'horrids' a-plenty and a 'dreadful' on every page. This special language of the shilling shocker – and it was common also, we might remember, to newspaper reporting until less than fifty years ago – was doubtless evolved in the first place as a means of gaining attention by frightening people. But so crude a technique cannot long have sustained its effect. Having been told a dozen times that a crime (or 'deed' – the preferred word in the terminology of sensation) was 'horrible', the simplest-minded reader must have ceased to respond with the intended tremor. Unfortunately, writers of popular fiction tend to be extremely conservative craftsmen. Their pleasant surprise at the success of anything that has worked once hardens overnight into dogmatic reliance. And so, well into the twentieth century crime literature continued to be laden with emotive adjectives and portentous synonyms that long since had ceased to scare anybody.

The Conan Doyle stories contain innumerable examples. Every murder Holmes investigates is dutifully dubbed 'foul' or 'brutal' or 'terrible' – as if to distinguish it from a fair, or elegant killing or from one occasioned by good-natured caprice. A blow is seen to have been 'frightful' and its victim 'unfortunate'. The bicycle in *The Adventure of the Priory School* is 'horribly' smeared with blood, while the agitated secretary has 'a face with horror in every lineament'. The duke of the same story, his duplicity revealed, turns not white but 'ghastly' white. Of course, all this is accepted today as characteristic Watsonian garnish. It is part of the fun that sophisticated readers derive from Doyle; part of the atmosphere cherished by successive generations of devotees. The fact remains that the creator of Sherlock Holmes was as ready as any of his penny-a-line contemporaries to lay hand to the hackneyed phrase in order to labour the obvious. A great entertainer he may have been, but he was a third-rate writer.

Why did the reading public continue to tolerate a heavy-handed style of depicting conflict between good and evil for so long after its counterpart on the stage had become unacceptable? Books were still being written and eagerly bought in the 1920s and 1930s which were only slightly less gauche in tone than *East Lynne*. Thus Horler, as late as 1939:

. . . the man in the mask spoke again. 'Tell me how it happened, Otto,' he said. The other worked his face into a series of horrible grimaces. 'It was easy enough,' he replied. 'The fool was asleep and I soon settled him.' For evidence he pulled from a sheath a long knife the blade of which was coated with a thick red smear, and placed it on the desk.

Part of the answer lies in the essential difference between literature and drama, the difference between private and public enjoyment. Apart from the special case of the theatre of the absurd, false or exaggerated emotion on the stage embarrasses and ultimately alienates an audience. The playgoer feels his intelligence and knowledge of life underrated. The confrontation is direct, and public; the many individual members of the audience who really would like to respond to crude emotional appeal (as they unhesitatingly do during a 'tear-jerking' film in the dark secrecy of the cinema) are inhibited by it. Those same people have no difficulty, in the sealed-off world of a book, in suspending criticism of style as readily as they suspend disbelief in the plot, so as to escape more completely from the pains and preoccupations of real life.

The villain of the old melodrama was identifiable at his very first appearance. He wore the face of wickedness and spoke in the approved accents of his kind. He was the Devil of the miracle plays with tail and horns concealed by frock-coat and top hat. The costume was significant. In the eyes of Victorian labourers and artisans it was the uniform of the man they believed they had most cause to hate – the man who, by reason of advantages of birth, education or wealth, was able to cheat them. He was generally a lawyer or a landlord. The distinction between him and them was one of calling or of station in life; no political issue was in question. And the cause of conflict had to be immediate and personal – a seduction, a piece of legal sharp practice, a fraud or injustice of some kind. Such matters were either within the experience of the audience or easily appreciable at second hand. In these plays there was nothing explicit for the comfort of a Karl Marx. Despite the inevitable indication of class differences, melodrama expressed no broad popular revolt, only fear and dislike as between individuals, dramatized in a moralistic way. Landlords, lawyers and financiers as such were not pilloried, only 'bad' ones. Nevertheless, the theme was repeated too often to allow any doubt of the audience's deep instinctive distrust of all who seemed to have manipulated their way into power over ordinary folk.

These performances were rather like burnings in effigy. They did members of the audience good by enabling them to discharge resentment of exploitation. The exploiters probably benefited too, if only indirectly. Booing the image of a landlord was preferable, from the landlord's point of view, to physical assaults upon real ones. But catharsis of a more generalized kind was involved. A pleasant feeling came from ranging oneself on the side of right against wrong, especially when it was easy to recognize which was which. Subtle, complicated or ambiguous wickedness would not serve this purpose. The villain had to be larger than life, and he had to act out in an obvious and familiar way social behaviour of which the audience disapproved.

Much the same convention is discernible in crime fiction from the mid-nineteenth century until the second world war. But because the readers and borrowers of books were predominantly middle-class, portraiture of evil required different models from those that aroused the enthusiastic hostility of poorer people. A civil servant or a bank clerk had too regular a salary and too thrifty a nature to be in much danger of incurring an eviction warrant. The doctor's wife whose dinner party guests occasionally included a solicitor was unlikely to feel implacable hatred for the legal profession. Nor were middle-class virgins commonly exposed to the attention of feckless young aristocrats: they did not work in ducal kitchens, and even if one had been 'got into trouble' by a sprig of the quality, her parents would have been more likely to try and force the acquisition of a titled son-in-law than to turn a daughter from their doors.

Who, then, were candidates for the role of villain in the escapist literature chiefly favoured by the respectable, comfortably-off middle section of society – the crime thriller and the detective story? The answer must tell something about the way such people thought, what they feared and what they despised.

At once a complication arises. The traditional detective story had no villain, only a murderer. And because the murderer's identity had to remain unrevealed to the very end of the book, it was necessary to hide his true character. The mystery, the puzzle, was what mattered, and in the interests of prolonging that mystery the behaviour of all the people concerned was understood to be potentially a sham. The game of bluff and double-bluff reached its most convoluted, and in a literary sense its most inane form, with the development of the 'least likely person' technique. No novel conceived on these lines could present in one character a set of qualities hateful to the reader. That would have given the game away. So the necessary identification of the author's attitudes with those of his public had to be accomplished in less direct ways. Some writers injected opinions into narrative. Others put them into the mouths of minor participants who did not qualify as suspects. A favourite method was to introduce a character with the sole function of appearing ridiculously or odiously at odds with accepted standards. Perhaps the most regrettable device, employed frequently by Dorothy Sayers, among others, was the description of an idiosyncratic detective 'humorously' taking a rise out of someone of another race or of different social loyalties.

No such circuitous means needed to be adopted by writers of thrillers of action, pure and simple. Their books often were published within the general 'mystery' category, but in fact there was about as much mystery in their plots as there is novelty in the contents of most packets marked 'new'. They depended for their appeal, which was much wider than that of detective stories, upon fast-moving events, exciting situations and colourful, not to say preposterous, characterization. Love interest was in order, so long as it did not hold up the action; and a descriptive purple patch or two might be interspersed between the fights and chases to convey exotic atmosphere. There was something boyishly exuberant about these novels and their enormous popularity testified to the readiness of most people, however sophisticated they may have liked to consider themselves, to surrender occasionally to their vestigial instincts of childhood.

Children know a bogeyman when they see one. He is a materialization of their own fears and antipathies. As they grow up in a world hostile to childish fancies, their belief in a personal bogeyman fades but there remains a need to objectify fear. Nothing is more distressing than to be unable to ascribe a cause to life's annoyances and setbacks. In extreme cases, the sufferer is liable to lose hold of reality altogether and to believe himself the victim of persecution by nameless beings armed with 'rays' or by conspirators from another planet, hovering invisible over his house. This sort of delusion is different only in degree from the very common persuasion that all one's troubles are somehow attributable to the political party in power, teenage indiscipline, immigration, water fluoridization, the Jews, television or Russia.

C. Day Lewis, in his introduction to *Murder for Pleasure*, by Howard Haycraft, associated the increase in the volume of crime fiction with the decline of religion after the death of Victoria. He suggested that the sacrificial aspect of religion was a continuation of primitive man's transference of communal guilt to the scapegoat, and pointed out that the pattern of the detective novel was as highly formalized as religious ritual. It embodied sin (the crime), its victim, a high priest (the criminal) and resolution by higher power (the detective). The action thriller does not lend itself to quite the same interpretation, for its villain could more truly be said to occupy the role of scapegoat than high priest. It is he – a reincarnation of the child's bogeyman – in whom the reader is invited to discern the causes of his unease, and with whose ultimate punishment or destruction he may feel those causes to have been removed.

Perhaps the most extravagant invention in the long gallery of crime fiction's bogeyman-villains is Fu-Manchu, the Oriental devil-doctor created by Sax Rohmer.

Of him it has been fitly said that he had a brow like Shakespeare and a face like Satan. Something serpentine, hypnotic, was in his very presence ... He came forward with an indescribable gait, cat-like yet awkward, carrying his high shoulders almost hunched. He placed the lantern in a niche in the wall never turning away the reptilian gaze of those eyes which must haunt my dreams for ever. They possessed a viridescence which hitherto I had only supposed possible in the eye of a cat ... I had never supposed, prior to meeting Fu-Manchu, that so intense a force of malignancy could radiate from any human being.

The original *Mystery of Doctor Fu-Manchu* appeared in 1913 and for the next thirty years sequels continued to be published in response to steady demand. They varied little from the prototype and the only serious problem they would seem to have presented their author was the devising, with every book, of some explanation of how the doctor had managed to escape the end so graphically described in the previous one. Rohmer, however, was sufficiently audacious a melodramatist to be able to make short work of such matters. When he ran out of ingenuity, he unashamedly improvised with a casual reference to 'certain methods that defy Western science' or to 'a secret of which Fu-Manchu alone was the master'.

The plots, such as they are, of the Fu-Manchu novels would be quite meaningless in paraphrase. They are a jumble of incredible encounters, pursuits, traps and escapes. Who is trying to accomplish what, and why – this is never explained. All that seems certain is that a titanic struggle is being waged by a man called Nayland Smith to thwart the designs of Fu-Manchu.

At last they truly were face to face – the head of the great Yellow movement, and the man who fought on behalf of the entire white race ...

Smith is in some unspecified way an agent of the British Government, whose interests he once served in Burma, Egypt and certain other countries. The police appear to be at his command and even an inspector must expect Smith to address him somewhat peremptorily:

'Too late!' rapped my friend. 'Jump in a taxi and pick up two good men to leave for China at once! Then go and charter a

116 · *Snobbery with Violence*

special train to Tilbury to leave in twenty-five minutes. Order another cab to wait outside for me.'

A man with authority to dispatch a pair of Scotland Yard operatives to China at twenty-five minutes' notice is a magnificent example of the sort of fictional go-getter that must have delighted readers who had no reason to hope that their own lives would ever cease to be hedged with petty prohibitions.

But what is Fu-Manchu up to that measures so drastic have to be taken by the indomitable Nayland Smith? The only answer to this question is rhetorical generalization pregnant with hints about a 'Yellow Peril'. Here is a typical reflection by the narrator, Dr Petrie:

> The mere thought that our trifling error of judgement tonight in tarrying a moment too long might mean the victory of Fu-Manchu might mean the turning of the balance which a wise providence had adjusted between the white and yellow races, was appalling. To Smith and me, who knew something of the secret influences at work to overthrow the Indian Empire, to place, it might be, the whole of Europe and America beneath an Eastern rule, it seemed that a great yellow hand was stretched out over London. Dr Fu-Manchu was a menace to the civilized world.

Passages like this abound throughout Rohmer's work. They link the action sequences and provide spurious justification for them. Credible motives are entirely lacking. Here is the forerunner – perhaps even the progenitor – of Ian Fleming and the espionage fiction of the 1950s and 1960s, the ancestor of the thriller of unreason.

It often has been said that stories of the Fu-Manchu type were devised purely as entertainment and that any attempt to subject them to serious criticism is misconceived. There is something too pat about this argument. No man writes entirely in a mental vacuum; however slight, however apparently automatic his work, it must proceed from ideas, traces at least of which will be carried to the reader. It is to instant rapport between these conveyed notions and the reader's existing prejudices, quite as much as to any quality of story-telling, that a book's success is attributable. The Fu-Manchu novels went into edition after edition. Their only clear message was one of racial vituperation. Had there not existed in the minds of many thousands of people an innate fear or dislike of foreigners – oriental foreigners, in particular – Sax Rohmer never would have become a bestselling author.

Before the second world war, the average middle-class man and woman in England had never seen a Chinaman. The few Chinese who lived and worked in Britain were to be found only in certain areas of the big cities and seaports, generally dockland districts such as London's Limehouse. Their communities were small, unobtrusive and industrious. They also had their own high standards of respectability and cleanliness. Chinese rarely came into conflict with the law and when they did it was as often as not in consequence of some trivial neighbourhood quarrel.

Such was the unexciting reality. No opium dens. No pad-footed assassins. No Tong wars nor kidnapping nor torture chambers. Seldom in the history of racial intolerance had a minority shown itself so unco-operative in the matter of getting hated. Fortunately for the great 'fiendish Oriental' myth, the majority of the British public had never walked down the neat, if dull, little streets of Limehouse nor had occasion to penetrate the harbour districts of Liverpool, South Shields or Cardiff. It did become briefly fashionable in the 1930s for groups of wealthy young Londoners to 'go slumming' in the East End, where they supposed that only their daring and their inbred superiority protected them from being doped, robbed or murdered, but they understandably refrained from admitting afterwards that nothing in the least degree thrilling had happened. Nor was the legend contradicted by the provincial and suburban sightseers whose charabanc tours of 'Chinatown' proved so consistently and disappointingly uneventful. They preferred to imagine that they had been into dangerous and forbidden territory, which doubtless they had glimpsed through eyes not unlike those of Rohmer's Doctor Petrie:

'The mantle of dusk had closed about the squalid activity of the East End streets as we neared our destination. Aliens of every shade of colour were in the glare of the lamps upon the main road about us now, emerging from burrow-like alleys. In the short space of the drive we had passed from the bright world of the West into the dubious underworld of the East.'

The vehemence of this prose is interesting. It is occasioned by nothing in the story itself, and indeed seems unrelated to experience of any kind. Why should street activity in a particular area be described as 'squalid' as if rendered so by a mere compass bearing? Why are alleys inhabited by 'aliens' specifically 'burrow-like'? And what has geography got to do with the distinction between 'world' and 'underworld'? Even the verb 'emerge', with its suggestion of secret and evil purpose, would seem a curious choice if the scene were not to yield at least one specific act of wickedness. But nothing happens. Rohmer's narrative, like the Limehouse touring coach, rolls on elsewhere. The readers have not been thrilled; they simply have been prompted to feel superior.

Historically, the British had been well conditioned to accept the myth of Asiatic guile. In common with other European countries during the nineteenth century, Britain had seized upon every commercial advantage offered by China's vast size and the divisions and weaknesses of her government. China was not colonized, but it was virtually partitioned. The Treaty Ports constituted an effective apparatus of exploitation, and Britain derived additional and special benefit from her control of the Chinese Customs with a consequent vested interest in the opium trade. Like all indefensible arrangements, this called for a virtuous attitude on the part of the beneficiary and a campaign of vilification against the unwilling benefactor – especially after the Opium Wars, in which the Christian forces of Queen Victoria had appeared to be compelling the Heathen Chinese to step up his drug consumption. By the turn of the century, the British had managed to convince themselves that with the exception of a handful of quaint converts, the Chinese were corrupt, untrustworthy, dirty, vicious and cunning. Connoisseurs prized their ancient art, of course, and chinoiserie continued to be a fashionable feature of middle and upper class drawing-rooms, but aesthetic appreciation was quite separate in the public mind from a dislike that verged on loathing for the race which had created that art.

Of all the fields of missionary endeavour that helped gratify the Victorians' desire to patronize the rest of mankind, China seems to have been regarded as presenting a special challenge. Its wickedness was not something negative, like the poor African's failure to realize that God was pained by the sight of a bare backside, but a conscious and systematic adherence to non-Christian – and therefore Satanic – traditions. The various rival churches, whose Missions to China unashamedly blackguarded one another and did as much poaching as proselytizing, were united in one respect: their propaganda had the common aim of destroying the idea that a civilization as ancient as the Chinese might actually possess enough merit to warrant its being left alone for a few more centuries. Congregations and, in particular, children at Sunday schools, were treated to harrowing accounts of a land of famine, banditry, infanticide and opium smoking, where only in the beleaguered mission compounds was there to be found enlightenment and joy. The theme was pursued in countless pamphlets and parish magazines, illustrated in magic lantern lectures, and worked into that peculiarly British manifestation of sadism, the literature of the Sunday School Prize. Thus – and not for the first or the last time – did actions dictated by political expediency receive the retrospective sanction of religion.

Before the nineteenth century, it was the traveller's tale that had provided people with their ideas about China. They pictured it much as the first readers of Marco Polo must have done – rich, strange and utterly remote. It inspired awe but also respect. The imperialist and religious propaganda of Victorian times rendered the mystery sinister and the writers of popular literature grasped eagerly this new opportunity of 'preaching to the nerves'. After the shock of the Boxer uprising in 1900, the reading public was ready to believe anything of the 'treacherous' yellow men, with their slant eyes and funny pigtails and evil secret societies. For the next forty years, the 'Yellow Peril' was a constantly recurrent theme of adventure and mystery fiction. Because China was so far away and was represented in Britain by only a tiny, scattered and uncommunicative immigrant population, it was possible to chill the blood of the credulous with the wildest inventions and the most absurd racial libels without fear of disproof or even contradiction.

The Chinaman-villain was a figure that might have been tailor-made for the use of crime novelists. He was readily associated in the minds of uninformed, insular people with vices that they conceived to be endemic in the East. He was what all the writers described as 'inscrutable' – in other words, a repository of unspoken thoughts and therefore dangerous. He was a drug addict himself and almost certainly a supplier of drugs to others (did not every newspaper reader in the 1920s know about 'Brilliant Chang' whose gang provided dope for the Society habitués of Mrs Kate Meyrick's '43' Club in the West End of London?). Worse still, it was part of the fiendish character of yellow men to desire sexual intercourse with white girls; this they accomplished by abducting their victims and putting them aboard junks that plied between Wapping and the water-front brothels of China. An intriguing incidental to this aspect of oriental villainy was the widespread belief that the labial plane of a Chinese vagina was horizontal instead of vertical and consequently less prized by native sensualists.

Sax Rohmer set a fashion that was to persist for thirty years when he fixed upon the Thames and the poverty-stricken Eastern boroughs of London as the main scene of the operations of his Chinese criminals. This was the sort of thing whereby the Lime-house thriller school sought to horrify their readers:

We stood in a bare and very dirty room, which could only claim kinship with a civilized shaving saloon by virtue of the grimy towel thrown across the back of the solitary chair. A Yiddish theatrical bill of some kind, illustrated, adorned one of the walls, and another bill, in what may have been Chinese,

completed the decorations. From behind a curtain heavily bro-
caded with filth a little Chinaman appeared, dressed in a loose
smock, black trousers and thick-soled slippers, and, advancing,
shook his head vigorously. 'No shavee, no shavee,' he chattered, simian fashion, squinting from one to the other of us with
his twinkling eyes. 'Too late! Shuttee shop!'

CHAPTER 10

Amid the alien corn

The fact of a public generally unaware of the ugliness of ethnic intolerance has to be accepted if one is to understand how so much popular fiction of racialist flavour came to be written without qualm and read without protest in the years before the second world war. Thrillers were packed with despicable and evil-intentioned foreigners, while even writers of the more sedate detective stories devoted some of their talents to remarkably splenetic portraiture of characters with dark complexions or gutteral accents. Foreign was synonymous with criminal in nine novels out of ten, and the conclusion is inescapable that most people found this perfectly natural.

Until the arrival from America of Earl Derr Biggers's Chinese detective, Charlie Chan, and his popularization through the cinema, the only thinkable role for an Asiatic in crime fiction was that of a felon. Ernest Bramah's Kai Lung did not count: he was a supposedly historical character and therefore inoffensive. Otherwise, 'yellow' men (this quite inaccurate chromatic distinction was insisted upon) were depicted as thieves, assassins, drug pedlars, white slavers and torturers. Sax Rohmer was the most single-minded propounder of Oriental wickedness, but the crude, repetitive and often comic fury of his style failed to disguise an almost total ignorance of the people and countries he affected to find so sinister.

The entire Fu-Manchu saga was on the level of infantile spider-fright. Would it have worked without constant reiteration of words like Eastern, yellow, Chinese, Orient? Almost certainly not. There seems to have been a deeply implanted association in readers' minds between Asia and things unclean and creepy, and it was exploited by many writers other than Rohmer.

Not all the reasons for the attitude are easy to determine. The most obvious – the spate of political and pseudo-religious propaganda in justification of British intervention in the Far East – was also the most important, but there were others that only an anthropologist or a psychologist could hope to evaluate. They possibly involved anxiety about stature (why were Asiatic murderers always lithe and tiny, torturers and executioners invariably gigantic?); sexual fears (the vertical vagina syndrome); doubt of intellectual competence (Eastern 'cleverness' was constantly being emphasized); and a fear of social corruption through drugs (another supposedly Oriental speciality).

'Drug' remained a strongly emotive word throughout the 1920s and 1930s. Quite forgetting that large numbers of their Victorian forebears had taken advantage of unrestricted sale of cheap laudanum to anaesthetize themselves and their fractious infants, people regarded the less extensive but more diligently publicized drug addiction that followed the 1914–18 war as a new and deadly threat to civilized society. The very mention of heroin or cocaine – now the two most favoured narcotics – was enough to send a shiver of excitement up the public spine. Newspapers, thankfully aware that the path of social duty ran parallel to that of self-interest, took good care that the shivers continued. Their task was facilitated by the fact that drug-taking, being expensive, was mainly the indulgence of wealthy and often well-connected people: it was a fashionable vice and thus could be covered by the same apparatus that Fleet Street maintained to indulge its readers' interest in Society. Stories about drugs and drug rings appeared every other day. Although they were seldom factual, repetition conveyed the impression that addiction was a national problem. Physical and moral consequences were never described; the implication was that they were indescribable. Every now and again, a top-drawer addict would 'tell all'. Behind the portentous language of these hack-ghosted confessions was singularly little information. It was all very vague, but in the compost of imprecision grew an almost superstitious dread which an innocent and ignorant public found very pleasurable.

The writers of crime fiction were quick to discern and to profit from it. Drug trafficking became one of their main themes, joining blackmail, legacy-grasping, larceny of necklaces and concealment of fraud in the canon of thriller motivation. Novelists did not suffer the inhibitions imposed upon newspapers by lack of facts and by the laws of libel. They could happily assume with their readers that 'the stuff', as they always termed narcotics in order to sound casually knowledgeable, was smuggled into London from Eastern ports by gangs directed by arch-criminals, usually Chinese; stored awhile in secret riverside warehouses under the guard of desperadoes; and then distributed by incredibly elaborate means to the opium dens of East London and to night-clubs and salons on the opposite side of the city, where languished twitching debutantes, desperate blue-bloods with pin-point pupils, wild artists whose pictures defied identification by normal people, and once brilliant surgeons now broken in mind and body and ready to perform plastic operations on fugitive gangsters as the price of another 'shot'.

Drugs were credited with near-magical powers thirty years before the word 'miracle' came to be appended to the sulphonamides and antibiotics. It was believed that they transformed the taker, more or less immediately, from a harmless and respected member of society into a monster of guile, violence and depravity. Perhaps the extravagance of this notion was an outcome of native puritanism; it was not very different from the pitch of much of the temperance propaganda in the previous century. People also remembered some of the horrifying accounts of opium addiction

SCENE—*Hotel Lounge.*

The Man. "GOING OUT WITH THAT GHASTLY DAGO AGAIN? YOU'RE GETTING YOURSELF TALKED ABOUT. WHY DON'T YOU

whereby the missionary societies had sought to prove the worthiness of their China campaigns. The great impression left by Robert Louis Stevenson's *Dr Jekyll and Mr Hyde* was of further encouragement to the idea that chemical intervention would have instant and drastic effect on personality. Curiously, none of Conan Doyle's readers seems to have thought the worse of Sherlock Holmes on account of his fondness for cocaine – with the exception of Bernard Shaw, who dismissed poor Holmes as 'a drug-addict without a single amiable trait'.

Lack of knowledge of what the various drugs actually did to people and of their degrees of harmfulness led to many misconceptions. Cocaine was generally implied in fiction to be a stimulant that criminals used as an aid to the planning of brilliant coups. Heroin, perhaps partly because of the suggestiveness of the name, was supposed to be the special weakness of Society women – languid ladies of means and title to whom supplies of 'the stuff' would be brought by backstair courier. What pleasures, corrupt or otherwise, heroin opened up for these women were never revealed: an omission that readers doubtless were expected to remedy from imagination. Far more sensational in tone were references to hemp, the Eastern name for which, hashish, was calculated to horrify people who thought heroin a comparatively innocuous indulgence of the idle rich and for whom cocaine had homely associations with dentistry. They thrilled to revelations of imported fiendishness such as this scene in Rohmer's *Si-Fan Mysteries*:

Upon the divans some eight or nine men were seated, fully half of whom were Orientals or half-castes. Before each stood a little inlaid table bearing a brass tray; and upon the trays were various boxes, some apparently containing sweet-meats, others cigarettes. One or two of the visitors smoked curious, long-stemmed pipes and sipped coffee. Even as I leaned from the platform, surveying that incredible scene (incredible in a street of Soho), another devotee of hashish entered – a tall, distinguished-looking man, wearing a light coat over his evening dress. 'Gad!' whispered Smith, beside me – 'Sir Byngham Pyne of the India Office! You see, Petrie! You see! This place is a lure. My God!'

In 1924, John Rhode's mystery novel *A.S.F.* was based on the proposition that

> despite the most desperate efforts of the Criminal Investigation Department and the police generally, the cocaine habit was alarmingly on the increase in England ... Some master-brain was directing the cocaine traffic.

Who, asked Rhode, was this figure and whence did he conduct his plan of operations? The answer was sensational indeed. The organizer of the ring was none other than the brother of the Home Secretary. Scandal was averted in a way that neatly foreshadowed the non-ethic of secret service fiction forty years ahead. The criminal confessed all, then lit a poisoned cigarette. 'One of the Home Office doctors' hurried into the room in time to declare "The man's dead, sir," whereupon a high official took him aside ...

> 'It's the Home Secretary's brother,' he whispered. 'He always had a weak heart, he's had to live in a warm climate and avoid exertion for years. There'll be no need of an inquest under the circumstances. It would be a great grief to the Home Secretary and Lady Westwood.'
>
> 'Oh, no, of course not. I can give a certificate,' replied the doctor readily. 'Dear me, how tragic!'

An interesting aspect of the use of the drug theme in crime novels of the period is the preoccupation with loss of will-power that it reveals. The fact that half the habitués of the Rohmer hashish house were foreigners was unremarkable; it was the presence among them of a British Civil Servant – a titled one, at that – which was intended to make the readers' flesh creep. If Sir Byngham Pyne had succumbed to the lure of an alien vice, who could say what secrets he might not betray to the enemies of his country?

In the *Moorcroft Manor Mystery,* a character says of another, a man of shifty aspect: 'Don't admire the old man's choice. Looks a regular doper from Limehouse.'

And in one of the popular 'Colonel Gore' detective stories, a woman of odd appearance excited the comment:

'I bet the old thing dopes . . . She's as yellow as a Chink. Weird old frump . . . gets up at three o'clock in the day, Sylvia says, and floats around in a dressing gown until she goes to bed again.'

These and countless similar references suggest wide acceptance of the idea that drugs not only delivered their users into the power of an alien race, but actually imparted to them some of the characteristics of that race. Here was a variation on the ancient belief that a person who had sold his soul to the devil acquired from his master certain diabolical trade-marks – the inability to cast a shadow, for instance. It was less disturbing to hold some outside agency responsible for the scandalous behaviour of one's fellow citizens than to have doubts about the stability of the social order. A similar desire to transfer blame would be evidenced by the spate of espionage fiction in the 1950s and 1960s. This was to feature 'brain-washing' rather than drugs as the evil device whereby foreign conspirators try to erode the will of free and decent people.

One of the true contributory causes of the growth of drug addiction in the 1920s was the return to civilian life of large numbers of servicemen already reliant on the morphia they had been given to relieve the pain of wounds. So it may fairly be said that war, and the feelings of disgust and guilt associated with it, contributed to the drug phobia so persistently reflected in crime novels. Perhaps reaction to the war, and in particular to the 'cold steel' aspect of bayonet fighting, was also responsible to some extent for the fascination that knives and daggers held for readers. The number of deaths by stabbing offered for investigation by the police and detectives of fiction was remarkably high in relation to actual crime statistics. Every second or third murder victim on the library shelves had died by puncture. Writers tried hard to re-concile this apparent indulgence of public morbidity with their duty to assuage public conscience. The most obvious device was to make the criminal a foreigner, but because it *was* obvious and therefore inimical to the mystery element, this method eventually fell out of favour. Emphasis came to be laid instead on the un-Englishness of the knife as a weapon. It was commonly termed 'wicked-looking' or 'evil' and some of the higher-flown prose of the thriller writers was reserved to describe the elaborate workman-ship of this alien cutlery and to convey the sense of revulsion it inspired:

> ... a long, fifteenth century Italian dagger. The hilt was an exquisite piece of workmanship, beautifully chased and en-crusted at the upper end with uncut jewels ... The blade ... was very slender and exquisitely graceful, fashioned from steel that had in it a curious greenish tinge which lent the whole weapon an unmistakably sinister appearance.

Margery Allingham, *The Crime at Black Dudley* (1929).

A catalogue of all the daggers meticulously identified in crime fiction would be a long one, embracing weapons from Italy, Spain, Corsica, France, North Africa, Arabia, Malaya, Mexico, China, Mongolia and even Ancient Egypt. There were poniards, stilettos, pangas, krishes, sacrificial knives – everything, in fact, but the good old-fashioned Sheffield carver (a leading choice, it may be noted, of the English domestic murderer in real life). Readers seem to have been invited to suppose that such weapons possessed some kind of compulsive quality, derived from the nasty nature of their original owners, which was more to blame for the crimes than the actual perpetrators.

> Sergeant Long compressed his lips beneath his heavy moustache. 'It was no accident, Colonel. He was stabbed in three places. It's an ugly business, this. I saw the knife myself, sir. A nasty little affair. I'd say it was a black man's or a yellow man's knife, myself. I saw a knife once something just like it with a stoker I had to take off a West African cargo boat ... A

native knife of some sort that was – the chap had got it from a
nigger, he told us.'

Lynn Brock, *The Deductions of Colonel Gore.*

Lynn Brock's real name was Allister McAllister and he was a
prolific writer of detective stories during the 1920s. The attitudes
he expressed were shared by scores of his fellow authors who, like
McAllister, saw no reason why they should not state them explicitly in novels of entertainment. Publishers presumably had no
fear of such sentiments being considered offensive by readers, or
they would have discouraged them. As it was, huge sales continued
to be enjoyed by 'Sapper', a rabid racialist; by John Buchan,
whose characters frequently made disparaging remarks about
Jews and Negroes; by the anti-Semitic G. K. Chesterton; and by
other equally famous and equally psychotic authors. Not even
Victor Gollancz, a man of international sympathies and a declared
champion of minorities, seems to have thought of trying to restrain
Dorothy L. Sayers from the snide remarks which she was always
slipping into the detective stories that Gollancz published, for
example:

This gentleman, rather curly in the nose and fleshy about the
eyelids, nevertheless came under Mr Chesterton's definition of a
nice Jew, for his name was neither Montagu nor McDonald,
but Nathan Abrahams, and he greeted Lord Peter with a hos-
pitality amounting to enthusiasm.

'I want you to come and dine at the Soviet Club with me
tonight.' 'Good God, Mary, why? You know I hate the place.
Cooking's beastly, the men don't shave, and the conversation
gets my goat.'

'... awkward little Italian fellow, with a knife – active as a
monkey.'

(*Lord Peter Views the Body*, 1928)

Margery Allingham became a highly accomplished and an unfailingly literate contributor to mystery fiction. Her later books

won the approval of the more serious critics and were read by professional and academic people. Here, though, are two of her early villians:

> He was a foreigner, grossly fat, and heavily jowled ... heavily-lidded eyes, broad nose, shock of hair, worn long and brushed straight back from the amazingly high forehead.

> The man was a foreigner, so much was evident at a glance; but that in itself was not sufficient to interest him so particularly ... He was white-haired, very small and delicately made, with long graceful hands which he used a great deal in his conversation, making gestures, swaying his long, pale fingers gracefully, easily. Under the sleek white hair which waved straight back from a high forehead his face was grey, vivacious, and peculiarly wicked.

> *(The Crime at Black Dudley)*

The descriptions are of a more skilful kind than the average thriller writer would have managed to produce, but they are calculated to chime with the same sort of prejudices as those cherished by 'Sapper' or Rohmer. Thus, the first man was not just fat – as a jolly English yeoman might be fat – but grossly so. He was, in fact, a German, or, as the author put it, a Hun. His hair being worn long was in 1929 a sure sign of 'artiness' and the high forehead betokened intellectualism, another extremely suspect affectation. Height of forehead was also a noticeable feature of the second villain, but in his case it went with long and graceful hands and a small, delicate body. Odd sexual proclivities are here implied. That these would have been Continental in origin readers might have inferred from the mention of the man's use of gestures in conversation. The phrase *'peculiarly* wicked' is made understandable by the preceding adjective 'vivacious'. An Englishman with white hair (which has strong sentimental connotations) is most unlikely to be wicked, but the possibility is just conceivable. That he should combine wickedness with vivacity, however, is altogether out of the question. Peculiar to foreigners, as Miss

Allingham's public well knew, is the capacity to sin and look pleased about it at the same time.

German villains were stock furniture of the crime novel from 1918 onwards, although few were as sophisticated as Miss Allingham's gentleman with white hair. The majority were scowlers and snarlers. They had 'bullet-shaped' heads and thick necks and were much given to muttering 'hein'. Their names were generally short and gravelly, like their tempers, and they treated their fellow malefactors with even less respect than they showed their opponents. Crude, two-dimensional copies of the wartime caricatures of the national enemy, the German crooks of fiction were plainly in the wrong profession. Their accents alone would have aroused the suspicion of the dimmest detective, while choleric disposition and sadistic habits must have been disastrous encumbrances in a calling that demands self-effacement above all things. The unconvincing behaviour of these evildoers suggests that writers continued to employ them simply because they felt that the hatred of Germans stimulated during the war was a normal and permanent public emotion. An element of laziness was involved too. Whole paragraphs of descriptions of sinister attributes could be dispensed with simply by calling a character Karl. Popular literature is full of mental short cuts, no less acceptable to author than to reader, and any convention or cliché which signals adoption of the appropriate attitude, tends to be self-perpetuating. For this reason, clumsy Teutonic criminals continued to swagger through crime fiction long after the passions of 1914-18 had cooled and the traditional pro-German sympathy of the British Establishment had begun to reassert itself. 'Sapper' hinted at the uneasiness aroused in some jingoistic writers by failure to let bygones be bygones and to find some new and politically more deserving object of vilification:

'I know they're Huns. I know it's just one's bounden duty to use every gift one has been given to beat 'em. But, damn it, John, they're men too. They go back to their womenkind.'

(*The Final Count*)

'Sapper's' recurrent arch-villain, it may be noted, was not a German. He was called Peterson, a name much more suggestive of Scandinavian origin.

Compared with the somewhat half-hearted presentation of Hunnish criminals, the supposed characteristics of some other nationalities were depicted in a way that left no doubt of the real dislike many authors felt for them. It is in the aside, the casual reference, the quoted remark of a character, that a novelist's true opinion is to be found, rather than in the main body of his narrative. William Le Queux, for instance, left to a minor figure in one of his stories the job of telling the public what an insufferable lot were the native inhabitants of the French Mediterranean coast. This man announced his intention to

> 'pitch my quarters in Cairo, where English-speaking visitors are protected, properly treated, and have their comfort looked after. . . . The Riviera has declined terribly these past five years. Why the people here actually hissed the Union Jack at the last Battle of Flowers!'
>
> *(The Gamblers)*

Dorothy Sayers also took a poor view of the French, who had no public schools. She deputed her Lord Peter Wimsey to point out that

> 'owing to the system of State education in that country, though all the French write vilely, it is rare to find one who writes very much more vilely than the rest.'
>
> *(The Nine Tailors)*

Wimsey was given further witty things to say about the bad quality of French envelopes, pens, ink and government departments.

Sydney Horler's special aversion was to 'stinking Italianos' but otherwise his contempt for non-Britishers was fairly equitably distributed. He considered the French dishonest, the Americans absurd. 'The Average Swiss,' he wrote, 'has a curiously wooden expression – but an alert look comes into his eyes directly you begin to move your hand pocketward.' As for European footballers, 'I suggest that if any more of these ridiculous international matches . . . are played, the visitors be searched before they go on the field; they may have a knife or so hidden in their stockings.' He addressed the following plea to Gilbert Frankau, bestselling romantic and adventure novelist:

'Let me implore you, with all the force at my command, if you write any more Secret service novels, not to give your hero the name of 'Marcus Orlando' and not to make him wear boots with cloth uppers. Levantines may have their place in fiction, but they should not figure as beaux chevaliers in British novels of adventure.'

(More Strictly Personal)

Horler's references to Jews, although sly, invariably had that self-congratulatory tone used by people who believe they are saying something agreeable to their hearers. He was only one of several popular authors of the period who put anti-Semitic sentiments into print and there is nothing to suggest that their assumption of the approval of their readers was misplaced. The Jew was, without question, the favourite object of British middle class scorn. His mere existence was felt to be an affront. Horler in 1933 had only to take a walk by the sea to be moved to protest:

The choicest collection of Hebraic types I have yet seen (even in New York) was to be observed; what it is about Bournemouth that attracts these pronouncedly Asiatic-looking Jews I do not know . . .'

(Strictly Personal)

while a few years earlier Allister McAllister described the similarly mortifying state of affairs that awaited a British Army Officer on his return from service abroad.

Two days after his forty-second birthday he had landed in England, spent a week interviewing solicitors and tailors and such things [*sic*], and, bored to extinction by a London which seemed

to him entirely populated by Jews, had fled westwards in search
of such of his kith and kin as still survived.

(Deductions of Colonel Gore)

It is a matter of conjecture whether the rise of fascism in Europe
and the outbreak of a second world war were helped along by the
attitudes of the large section of British society that found echo in
Mr McAllister's books. About one thing, though, there can be no
argument. By the time the Nazis had had their way, it was a vastly
greater multitude of mankind than the kith and kin of a bored
British officer whose survival was past praying for.

CHAPTER 11

Below Stairs

When Bulldog Drummond was making inquiries in the London suburb of Peckham about a gang of international criminals, one of the first questions he put to a householder was whether anything suspicious had been seen by her servants. The house was shabby, the woman down-at-heel, the neighbourhood seedy. And yet, because the woman was the owner of property, Drummond took it for granted that she employed two or more servants.

The assumption was not a piece of simple-mindedness in the tradition of Marie Antoinette's 'Why don't they eat cake'? 'Sapper' might have been a lieutenant-colonel, but he was no aristocrat, insulated from the realities of life. He expected a woman living in her own house to keep servants. It was the rule, even in Peckham.

During the first world war, nearly half a million men and women left domestic service to enter the armed forces or industry. Few of them returned to their old jobs. And yet, in 1921, one third of all employed women were still classified as being in service. The number was three times as great as that of women in the textile industry. Women servants outnumbered women teachers by nine to one. Ten years earlier, in the final glow of Edwardian self-indulgence, every fourth middle-class family in London had equipped itself with a resident servant. Only one family in eight could boast this advantage in the early 1920s, although in the wealthier areas the proportion was as high as 50%.

These were households whose servants actually lived on the premises, in their own quarters 'below stairs', over stables or garages, and in attics. A far greater number of families was served by 'maids' and charwomen who hired themselves out at an hourly or weekly rate. This varied considerably according to district, the age of the worker, and the amount of unemployment at the time. A shilling an hour was considered very generous indeed. Sixpence or eightpence was more commonly offered. Many young and comparatively inexperienced girls could be found willing to do a whole week's housework for as little as four or five shillings. There was an influx into the relatively prosperous South East of girls whose families in depressed industrial areas were only too thankful to have one less mouth to feed. They worked as mothers' helps, runners of errands and general skivvies in return for their keep and a little pocket money.

Male casual labour was plentiful and cheap. Men called from door to door in the suburbs offering to dig gardens, mow lawns or do any other jobs that could be found or devised. They mostly were honest, if increasingly wretched men, and the woman who peered apprehensively at the latest in the never-ending stream of doorstep petitioners was generally a kindly enough person, embarrassed by the distress and lost dignity of others. But she was also instinctively wary of strangers, having read and heard terrible stories about tramps and gypsies. Itinerant odd-job men therefore encountered a good deal of hostility and needed to keep the price of their labour low enough to counter it. Some had to be content with payment in kind – perhaps a cup of tea and a cast-off coat, in return for half a day's digging.

It might be supposed that those people who benefited from the existence of a large pool of cheap labour were grateful for the advantage that even a modest regular salary conferred in terms of the availability of domestic help. Never before had so many enjoyed the social cachet of being able to drop references to 'the servants' or, at least 'the maid'. But their minds seem not to have been easy. If they had been, one might expect to find less evidence in their favourite escapist literature of a preoccupation with servant-master relationships. Why were detective stories populated with quite so many butlers and footmen and gardeners and cooks and chambermaids? They were providers of testimony, admittedly, with which to feed the plot. Servants were always closely questioned by the police or private investigator. They tended, by reason of long hours and closely supervised duties, to be natural discoverers of bodies. They noticed other things as well, including some curious aspects of the private lives of their employers and the unorthodox behaviour of house guests. And yet, as writers in a later, more economical epoch were to demonstrate, witness to such matters could equally well be borne by a very much smaller domestic staff, or even by the suspects themselves. Explanation of those hosts of menials must lie elsewhere than in plotting strategy.

Press, cinema and theatre, no less than popular literature were pervaded by supposedly upper-class norms. At one time, there were so many plays with the curtain rising to show a parlourmaid pottering around the stage that even London's undiscriminating audiences began to suffer a sense of *déjà-vu*. Actors and actresses delivered their lines in the theatre and later in Britain's first terrible talking films in a standardized combination of gush and drawl that was meant to sound like conversation in society drawing-rooms. Newspapers slavishly reported every detail of the most trivial perambulations of anybody with a title, while in every doctor's and dentist's waiting-room in the country there was a *Tatler-Sphere-Sketch-Bystander* roll-call of that section of the population engaged in permanent attendance at point-to-point meetings and hunt balls. Very white, ethereal females with tasteful gauze neckerchiefs and treble-barrelled names were reverently featured in advertisements for Pond's face creams. They all looked like members of the Usher family, on loan from the vault. Then there were the Best People's goings-on in public. Their involvement in night-club raids, their stunts for charity, their bouts of hooliganism on such occasions as Boat Race night, were reported in newspapers in a tone of cheery approbation very different from the comment aroused forty years later by violence in another quarter.

The true reason for all this obsessive preoccupation with the top layer of the class structure was almost certainly anxiety. People who thought of themselves as middle-class believed that they had nothing to gain from social change and a great many things to lose. As they worried, in their traditional way, about 'times' being unsettled, they began first to entertain an exaggerated estimate of their own advantages, then to identify them with the interests of the ruling class (delusions of grandeur are detectable at this stage) and finally to see working class people as envious, unreasonable and vicious, but too stupid, fortunately, to constitute a real menace in any political sense.

Not even in the great days of Victorian certitude had the 'lower orders' been treated with such contempt as they received between demobilization after the first world war and the requirement of new levies for the second. In the literature of entertainment, many writers made no attempt to portray working people save as cringing menials or ill-educated buffoons. It is almost impossible to find a crime novel of the period in which opportunity is not taken to make fun of 'common' ways of talking. Even Freeman Wills Crofts, one of the least spiteful of authors, felt constrained occasionally to use the outrageous pseudo-Cockney that thriller writers had evolved as a standard mode of indicating working class speech.

'But lor, guv'nor, it's easy for lydies as wot 'as lots o' money to be pleasant. W'y shouldn't they be?'

Homely philosophy, sans aspirates.

And here, conveyed in the same mythical argot by Agatha Christie, is the grief of a female domestic on losing her employer:

'There ain't a many like her,' sobbed Alice when the train had finally departed. 'I'm sure that when Charlie went back on me with that girl from the Dairy, nobody could have been kinder than Miss Grey was, and though particular about the brasses and the dust, she was always one to notice when you'd give a thing an extra rub. Cut myself in little pieces for her, I would any day. A real lady, that's what I call her.'

(*The Mystery of the Blue Train*, 1928)

Alices abounded in crime fiction. They were undersized, had chronic sniffs, and were very easily moved to tears. They frequently broke things and were remarkably obtuse as witnesses. We know what Alices looked like, for they were pictured, week in week out, in *Punch* cartoons: comical little drabs whose malapropisms and physical clumsiness must have struck the readers of that risible journal as most droll. It seems not to have occurred to them that physical underdevelopment, constant colds, confusion and awkwardness might have been due to living in a wretched home and going short of food and sleep. Such a reflection would have been sordid and there were enough unpleasant things in life without imagining more. Pleasant fancies, on the other hand, were quite in order, as was this speculation about the elderly butler in *The Moorcroft Manor Mystery:*

There was something remotely aristocratic about the man. It was not expressed so much in the manner of his speech as in the general atmosphere of him. Most butlers ... were rather like that. Perhaps it was their constant contact with gentility, through which they unconsciously absorbed the mental ether of higher spheres, that was responsible ... A ghost of a smile flitted across the old man's face. 'A good butler, sir, is never out of a situation for long,' he replied, with quiet confidence.

Being 'in service' was clearly a way of life, even after the great war which had rooted 400,000 servants out of their kitchens, pantries, sewing-rooms, nurseries, stables and gardeners' cottages. Lynn Brock's *The Deductions of Colonel Gore*, a detective story of the mid-1920s, provides interesting evidence of the servant-mistress relationship as it still existed less than half a century ago.

'Flora was my name then, sir, though I had to change it to Florence afterwards, because of ladies I've been with not thinking Flora suitable to my station ... I'm leaving today, sir, with my wages or without them, and my box is packed and ready to go with me ... I'm going at eight o'clock, sir, soon as some of my things as were with the washer-woman come back, if you'll excuse me mentioning them, sir.'

This passage is shocking in its implication of a body-and-soul subservience. The woman lacked a right to the most elementary possession of all, her own name. Her one freedom – and that was subject to the possible loss of whatever wages were owing – was to pack her box and depart. The reason for her leaving, incidentally, was nothing to do with the terms of her employment; she simply disapproved of certain marital irregularities in the household. Servants did tend to have a more highly developed or at least a more rigid moral sense than their employers (note the apology for mentioning personal laundry).

Dignity, of the kind we detect in Florence (formerly Flora), is very seldom permitted the menials of crime fiction. They tend to preface every utterance with 'Please, Mum ...' and panic very readily, despite the religious upbringing suggested by their frequent use of the phrase 'Lor bless yer, sir/mum ...' The 'mum' by the way, is not a familiarity but working-class pidgin for 'Madame'. Policemen and other investigators seldom get much sense out of them. In any case, their evidence is widely regarded as unreliable because lowliness of station renders them especially susceptible to bribery or threats.

When James Agate put an advertisement in the *Daily Telegraph* for a new chauffer-valet in 1932, there were 211 replies. He interviewed the odd eleven before finding one who could drive. Three years later he was without a chauffeur once again and described in *A Shorter Ego* how he 'sent round to the Labour Exchange'. One of the applicants, from the depressed area of Durham, said he was willing to accept any wage that was offered and to work for it all hours that his employer required. In 1936, yet another of Agate's chauffeurs 'nearly fainted on hearing he was engaged, owing to two and a half months' semi-starvation'. The ferocity of competition for jobs in domestic service allowed of few ethical niceties. Men seeking appointment as chauffeurs, Agate learned, would do anything to conceal the existence of their wives and children because the post was traditionally occupied by a bachelor. Conversely, it was common for a 'married couple' going to a house as butler and cook never to have seen each other previously.

Sydney Horler had a very low opinion of chauffeurs. He dismissed one, whom he was paying £2 15s a week, on the grounds that he had become careless and insolent. When Horler went to 'one of the biggest garages in Surrey' to engage a replacement, the works manager told him: 'Chauffeurs as a class are the least dependable of all servants. They are rank socialists to a man. They bleed their masters, levy blackmail on garage owners, have no sense of loyalty to their employers, and are generally contemptible. The fact of the matter is that since the War it has become the most difficult thing to find a good chauffeur. Easy money and easy hours are the principle factors in their disgraceful conduct. These causes demoralize them.' (*More Strictly Personal*)

Antipathy towards chauffeurs as a profession is to be discerned in the work of a surprisingly large number of Horler's fellow writers. For every sympathetic portrait of a chauffeur (generally as a kind of bodyguard-confidant – a reformed criminal or a still grateful other-ranker rescued from No-Man's-Land by the officer who now employs him) there were a dozen of shifty or sinister character. These were inclined to be morose and contemptuous of authority and might be detected, if watched carefully, in conversation with evil-looking strangers behind the garage or under the bonnet of the car while pretending to trace an engine fault. It was a chauffeur, as often as not, who undertook the abduction of the heroine ('I have instructions to take you to see Sir Robert at Scotland Yard, miss.' 'But surely *this* isn't the way to the Yard?'). He also was useful as a courier between one criminal establishment and another. In some stories, he was even employed as an agent to gain access to victims' houses by way of the servants' quarters. Violence from a chauffeur was often called for: his speciality was dealing surprise blows with a heavy spanner, a tyre lever or a starting handle.

A possible clue to the reason for middle-class chauffeur-phobia is to be found in a mystery by Lynn Brock. It is perhaps the only novel in which a chauffeur is permitted the distinction of turning out to be the murderer. The reader is told that the man had been assistant science master at Tenbury Grammar School before the war, in which he '*ended up with three pips*' and the Distinguished Service Order.

Nothing is more likely to arouse hostility in someone with the means to employ a servant than the discovery of that servant's possession of qualities or qualifications superior to his own. This was a frequent embarrassment in the 1920s and early 1930s. Among the huge multitude of unemployed were many men of good education who had failed to get their jobs back after their war service. Others, including teachers and local government employees, had fallen victim to the various 'economy' measures dictated by the deflationary policies of the time. In some respects, the fate of these people was more pathetic than that of the workless in the hard core industrial areas. Their poverty was a peculiarly lonely affliction. They lacked the one solace available on Tyneside or in South Wales – the companionship of mass misery. At the inquest on a man found dead on the railway line in the respectable North London suburb of Mill Hill in 1933 it was revealed that he had lost his job the year before but had continued to leave the house every morning at his usual time ever since in order to keep the fact of his unemployment a secret. Had he been able to drive a car (or even if he had not) this man might well have been one of the 211 who replied to James Agate's advertisement. It was from the pool of professional men without a profession, casualties of business contraction, temporarily embarrassed ex-officers, public school men awaiting an opportunity, that luckier members of the same class recruited their valets, general body servants and chauffeurs. They had not much choice if they insisted, as most of them did, on the applicants being well spoken and of presentable appearance. But a risk inseparable from the engagement of such people was that of their adopting an attitude of familiarity. Many a modestly successful merchant or broker or shopkeeper nursed the dread, in his heart of mock-Tudor hearts, of being suddenly addressed as 'Bill' or 'Cock' or 'Old chap' by a normally taciturn but never quite convincingly respectful man in cap and leggings.

The heroes of crime fiction were as nearly infallible in their choice of servants as in other matters. The Saint, for instance, had a man of whom Leslie Charteris declared:

> There was only one Orace – late sergeant of Marines, and Simon Templar's most devoted servant.

We may be sure that Orace, presumably so chronic an aitch-dropper that he did not rate an apostrophe, would never have embarrassed Mr Templar by sudden revelation of having been to the same school.

Reggie Fortune's manservant, Sam, enabled him to have 'late and lazy' breakfasts. He could serve the sort of tea that moved an enraptured girl caller to ask 'But do men always make teas like this?' And it was into the arms of Sam, not a patient wife, that Dr Fortune subsided limply after battling through a London winter's day to his rooms in Wimpole Street.

The various detectives invented by Edgar Wallace contrived to emerge unmarried from adventures that always involved pretty and amiable young women. Not even the intimate association imposed by sharing a flooded cellar or a locked attic persuaded them that female company might be an even better thing out of business hours. Were they, then, misogynists? Not at all. Each had waiting for him at home one of those unobtrusive, reticent and supremely efficient male ministrants who symbolized, perhaps more than any other figure in contemporary literature, the popularly conceived advantages of wealth. John Rhode in *Tragedy at the Unicorn* (1928) provided some simple rules for recognizing the genus:

Ferguson was so typically the valet and confidential servant
that he could not by any possibility have been mistaken for
anything else. He was always dressed soberly in black and had a
quiet and respectful manner which was entirely natural . . .

but this description conveys nothing of the reserved omniscience,
the potentially devastating familiarity with 'the correct thing',
which the manservant of popular fiction was ever prepared to
deploy to the greater glory of his master or to the discomfiture of
his enemies.

The most famous servant created by any detection writer is
Bunter, Lord Peter Wimsey's man – if man, indeed, is the word
for a being who epitomized everything that Dorothy Sayers considered desirable in a director of worldly affairs. Nowhere does
Miss Sayers indulge in lyrical prose at greater length than when
the qualities and talents of Bunter are being proclaimed.

On the morning of the wedding-day, Lord Peter emerged from
Bunter's hands a marvel of sleek brilliance. His primrose-
coloured hair was so exquisite a work of art that to eclipse it with
his glossy hat was like shutting up the sun in a shrine of polished
jet; his spats, light trousers, and exquisitely polished shoes
formed a tone-symphony in monochrome. It was only by the
most impassioned pleading that he persuaded his tyrant to allow
him to place two small photographs and a thin, foreign letter in
his breast-pocket. Mr Bunter, likewise immaculately attired,
stepped into the taxi after him. At noon precisely they were
deposited beneath the striped awning which adorned the door
of the Duchess of Medway's house in Park Lane. Bunter
promptly disappeared in the direction of the back entrance,
while his lordship mounted the steps and asked to see the dow-
ager.

(*Lord Peter Views the Body*)

Bunter's sartorial sense is perfect, but there is more to it than
that. He is a sort of priest, charged with the maintenance of ritual
and ornament which reflect the immutability of the social struc-

ture. Fashion is a word Bunter would have disdained. Fashion implies change, and change is not to be thought of so long as duchesses are receiving at Park Lane and a Duke dines still at Denver. Bunter is concerned not with fashion but with style – a very different thing. And in this, his instinct is never faulted. Nor is it wanting when the capricious appetites of his master need to be divined:

> 'Bunter!'
> 'My Lord?'
> 'No bacon this morning. Quite the wrong smell.'
> 'I was thinking of buttered eggs, my lord.'
> 'Excellent.'

One has seen how Bunter's sense of propriety automatically sent him to the back entrance of the Medway residence in Park Lane. A more difficult test awaited him one Sunday afternoon 'in that halcyon summer of 1921' when he accompanied Lord Peter to the altogether unfamiliar milieu of Bloomsbury. It was a poor district in those days, to judge from the declaration by a resident 'struggling general practitioner' that 'there are times when even a half-crown visit makes all the difference between making both ends meet and having an ugly hiatus' and also from the author's mention of the Bloomsbury 'swarm' of infants, 'presumably within-doors, eating steamy Sunday dinners inappropriate to the tropical weather.'

> Lord Peter Wimsey and his host sat down to table, and the doctor expressed a hope that Mr Bunter would sit down with them. That correct person, however, deprecated any such suggestion. 'If I might venture to indicate my own preference, sir,' he said, 'it would be to wait upon you and his lordship in the usual manner.'

And so he did, handing the salad (no steamy, unseasonable food would get past *him*) and pouring out water 'with a grave decency appropriate to a crusted old tawny port'.

It would be naïve to suppose that Miss Sayers span out her

high life fantasies without once slipping tongue in cheek. She was an intelligent and educated woman and, although her sense of humour was deficient and sometimes unattractive, her phrasing of many of the Wimsey and Bunter passages shows that she enjoyed writing them and intended them to entertain. Was John Strachey missing this point when he declared that by 1930 she had almost ceased to be a first-rate detective writer and had become 'an exceedingly snobbish popular novelist?' His error, if he was making one, was to assume the two states to be mutually exclusive. If Miss Sayers was a first-rate writer of detective stories in, say, 1928, when she was considered a sufficiently eminent author to be entrusted with the selection for Gollancz of *Great Short Stories of Detection, Mystery and Horror,* she surely had not fallen far from grace by 1934, the publication year of *The Nine Tailors,* which was to be reprinted twenty-two times in the following twenty years. Of course she was snobbish: the fun she allowed herself in putting into Bunter's mouth the pomposities of a late Victorian butler is altogether innocent of social criticism, while she treated Wimsey, even at his most inane, with an auntie-like indulgence that amounted almost to fawning. But her public showed by continued support that they found nothing reprehensible in her attitude. The probability is that they rather enjoyed a bit of snobbery themselves and were more inclined to identify with a clever lordling and his resourceful valet than with characters who suffered, as they did, the limitations of real life.

If Bunter was an entertaining myth for readers, he also perhaps was a compensatory one for his author. More than once in her correspondence Miss Sayers blamed slowness of progress with her latest novel upon domestic crisis. Having sacked the current set of servants, she was obliged to do all the cooking herself until she could get some new ones. The vision of an imperturbable, ever reliable Bunter must have shimmered above her hot stove like a Saharan mirage.

Not all thriller writers were able entirely to sublimate their concern over the servant 'problem', as it was called, into the creation of an idealized factotum. Sydney Horler provided his hero, Tiger

Standish, with a faithful valet but he could never dismiss one of his own domestics without an outburst of righteous indignation.

One takes these people from their back street hovels, one gives them every comfort, the best of food and even doctors, and after that they'll spend all their time in trying to take fresh advantages. If I had my way, I'd see that every maid who was dismissed for one of the many gross faults peculiar to the tribe was sent to earn her living in a North of England cotton factory or some such place for a period of not less than three months.

Strictly Personal

Servants could be difficult about money, too. This won them no friends among those whose natural thrift enabled them to be instrumental in providing employment for others. In an article in the *Daily Mail* entitled 'The Life of the New Poor', E. Phillips Oppenheim drew attention to the plight into which he had been forced by the cupidity of the lower orders.

My chauffeur, content with thirty shillings a week before the war, now demands a weekly wage of three pounds ten. My indoor servant, to whom I paid a pound a week, now requires two . . . It is the class representing the brains of the country who, faced with an income tax eating into the very vitals of their earnings and an exorbitant increase in the cost of living and wages, must languish and decline under an impossible burden.

These words were written in all seriousness by a man whose income from American sales alone averaged three hundred pounds a week during the eight worst years of the Depression.

CHAPTER 12

Girls who kept cool

The role of heroine in crime fiction has never been an altogether comfortable one. She tends to be an encumbrance. Until very recent times, it was deemed that women could not run fast enough nor hit hard enough to keep up with the male characters. Their parts were passive. A woman might inspire and, within limits, sustain a hero – perhaps cut a bond or two for him at an opportune moment – but she was barred from violent intervention on his behalf. In return, she enjoyed immunity from vulgar assaults such as kicks, punches and blows on the head. Being locked in cellars, attics and crypts was in order; so was abduction by homicidal maniacs. But no matter how desperate or unprincipled her captors were supposed to be, it was never suggested for a moment that sexual conquest figured among their plans.

There was strong objection until the end of the 1930s to the introduction into mystery stories of what is now understood by 'love interest'. Several critics, including W. Somerset Maugham as we have seen, denied the possibility of a good thriller being able to support a romantic theme. This contrasted with Victorian tradition. Through the dark convolutions of the gothic thriller, there always had been discernible a golden thread of true love. A book without a heroine would have been as dubious a publishing proposition before 1914 as would one with an anti-hero. At least two highly successful mystery-adventure writers whose work bridged the Victorian and Edwardian and the post-war eras – William Le Queux and E. Phillips Oppenheim – never did abandon their faith in the necessity of a heroine. Yet there is noticeable evidence in this description in *The Gamblers* by Le Queux of compromise with a new fashion:

> Ulrica was a typical woman of the up-to-date type – pretty, with soft, wavy, chestnut hair and a pair of brown eyes that had attracted a host of men ... yet beneath her corsets, as I alone knew, there beat a heart from which, alas! all love and sympathy had long ago died out.

By 1920, hard hearts and shrewd little heads were the mode. A certain world-weariness was acceptable. It perhaps was felt to go well with emancipation. Romantic love was liable to be consigned to the area designated in the new jargon of the day as 'all that rot'. Of course, a fashion, if not a virtue, was being made of necessity. The war had slaughtered a million more or less virile men and maimed or driven mad at least another million. There were far more women in the country than could hope to obtain partners. The pretence that marriage was an irrelevant indulgence was a comfort to the deprived. It appealed also to the increasing number of working women. A big proportion of these owed their jobs to their mobility and their willingness to work for less money than men. In the eyes of employers, including local authorities, a married, and therefore potentially pregnant, woman was an unreliable piece of equipment. In the industrial areas there was strong resentment among male workers against women whom they considered not only to be helping depress wage standards and contributing to unemployment but to be doing these things without even the excuse of having to support themselves. White-collar workers were only slightly less rigid in their opposition. Office collections for wedding presents expressed goodwill of a decidedly valedictory kind. Many private firms and all education committees automatically dismissed women employees when they married.

Economic discrimination was hard enough to bear, but women who wanted to take advantage of new educational opportunities in order to enter professions were also liable to encounter political hostility and moral indignation. Dorothy Leigh Sayers must have been well aware of this unsympathetic climate by the time she created Harriet Vane, the fictional projection of herself who symbolically avenged womankind in general by snubbing in book after book the zealous, if rather supercilious courtship of Lord Peter Wimsey.

Born seven years before the death of the Good Old Queen, Dorothy Sayers was the daughter of a clergyman-schoolmaster. After a childhood in East Anglia, she went to Somerville College (the model for her *Gaudy Night*) and was one of the first women to receive an Oxford degree. To take top honours in mediaeval literature cannot have been regarded in 1915 as a normal feminine accomplishment. Nor was there anything conventional about her choice of job on coming down from university: she became a copywriter in a London advertising agency. She married in the year of the General Strike, 1926, but Lord Peter had been at large for three years by then and the money was beginning to come in. In 1930, Wimsey cleared Harriet Vane of a murder charge in *Strong Poison* and there began the long tussle for Harriet's agreement to become Lady Wimsey that some readers deplored as getting in the way of the detection.

Miss Vane, resolutely unwed, continued to voice her creator's opinion concerning the modern role of women in society. In *Have His Carcase* (1932), a tea-dance in Victorian costume moved her to the reflection that

> the slender-seeming waists were made so not by savage tight-lacing but by sheer expensive dressmaking. Tomorrow on the tennis court the short, loose tunic-frock would reveal them as the waists of muscular young women of the day, despising all bonds.

Were men really stupid enough, Harriet wondered, to believe that milliners' fashions could bring back the old days of submissive womanhood?

Lord Peter, who carried ten gold sovereigns in his pocket – not to spend, but because 'they feel pleasant, don't they?' – had his own methods of winning a girl's acquiescence. If the girl was of good family, as was Harriet Vane, he had only to draw on his past experience with the Quorn and the Pytchley and get into a saddle.

> Harriet was silent. She suddenly saw Wimsey in a new light. She knew him to be intelligent, clean, courteous, wealthy, well read, amusing, and enamoured, but he had not so far produced in her that crushing sense of utter inferiority which leads to prostration and hero-worship. But now she realized that there was, after all, something god-like about him. He could control a horse.

If, on the other hand, the intended conquest was of a working-class girl, the advice of the omniscient Bunter was necessary.

> 'I wish to appear in my famous impersonation of the perfect Lounge Lizard – imitation très difficile.' 'Very good, my lord. I suggest the fawn-coloured suit we do not care for, with the autumn-leaf socks and our outsize amber cigarette-holder.' 'As you will, Bunter . . . we must stoop to conquer.'

Lord Peter's object in the second instance, it need hardly be said, was information and not venery. His highly developed detective instinct could always be relied upon to protect him from involvement in a misalliance. Witness how, in *Have His Carcase*, he divined from the evidence of a single piece of notepaper the true social origin of its sender:

> Wimsey took the blue sheet of paper and cocked a knowing eye at it. 'Very dainty. As supplied by Mr Selfridge's fancy counter to the nobility and gentry . . . Olga Kohn – who sounds like a Russian Jewess – is not precisely out of the top drawer, as my

mother would say, and was obviously not educated at Oxford
or Cambridge . . .'

Miss Sayers, of course, was; and passages such as this suggest
that she never quite overcame the need to remind herself of the
fact. Nor could she resist making the kind of observation that
was calculated to reflect her own intelligence, good taste, and
racial purity. Thus, Olga Kohn's room was described as having a
general air of semi-artistic refinement and containing, before its
empty fireplace, *a dark-haired young man of Semitic appearance,
who acknowledged the introductions with a scowl* and subsequently failed miserably to understand Wimsey's subtle jokes
about the Second Law of Thermodynamics.

Harriet Vane was no heroine in the romantic sense. For one
thing, she was supposed to be a detective novelist and therefore
more interested in people as potential book characters than as
human beings. She was aware of the value of publicity and lost no
opportunity of getting herself interviewed by the journalists assigned to cases that Lord Peter was investigating. Bodies held no
horrors for her. On one occasion she searched with absolute im-
passivity the pockets of a corpse whose neck had been hacked
through to the backbone with a razor. She later shared in
Wimsey's heavily facetious jesting about the victim's lack of dress
sense (he was a foreigner) and abominable taste in shoes. Even the
cut throat was made the subject of humorous back-chat. A police
sergeant,

> who had gaped in astonishment at the beginning of this ex-
> change, now burst into a hearty guffaw. 'That's very good,' he
> said indulgently. 'Comic, ain't it, the stuff these writer-fellows
> put into their books?'

Comic, indeed – or so it must have been generally agreed at the
time, for the sales and reputation of Miss Sayers rose steadily, with
scarcely a single dissenting voice among the critics. The *Daily
Express* was inspired to announce in 1934 that she had already

'eclipsed Edgar Wallace and Conan Doyle as the master writer of detective fiction'.

Other authors of the period were less severe in the delineation of heroines. They lacked, perhaps, the toughening effects of a Somerville education. Agatha Christie was too busy perfecting her formula of the Least Likely Person to create unconventional young female characters. Sydney Horler, who suggested acidly that Miss Sayers spent 'several hours a day watching the detective story as though expecting something terrific to happen', did not approve of any deviation from the English Rose standard of womanhood. Nor did Edgar Wallace, although his heroines needed to be rather more athletic than most in order to survive encounters with mad master criminals, escape from collapsing caverns, and extricate themselves from gas-filled pits. One curious feature of the typical Wallace heroine is her close family relationship to the villain or one of his henchmen. The theme of guilty father and innocent daughter is one that seems to have haunted Wallace. George Orwell thought he detected 'a fearful intellectual sadism' in Wallace's plots, which, according to Orwell, commonly included arrangements for the villain to be hanged on the same day as the heroine was married. This may be a misinterpretation. Hanging did fascinate Wallace but more probably for the right than the wrong reasons: he was a gentle and generous-hearted man, and in more than one passage describing prisons and the execution shed the impression is given that the obscene paraphernalia of capital punishment revolted and distressed him.

If not actually immortal, like her evil master, Fu-Manchu, Sax Rohmer's heroine was wondrously durable. Only a slave girl was Karamaneh, but

seemingly, with true Oriental fatalism, she was quite reconciled to her fate, and ever and anon she would bestow upon me a glance from her beautiful eyes which few men, I say with confidence, could have sustained unmoved. Though I could not be blind to the emotions of the passionate Eastern soul, yet I strove not to think of them. Accomplice of an arch-murderer she might be; but she was dangerously lovely.

(*The Mystery of Dr Fu-Manchu*)

In book after book she appeared and reappeared in order to set Dr Petrie's senses reeling (on no recorded occasion did he get them under sufficient control to achieve physical contact with her) and to lead him and Nayland Smith out of the latest trap patiently prepared by the diabolical Doctor. How so perversely inclined an accomplice as Karamaneh could remain so long on the Fu Manchu payroll is one of the enduring mysteries of crime fiction. Perhaps she kept her job through the personal representation of Arthur Sarsfield Ward, whose Irish charm and chivalry impressed his friends much more favourably than did his literary style. Ward, when he was not being Rohmer, wrote for the theatre, travelled – chiefly in America but significantly little in the East, and was happily married.

E. Phillips Oppenheim bequeathed no memorable heroines. He seems not to have been much interested in personality; with him, plot and furnishings were all. His enormous readership, which for many years included the most substantial section of the magazine public in the United States, did not complain. It was enough for them, apparently, that women should exist in Oppenheim's novels as creatures so refined by wealth and gracious living as to have become virtually disembodied. Those elegant, perfumed wraiths were described as doing all sorts of impressive-sounding things. They could capture hearts, make pulses race, command the attention of an entire assembly, wither by a glance, melt (very, very occasionally) into arms. Yet none was ever depicted in a way that brought her to life as a human being. Oppenheim was not, of course, the only popular author who was unable or unwilling to portray characters in terms that had any relevance to common experience. But he was a vigilant businessman and a hard worker: he would not have left unremedied any deficiency of style or construction that demonstrably affected his sales. We may be sure that the Oppenheim heroines remained impossible because his customers preferred them so.

Why did they? Why, for that matter, did the readers of Sax Rohmer continue to be entranced by his 'slave girl' fantasies? And why, in a different sphere of escapist fiction, did Ethel M. Dell's devotees follow so eagerly the fortunes of one utterly incredible woman after another?

Several reasons are suggested by cross-reference, so to speak, between the books and their times, between the authors and the kind of people known to have read their work.

The times, economically, materially, were hard times. For the overwhelming majority of people there was no wealth and very little protection from the effects of poverty. The books, in the main, were bought or borrowed or rented by that section of the community that lay between the very rich and the diligent but chronically hard-up 60 or 70%. To this middle section the writers themselves belonged – by origin and allegiance, if not always by standard of income. The constant preoccupation of most of its members, naturally enough, was the preservation of the structure of society as a whole. They nursed no hopes of climbing into the seats of power, but their contentment always was tinged with the fear of falling. They prayed for a three-fold stability: the stability of the country in relation to the rest of the world, political stability within the country, and moral stability – the continued prevelance of those rules of behaviour which they had been brought up to revere.

From the turn of the century until the second world war, writers of crime and detection stories took care never to offend patriotic susceptibilities. The political tone was conservative save in a handful of instances. As for morals, it would be difficult to point to any other single branch of popular entertainment that conformed more strictly to current notions of decency.

'Shut the door, Wick,' she commanded. 'And then come and sit down here. I want you not to look at me. That's why I've switched off the lights . . . You're such an old dear that I know you'll hardly believe that I could be capable of the limit. I'm afraid I am, or rather, was. On a certain night in December I

got as near to it as doesn't matter. I was fool enough, mad
enough, to stay a night at an hotel in Bournemouth – with Mr
Barrington.' Gore stared at her blankly. 'Hell, Pickles,' he said
at length, softly, 'what did you do that for?'

(The Deductions of Colonel Gore)

Lynn Brock's readers did not require 'the limit' to be physi-
ologically specified. Such public school euphemisms were familiar
to them. More than that, they were literally meaningful. Extra-
marital copulation – and in Bournemouth, of all places – really was
beyond the bounds, and it was a daring writer who for purposes of
plot allowed a character to confess to it, however obliquely. Only
thirty years later, commentaries on coital encounters were to be a
commonplace of the crime novel, but in the 1920s ruttish imaginations had to conjure what they could from passages such as
this :

From the tip of her sprucely-waving golden head to the toes of
her smartly-sensible shoes, her orderly freshness and daintiness
were without blemish – an estate of jealously guarded, minutely
vigilant propriety – sweet, sound English womanliness, scrupulously groomed, meticulously decked for the afternoon.

The heroine of another thriller of the earlier part of the inter-
war period was described as walking

with magnificent self-assurance and an easy grace. Her flaxen
hair was neatly shingled, revealing the contour of a perfectly
shaped head; her intense blue eyes danced with the divine fire
of youth.

Blondes – already out of favour with serious novelists, for whom
perhaps they represented too brash a taste – were openly preferred
by the thriller writers. So were blue eyes and neat hair. It was,
after all, the age of the cloche hat. 'Naturalness' was frequently
emphasized, with a wealth of horticultural simile. 'This fragrant
blossom,' enthused Ralph Trevor, 'from the garden of womanhood

who sat opposite . . .' Less extravagant, but reflecting a similar distrust of cosmetics, was E. R. Punshon's description of the heroine of *The Unexpected Legacy* (1929).

> She was about the middle height, with a very light and graceful bearing, and her small face was of a lovely oval, with small, exquisitely shaped features and two very serious, thoughtful, and extremely bright blue eyes. Her complexion was as pure as that of a little child, and evidently owed as little to any artificial aid.

Two years later, in *Proof Counter Proof,* Punshon had a character lament the difficulty of telling a woman's age because, with all of them using make-up, 'you can't tell a grandmother from a schoolgirl, except by the schoolgirl knowing so much more'. Discernible here is the resentment aroused in settled and respectable people by the precociousness, as it seems to them, of a younger generation. This was frequently expressed in detective fiction, as was disapproval of overt sexuality. Punshon's woman of indeterminate age, for example, 'had dark hair and eyes, dressed up to the nines, and you could smell her from one end of the shop to the other'. She had *a sort of foreign way with her* and wore her hair long, not shingled or cropped in the current style.

Long hair was commonly associated with moral laxity until the later 1930s, when it became fashionable once again. *A bunch of black ringlets* was part of Harriet Vane's ordinance of seduction when she set off to turn the head of a suspected criminal and to extract information from him. She selected a *slinky garment . . . with a corsage which outlined the figure and a skirt which waved tempestuously about her ankles*. An oversized hat hid half her face, while *high-heeled beige shoes and sheer silk stockings, with embroidered gloves and handbag, completed this alluring toilette.* The ringlets, Dorothy Sayers was careful to add, had been *skilfully curled into position by the head hairdresser at the Resplendent.*

Miss Vane obtained the information she was after, then calmly disengaged from the suspect without having allowed him the slightest liberty in return. It may be objected that a branch of fiction

that always had enshrined the ideals of fairness and sportsmanship
was no medium for sexual sharp practice by a heroine ruthless
enough to wear a tight corsage and a floppy hat. But the victim of
the subterfuge had even more to suffer. When, understandably, he
spoke later of his experience in ungentlemanly terms, there was
revealed to him that side of the British aristocratic character
which normally is glimpsed only by fleeing foreign soldiery or by
importunate tradesmen:

'Manners, please!' said Wimsey. 'You will kindly refer to Miss
Vane in a proper way and spare me the boring nuisance of
pushing your teeth out at the back of your neck.'

The fact is that there was a certain elasticity in the ethical
posture of Miss Sayers and the people for whom she wrote. This
permitted acceptance of the ineligibility of certain classes of
people to receive the benefits of fair play. Lord Peter once listed
such outsiders as 'liars and half-wits and prostitutes and dagoes'. It
was a hasty, off-the-cuff inventory, but it can be elaborated in the
light of extended reading of Miss Sayers's novels. Liars would include all who failed to observe the law, particularly those substantial sections of it devoted to the protection of property and
privilege. Into the half-wit category would be put anyone who fell
down on jokes about the Second Law of Thermodynamics, also
people guilty of sartorial gaffes and errors of pronunciation and
mistakes with fish knives. Prostitute presumably applied to any
woman who exploited her sexual attractions for money, as distinct
from social advancement; while dago would be a generic term for
all non-British persons and particularly those of swarthy com-
plexion.

To cheat or treat shabbily anyone in these categories was permissible. One did not lose caste by doing so. Nor did a lady – a real
lady – put her reputation at risk by associating with such people
for the purpose of worming confidences out of them in a good
cause, as when

Miss Harriet Vane, in a claret-coloured frock, swayed round

162 · *Snobbery with Violence*

the dance floor of the Hotel Resplendent in the arms of Mr
Antoine, the fair-haired gigolo . . . who was rather surprisingly
neither Jew nor South American dago, nor Central European
mongrel, but French.

This and Miss Vane's earlier encounter of a similar nature were
in public, needless to say. Thriller writers were more circumspect
on behalf of heroines who found themselves alone with a man of
unpredictable or evil intent. The possibility of sexual molestation
was one that had to be treated carefully. Commenting on what he
called the 'mealy-mouthed' quality of detective fiction, Cyril Hare
observed that this was to be expected of the 'favourite reading of
the very classes who are most easily shocked by frankness in such
matters as sexual behaviour'. An almost Victorian reticence continued to be observed in crime fiction for decades after treatment
of unsavoury topics had come to be accepted, within limits, as a
legitimate feature of the straight novel.

John Rhode, who turned to writing solid, workmanlike detective fiction after retiring from a military career as Major Cecil
John Charles Street, was not ashamed to declare one of his heroines 'as straight as they make them'. In his *Tragedy at the Unicorn*
(1928) a girl is included on a list of suspects simply because the
murder victim had, on one occasion, caught her in his arms and
tried to kiss her.

Edgar Wallace was constantly putting his women in desperate
straits, but lascivious hands were never laid upon them. It could be
argued that the pace of the action never gave venery a chance.
Seduction, even ravishment, does take time; the instant rapists of
the Chase–Spillane–Janson school were yet to be unloosed upon
an age of even greater credulity than the 1920s. However, what in
that coming time would be termed programming difficulties were
not the reason why Wallace and his contemporaries spared their
heroines' maidenheads. They simply did not feel any compulsion
to treat of sensuality in the context of the thriller. Margaret
Belman removed her skirt readily enough at the behest and in the
presence of Mr J. G. Reeder, but this was only because the water

in the cellar where they were trapped had risen to a level which made swimming unavoidable. The public, Wallace considered, was more interested in the couple's survival and ultimate escape than in the reaction of the hero to the baring of his beloved's thighs.

A theme that often recurred in the tales of Wallace and others was that of a girl physically held under duress or intimidated by other means, including threats to injure or expose someone dear to her, until she acceded to her tormentor's demands. It was a very old, one might almost say venerable, theme, but it was acceptable only so long as a woman's 'honour' was deemed to be a commodity, and a negotiable commodity at that. Few readers now would accept seriously the idea of a villain restraining not only the girl but his own appetite until after the wedding. The modern conception of a criminal is that of an utterly amoral opportunist. He is witty, photogenic, sadistic, sexy and clever. That is how the public, conditioned largely by television, likes him to be. Wallace's public, many of whom were also readers of Oppenheim and Anthony Hope, Sabatini and Conan Doyle, John Buchan and William Le Queux, cherished a different kind of fantasy. The preferred criminal was daring, dangerous and vaguely anti-social; but he was honourable according to his lights, a giver and taker of sporting chances, and, on all the evidence, as highly sexed as a muffin. Girls were abducted by him or his hirelings but never for on-the-spot enjoyment. Either the object was to put pressure on a father, husband or fiancé, or it was to get the girl herself to the altar, with benefit of clergy and a photograph in *The Tatler*.

Respectability, such stories implied, was a universal currency that not even a burglar or a bank robber would think of debasing. In books without number its defence was propounded as a motive for murder. And what is blackmail, the second most common crime in the detection calendar, if it is not a means of putting respectability at hazard?

Even the pulp magazine market was sensible in the 1930s of the need to preserve a certain decorum for the benefit of those whom the publishers of *Spicy Detective* rather nervously called 'certain groups of people in different parts of the country'. In a circular to contributors on both sides of the Atlantic, they laid down, *inter alia*, the following rules:

In describing breasts of a female character, avoid anatomical descriptions. If it is necessary for the story to have the girl give herself to a man, or be taken by him, do not go too carefully into the details ... Whenever possible, avoid complete nudity of the female characters. You can have a girl strip to her underwear, or transparent negligee or nightgown, or the thin torn shreds of her garments, but while the girl is alive and in contact with a man, we do not want complete nudity. A nude female corpse is allowable, of course. Also a girl undressing in the privacy of her own room, but when men are in the action try to keep at least a shred of something on the girls. Do not have men in underwear in scenes with women, and no nude men at all. The idea is to have a very strong sex element in these stories without anything that might be interpreted as being vulgar or obscene.

CHAPTER 13

The little world of
Mayhem Parva

In 1925 A. E. W. Mason wrote: 'All the great detective novels are known by and live on account of their detectives.' This is true. For every person in the world who has heard of Sir Arthur Conan Doyle there are scores to whom the name of Sherlock Holmes is familiar and that of Doyle quite meaningless. Father Brown exists vividly as a podgy, innocent-looking priest in imaginations that retain only the dimmest image of his very solid creator. Wimsey, Poirot, Dr Thorndyke, Albert Campion, Roger Sheringham, Dr Fell, Sir Henry Merrivale were – and still are – asked for by name in libraries, as though they were waiting friends rather than characters in books.

Towards the end of the first world war, the young wife of an English officer amused herself by writing a story about the investigation of a crime in a country house. She called it *The Mysterious Affair at Styles*. The book was accepted by the seventh publisher approached and was printed in 1920. The career of Agatha Christie had been launched. So had that of Hercule Poirot.

Public acceptance of Poirot meant for Agatha Christie the difference between remaining a competent but only moderately well-paid member of the detective story industry and promotion to that small group of writers who, because their names or those of their creations are universally familiar, enjoy self-proliferating success. For half a century after the publication of *The Mysterious Affair at Styles*, readers continued faithfully to follow the adventures of the egotistic, moustachioed little man who had quit the Brussels Police in 1904 and devoted a retirement in England to the pursuit and unmasking of criminals. Poirot novels have been published at an average rate of nearly one a year; nineteen were written between 1920 and the outbreak of the second world war.

Poirot, one might imagine, was not a character calculated to win the confidence and affection of the British library public of the 1920s. For one thing, he was an alien. Apart from A. E. W. Mason's Hanaud, no foreign detectives – not even Arsène Lupin – had been thought of very highly; Charlie Chan, Mı Moto and other exotics would not cross the Atlantic for several more years. Poirot was short and had a noticeably egg-shaped head. Neither feature would have commended him to a people at once sensitive to deficiency in stature and readily amused by minor deformities. His eyes went green when he was excited and he was an incorrigible moustache-twirler. He carried a cane, smoked sissy cigarettes, was a somewhat fancy dresser, dyed his hair and spoke English with comic literalness. Without doubt, a Froggie and an effeminate Froggie at that. Was it not natural enough that six publishers had turned down *The Mysterious Affair at Styles*?

But of course Poirot was not a Froggie. He was a Belgian. The distinction was an important one in 1920. Not only had the British unaccountably neglected to coin a derogatory epithet for the inhabitants of Belgium but they still were inclined to think of that country as the military propagandists of five or six years earlier had encouraged them to think – with indulgent sentimentality. Poirot's five-feet-four, his slight limp, his aggressive moustaches – these, in the context of 'gallant little Belgium', were admirable. So was his fastidiousness, which would have been deemed odious affectation had he been one of the French, those unreliable allies who now were making a thorough nuisance of themselves just when England wanted only to put a poppy wreath on the nice new Unknown Soldier's Tomb at Westminster Abbey and then settle down to crosswords and detective stories. For the detective story was playing an increasingly important part in the attempts by the middle class to restore its nerve and to take its mind off the irrational and disconcerting things that other people, in other places, continued so wantonly to do.

In essence, Poirot was neither French nor Belgian. He was an altogether English creation – as English as a Moorish cinema foyer or hotel curry or comic yodellers. He personified English ideas about foreignness and was therefore immediately familiar to readers and acceptable by them. As a detective he had special qualities calculated to make him an enduring figure of fiction. He was knowing. He had an instinct for discovering the truth. He could, by a quick twist of his nimble mind, dispose of an alibi or uncover a guilty secret. If only there were more Poirots about, one felt, life and property would be much safer. And yet his extraordinary capacity for thwarting criminals and the predictable, if elaborate, triumphs of his intellect did not impose – as they well might have done – too great a strain upon the goodwill of a public traditionally impatient of the over-clever. Mrs Christie had forestalled this danger by emphasizing one of Poirot's characteristically 'foreign' qualities – his cockiness – to a point of amiable absurdity.

'Ah, it was a clever plan, but he did not reckon on the cleverness of Hercule Poirot!'

Once a vice has been rendered ridiculous, it somehow is felt to be endearing. Conan Doyle did Holmes a similar service when he made his display of superiority so theatrical that failure on his part to produce an arrogant remark at the right moment would have seemed a let-down. And in the cases both of Holmes and of Poirot a foil was provided, a companion-chronicler so obtuse, so good-naturedly dense, as to swing the reader's sympathy firmly to the detective. The device was cunning. It meant that one either was tolerant of the monumental priggishness of Holmes or risked being equated intellectually with poor old Watson. The alternative to allowing Poirot his air of omniscience was admission to being no smarter than a Captain Hastings.

Another means of strengthening the detective in the public regard was to contrast the success of his methods with the failure of those of the regular police, the representatives of established authority. Many crime writers adopted this method. It was favoured chiefly by the amateurs, who felt perhaps that it absolved them from the task of learning the facts about real-life investigation and legal process, but from Conan Doyle onward some of the most respected authors persisted in glorifying their own characters at the expense of stupid, pompous policemen. In the Sherlock Holmes stories, the propensity of men like Inspector Lestrade and Inspector Athelney Jones for misunderstanding the simplest clue and consequently committing heinous blunders was equalled only by Holmes's generosity in letting them take the ultimate credit for his inspiration. Mrs Christie's men from Scotland Yard were more responsible figures than the capering idiots propounded by Conan Doyle, but they clearly were not in the same league as Poirot.

Mrs Christie's detective-hero was intended to personify an orderly and methodical approach to life's problems. Order and method were words he used a good deal in conversation, and he never tired of emphasizing the virtue of employing 'the little grey cells'. His quaint form of speech helped to establish him as a character who would be remembered easily from book to book, and the impression grew that here was cleverness of an authoritative kind. As salesmen of encyclopaedias know well, the public is inclined to be in awe of knowledge but to distrust intelligence. In Poirot, though, seemingly disparate qualities existed side by side. He had an appealing continental politeness, was whimsically aware of the comic element in being foreign, respected True Love, British Justice and le Bon Dieu, and was just human enough to preface his brilliant solutions with the occasional faulty deduction

('Hurry, Hastings, and let us hope we are not too late!'). It did not matter that a great deal of his apparently deeply significant commentary turned out to have had only the most tenuous connection with the case. The red herring convention had not yet become discredited and crime writers were getting away with much worse than murder in their manufacture of distraction, false trails, unlikely motives and long coincidence. Even the great Holmes had been involved in more than one corny situation, so Mrs Christie's readers presumably saw nothing preposterous in Poirot's feigning death (after pouring his cup of poisoned camomile tea 'into a little bottle' for later analysis) in order to deceive his would-be assassin; or entrapping a murderess by confronting her with an actor made up as her dead husband, phosphorescent paint and all. Ironically, it was a Christie character who delivered the opinion: 'I myself think the Sherlock Holmes stories grossly overrated. The fallacies – the really amazing fallacies that there are in those stories . . .'

If the little Belgian invariably scored with intuitive brilliance, it was because most readers were not inclined to examine closely his lines of reasoning. The stories, after all, had been written not as academic exercises in logic but as escapist entertainment. For the customers of Phillips Oppenheim and Anthony Hope and William Le Queux, escape had meant transference into a world of riches and romance, of beautiful women and handsome men where duellists and maîtres d'hôtel and millionaires abounded but where no one, apparently, ever delivered milk or drove a tram or went back to Oldham or Milwaukee. Agatha Christie and her imitators offered something very different. It was a dream, but not of marble halls. The picture was of familiar homeliness and it was populated with stock characters observing approved rules of behaviour according to station, and isolated utterly from all such anxieties and unpleasantness as were not responsive to religion, medicine and the law.

The setting for the crime stories by what we might call the Mayhem Parva school would be a cross between a village and a commuters' dormitory in the South of England, self-contained and largely self-sufficient. It would have a well-attended church, an inn with reasonable accommodation for itinerant detective-inspectors, a village institute, library and shops – including a chemist's where weed killer and hair dye might conveniently be bought. The district would be rural, but not uncompromisingly so – there would be a good bus service for the keeping of suspicious appointments in the nearby town, for instance – but its general character would be sufficiently picturesque to chime with the English suburb dweller's sadly uninformed hankering after retirement to 'the country'.

There would dwell in Mayhem Parva a number of well-to-do people, some in professional practice of various kinds, some retired, some just plain rich and for ever messing about with their wills. The rest of the population would be working folk, static in habit and thought. Their talk, modelled on middle-class notions of the vernacular of shop assistants and garage hands, would be a standardized compound of ungrammatical, cheerful humility. Characters would not be easy to distinguish as individuals, but class would be easily identifiable and the sheep would be separable from the goats without much trouble.

> Four people were in the room: a somewhat flashily dressed man with a shifty, unpleasant face to whom I took an immediate dislike; a woman of much the same type, though handsome in a coarse fashion; another woman dressed in neat black who stood apart from the rest and whom I took to be the housekeeper; and a tall man dressed in sporting tweeds, with a clever, capable face, and who was clearly in command of the situation. 'Dr Giles,' said the constable . . .
>
> (*Thirteen for luck,* 1966)

A brigadier would talk like a brigadier, a vicar like a vicar, a wealthy hypochondriac would be unmistakably given to spite and self-pity, and her paid companion would be as meek and dowdy as are all paid companions. There would exist for these people no really sordid, intractable problems, such as growing old or losing faith or being abandoned or going mad. One or more would get murdered; the rest would be suspected for a while; one of them would ultimately be trussed for the gallows, if he or she had not first bitten on a pill smelling of bitter almonds or fallen from a train or something. And then, the air cleared, everything would be set to continue as before, right, tight, and reliable.

Such was England as represented by Mayhem Parva. It was, of course, a mythical kingdom, a fly-in-amber land. It was derived in part from the ways and values of a society that had begun to fade away from the very moment of the shots at Sarajevo; in part from that remarkably durable sentimentality which, even today, can be expressed in the proposition that every church clock has stopped at 14.50 hours and honey is a perpetual comestible at vicarages.

It offered not outward escape, as did books of travel, adventure, international intrigue, but inward – into a sort of museum of nostalgia. The word 'cosy' often has been applied, and in no pejorative sense, to the Mayhem Parva writers. Their choice of scene is held to have been calculated on the principle that the eruption of violence in the midst of the ordinary, the familiar, the respectable, is more shocking and therefore more satisfying than the older-fashioned presentation of villainy in surroundings unremittingly sinister. But was this their plan? Did they really expect readers to be horror-stricken by the discovery of a corpse in the tea tent at the church garden fête? The answer would be yes only if crime at Mayhem Parva had been the province of writers concerned with reality, writers such as Francis Iles, Raymond Postgate and C. Day Lewis before the second war and Julian Symons, William Mole and Mary Kelly after it. Real murder arouses in ordinary people terror, revulsion and dismay. Description of how the members of a small isolated community would in fact react to violent death in their midst is an altogether different matter from the presentation of an entertaining puzzle. And it was the puzzle-setters who dominated the field of crime fiction up to the 1940s and beyond. Their policy was to keep the griefs of their characters short and formal and to hurry everyone along to the interviews in the library in good time for them to dress for dinner – a social obligation that not even the most extravagant multiples of homicide were allowed to disrupt.

So long as such conventions ruled it was quite impossible to believe in the commission of a crime in the sense of finding room in the mind for the true blackness of spilled blood, the obscene vacuity of a murdered face. One noted instead the game's familiar counters and symbols; its clues, harmless as play money – gun, dagger, paperweight, poisoned thorn, spreading stain, body slumped, acrid reek of cordite, expression of terror as if, clutched in stiffening fingers, not a pretty sight, watch-glass smashed at 3.27 . . . Who was supposed to be dead, anyway? More often than not someone of wealth or of substantial expectations, a blackmailer perhaps, or a business rival, or somebody about to expose a piece of trickery, or simply a man or woman hated by everyone in sight. Very rarely was the corpse that of an innocent or venerated person. A young girl, other than one of specified immorality, was seldom the victim, a child never. Religion played no part in these crimes, save when the faith concerned was non-Christian, in which case it was described as a 'cult'. In short, sympathy for the departed was not solicited; rather was there an implication that getting murdered was, if not actually culpable, at least a misfortune involving contributory negligence. Agatha Christie's view of the casualties in her stories is a consistently detached one. The plot, the puzzle, is all, and apart from an occasional reiteration by Poirot of his own basic principle ('*I have a bourgeois attitude to murder. I disapprove of it*') no one wastes time on moral argument. The employment of the least-likely-person technique would nullify such statements, anyway. Appearing to be cynical is one of the occupational hazards of mystery authorship.

To characterize the fiction of the Mayhem Parva school as 'two dimensional' is not to question its adequacy as entertainment. It could not have offered what it did – relaxation, diversion, reassurance – if it had possessed that third dimension which gives a story power to affect the reader in much the same way as actual experience. Here was a plain, an area of immense contentedness and what people who do not care much for explorative thought call 'common sense'. It featured no dramatic heights, no chasms of desperation – just the neat little box hedges of the maze, the puzzle, at whose centre awaited a figure labelled Murderer. One was not afraid of meeting this unknown. There was in one's pursuit of the winding paths a sort of cheerful curiosity, quite unmixed with that feeling which the anonymous slayer inspires in reality, whether from Whitechapel in 1888 or from London left luggage offices in the 1930s – the feeling of dread. One cumulative effect of regular reading of this kind of fiction might have been to blunt temporarily the fear of death. Sympathy was not being solicited: that was a relief to start with. Then the method of murder was often bizarre, occasionally gruesome, but seldom credible enough to be really shocking. Pronouncement that the victim's death had been 'instantaneous' was made in enough books to encourage a personal hope that lingering ends were exceptional.

The atmosphere throughout the case usually was businesslike, with too much going on to allow of brooding. The detective did not stray beyond questions of time-tables, poison analyses, shoe prints, and so on, except when opportunity occurred for him to emphasize one or another of the idiosyncracies calculated to make him seem amusing or likable. Otherwise he kept his counsel and thereby the reader's confidence, venturing fragments of the most homely and unexceptionable psychology only to lend significance to clues or to cast doubts upon alibis. The detective was far too occupied with serving justice to indulge in the morbid philosophizing that constant encounters with corpses might have induced in less dedicated operators. Most important of all, the inevitable solving of the crime, the identification and rendering harmless of the murderer at the very end of the book, somehow had the effect of cancelling out the death or deaths which had gone before. It was as if murder had been merely an engine that had set the story going and then been jettisoned. In more than one novel, the reader needed to glance back from the denouement to remind himself of who had been murdered in the first place.

Agatha Christie maintained, after her very earliest books, an air of slightly sardonic detachment from the events of which she wrote. One feels it to be an attitude characteristic of an astute professional author. The sellers' market in crime fiction which lasted throughout the 1920s and 1930s permitted the publication of many books that not only lacked literary merit but, by being gauchely imitative, brought into ridicule a number of contrivances that had been used with discretion and therefore effectively by more capable writers. By 1926 when *The Murder of Roger Ack-royd* consolidated Mrs Christie's reputation, already it was inadvisable to postulate crimes committed by hypnotists, men armed with South American blowpipes, purveyors of untraceable poisons, and butlers. Murders of, or by, identical twins and long lost brothers were also questionable propositions. The last chapter gathering of suspects calculated to encompass the dramatic self-betrayal of the guilty party was not yet discredited, but a few sophisticated readers were beginning to wince at each recurrence of the device.

A less shrewd practitioner than Mrs Christie would have been tempted to bar all those elements of crime fiction that had become absurdities in the eyes of intelligent people. But she seems to have been well aware that intelligence and readership-potential are quite unrelated. So she hedged her bets. While preserving the essential artificialities, unlikelihoods and clichés of the bestselling whodunnit, she evolved a style of narration that hinted, just delicately enough not to offend British sensitivity to 'sarcasm', at self-parody. Here is her description of a rich foreigner, soon to be murdered:

> He was tall and thin, his face was long and melancholy, his eyebrows were heavily accented and jet black, he wore a moustache with stiff waxed ends and a tiny black imperial. His clothes were works of art – of exquisite cut – but with a suggestion of bizarre. Every healthy Englishman who saw him longed earnestly and fervently to kick him. They said, with a singular lack of originality: 'There's that damned Dago, Shaitana!'
>
> (*Cards on the Table*, 1936)

The passage shows Mrs Christie's awareness of how widespread in the England of 1936 was xenophobia, her own disapproval of which she implied in the phrase 'with a singular lack of originality'. But it would have taken someone with a little more subtlety than that of the average reader to notice that here was not just another routine sneer at the foreigner.

In *Death in the Clouds,* published the year before, Mrs Christie had included in the plot a figure traditionally venerated by the public and therefore not to be presented facetiously by any novel-ist who valued sales – a lord. One sees him first standing by the ancestral sideboard at breakfast time and helping himself to kidneys. Then, riding on the estate, he happens to meet the girl, not his wife, who has

> always loved Stephen, always since the old days of dancing classes and cubbing and birds' nesting. . . . Pictures floated before his eyes: hunting – tea and muffins – the smell of wet earth and leaves – children. . . . All the things that Cicely could never share with him, that Cicely would never give him. A kind of mist came over his eyes.

This sounds like a send-up of the middle-class conception of upper-class romance but one cannot be quite sure. After all, reams of exactly similar stuff were, and still are, being turned out by writers profitably equipped with the sort of fire-and-water-proof ingenuousness which their publishers call 'sincerity'. And so there existed no serious danger of alienating loyal if somewhat simple-minded aristophiles so long as tongue went no more obtrusively into cheek than:

> Aloud she said. 'So there's nothing doing?'
> He shook his head. Then he said. 'If I were free, Venetia, would you marry me?'
> Looking very straight between her horse's ears, Venetia said in a voice carefully devoid of emotion, 'I suppose I would.'

CHAPTER 14

Gifted amateurs

When Sherlock Holmes solved the mystery of the disappearance of the son of the Duke of Holdernesse in the *Adventure of the Priory School,* he named as his fee six thousand pounds. His Grace, aware that Holmes had traced not only his son but a skeleton in the family cupboard, made out his cheque for twelve thousand. Holmes admonished him about the skeleton but took the cheque. 'I am a poor man,' he said, with one of his very rare flashes of drollery.

Rewards are seldom specified in stories of private detectives. Philip Marlowe, of course, was a genuinely poor man. No one in the Holdernesse class would have persevered past that dingy little waiting-room. Marlowe's clients had the unprofitable tendency to become either broke or dead. But his terms were clearly enough stated. Forty bucks a day and expenses. To judge from Marlowe's case, the rate for the job had considerably diminished in the forty-three years since Holmes's little commission for the Duke. What had other investigators been making during that same period? There is scarcely any evidence. The policemen, from Inspector French to Sir John Appleby, would have received the pay appropriate to their rank and nothing else. Poirot had his Belgian pension; perhaps wariness on this score dictated his silence about the fees he presumably received on being called in to solve English crimes. Mrs Bradley always managed to do her detecting in her professional role of a Home Office consultant psychiatrist. Father Brown sleuthed exclusively for the salvation of souls, and blind Max Carrados because, as he put it, 'I am just interested in things'. The reformed criminal, Blackshirt, followed up the crimes of others simply for adventure; his new profession of authorship had made him independent of burgling. Criminology was in the way of being a relaxation from Dr Priestley's more serious work ('a monograph upon the nature of the human mind') and he was stated to be not a bit interested in justice as such.

There is, in short, a very strong presumption of amateurism throughout almost the entire range of British fictional detectives and adventurers in crime. Only a handful of the investigators had any official status, although some of the others appeared to enjoy facilities at Scotland Yard. In a few cases, these clearly were of a special order. Nayland Smith, it will be remembered, had a pair of C.I.D. men dispatched to China as simply as another man might have ordered a pie from the staff canteen. He did have Foreign Office connections, though. Less easily accountable was the readiness of Chief Inspector Parker to work with Lord Peter Wimsey in preparing the defence of the Duke of Denver on the murder charge which one would have thought it was Parker's duty to make stick. Dr Thorndyke was always able to order the local police force around wherever he set up his travelling microscope. His was a powerful personality, as was Dr Priestley's, and in both cases the medical title must have carried some weight. Other detectives had to depend on a co-operative friend or relative in authority – Miss Marples's nephew, for instance, or Poirot's colleague Japp – if they were to be allowed a hand in the case.

As crime fiction grew less crudely independent of probabilities, it became increasingly difficult to justify the presence of an interfering outsider on the scene of the crime. All kinds of device were used, but the object was the same as it had been from the days when Lestrade made his first heavily ironic remarks about the theorizing of the amateur Holmes. It was to secure the attendance of some gifted person with idiosyncracies that would be interesting to read about. Ideally, he would be unfettered by Judges' Rules, able to adopt unorthodox methods, talk as much or as little as suited the author's purpose, intervene physically if need be, and generally be at the core of the story in ways that could not logically be allowed even the most enterprising or eccentric policeman.

Occupations supposedly offering some entitlement to the tolerance of the authorities have included from time to time insurance assessing, medicine, teaching, librarianship, footballing, vintnery and (most optimistically of all) journalism.

None of these dually employed detectives has ever been really convincing. For a tale or two it did not matter greatly that the oceanographer, say, seemed to have an unreasonable amount of time away from work in order to solve the *Mystery of the Scuttled Bullion Ship* or the *Case of the Drowned Diver*. But when the author pleaded need for an expert on currents in order to secure his hero's attendance at the investigation of *The Brewery Vat Murders*, even the most faithful readers had the uncomfortable feeling that the plot was being rigged. A writer of the calibre of G. K. Chesterton could get away with a great deal of unlikelihood and inconsistency because he was bold enough to pretend that he had introduced them deliberately in order to illustrate some deeper theological truth. Even so, it required considerable sympathy for Chestertonian views on paradox to accept the saintly Father Brown's knack of always being around when a crime was about to be discovered. Less skilled authors, imagining that specialized or esoteric knowledge was enough to make a detective story intriguing, persisted in having their pet experts 'called in' until the whole thing became ridiculous.

There were two ways of avoiding such difficulties without leaving the investigation exclusively to the police. One was to make the crime or crimes political, thus justifying their solution by a hero (most recently, an anti-hero) with no specified obligations or inhibitions other than the vaguest sort of patriotism. He was the spy, the special agent, the counter-espionage man: a Saint George *in Vacuo*, having to render no account of means so long as ends were achieved.

The second and far more venerable method was to call on patronage. It dated from the old master himself. When Edgar Allan Poe was inventing and setting the form of the detective story in the early 1840s, he created for his purpose not a policeman, not an agent of government, but an eccentric gentleman of independent means, an aristocrat, le Chevalier D. Auguste Dupin, no less. Dupin had his conveniently available chronicler, who recorded the Chevalier's habit of living behind closed shutters in a room illuminated dimly by perfumed tapers. Here, in chambers in the Faubourg Saint Germain, the pair 'gave the Future to the winds, and slumbered tranquilly in the Present, weaving the dull world around us into dreams'. Besides being a philosopher and something of a sensualist, Dupin displayed a notable grasp of psychology. This enabled him on one occasion to solve a murder – that of Marie Roget – without leaving his chambers. He studied newspaper reports of the crime and deduced the truth from what witnesses had said, in the light of his knowledge of the probabilities of human behaviour.

Much has been written, especially by Americans, pointing out similarities between Dupin and Sherlock Holmes and thus implying that Conan Doyle based his detective on the creation of Edgar Allan Poe. Apart from the question of national kudos, the relationship is not of much importance. Both Dupin and Holmes were portrayed as intellectuals with highly developed powers of observation and logic. Both were aristocratic in manner and outlook, although only the Frenchman could boast an actual title. They shared a taste for nocturnal expeditions and were commonly antipathetic to domestic ventilation. So far can they be said to resemble each other. The essential difference – the division between a classical original, familiar now mainly to scholars, and a character, however derivative, that has become a part of international mythology – is due to Doyle's possession of a quality the American author lacked. He was able to make Holmes a live, palpable, human being and invest him with faults and virtues which, though not altogether credible, were unfailingly intriguing. Holmes was a crisp and intelligible talker; his air of infallibility was not only impressive but curiously endearing; and he got on with things. Dupin was unconscionably wordy, affected and static.

Poe had few direct imitators. Conan Doyle had many. The most painful results were the books of those admirers who tried most diligently to reproduce Holmes's eccentricities and scientific showmanship. Wiser were those who were content to borrow only general shapes of construction and presentation within which individual style and inventiveness might be freely developed. One such shape was the conception of the detective as a consultant, independent of authority yet in himself authoritative; less a practitioner in, than a patron of, criminology. It was this conception that had paramount influence upon the intellectual half of crime fiction – the whodunnit as distinct from the thriller – from the turn of the century onwards.

Into the Baker Street set-up may be read quite easily Doyle's own professional background and ideals. The fact of Watson's being a doctor is not the point; it is the manner, method and way of thought of Holmes which derive from the training of a medical man. His clients are like patients: after being duly amazed and gratified by the Holmesian conjuring trick of snap deduction, they proceed to describe the mysterious circumstances that trouble them, much as if they were illness symptoms. Holmes is sympathetic – save when he suspects fraud – and prompts and probes either kindly or with sharpness in order to draw out the data he needs for diagnosis. If he can see a likely solution, he does not commit himself yet nevertheless sends away his caller with the firm feeling that Mr Holmes has the measure of the problem and will put all right in good time. If, on the other hand, he is hopelessly flummoxed, he remains looking gravely confident until the patient/client has been shown out by receptionist/landlady Mrs Hudson before expressing apprehension that 'these are deep waters, Watson'. Doyle certainly knew the tricks of the medical profession.

He was also aware of the veneration in which doctors are held by ordinary people, and it is noticeable that Holmes is treated with respect, not to say awe, by all who come in contact with him except the most brutalized criminals and the occasional irascible lord (whom he is sure to humble sooner or later, anyway). Holmes has authority. It is his most noteworthy characteristic. Perhaps it is the most important feature of any detective who is to prove a success with the reading public. For if anything distinguishes crime fiction from other forms of story-telling, it is the hero's implicit instrumentality in restoring the rule of right over wrong. He is not concerned, as are the heroes of novels of romance or adventure, with such personal and trivial objectives as winning the girl or making a fortune or escaping from his enemy. Establishment of the truth, vindication of the innocent, exposure and punishment of the guilty: to ends no less formidable than these is he dedicated. The task demands authority and at the same time confers it, and it ought to be seen to do so if the book is to satisfy convention.

How does an author set about the investment of his hero with qualities that the majority of readers will see as admirable and consistent with high moral purpose and yet keep him human enough to retain their sympathy? The balance is by no means easy to achieve. People enjoy being impressed by the acrobatics of giant intellects, but once an argument becomes too complicated or a display of knowledge too recondite they lose interest. Championship of law and order commands support up to a certain point: a grain too much zeal arouses suspicion of officiousness or worse. The over-clever detective grows as tiresome in the long run as the most uninspired plodder.

Doyle's formula was an almost perfect solution of all the difficulties. He gave Holmes a dozen enviable attributes, including personal independence, financial sufficiency, an intelligence of moderately high order that was combined with a flair for showmanship and just enough wit to flatter but not to tax the average reader's sense of humour. He made him as loyal to God, Queen and country as any parson or any patriot could have desired, but allowed him pride and an occasional flash of bloody-mindedness that would appeal to the gallery as surely as would his skill at fisticuffs. At the same time, readers were invited to watch this extraordinarily strong-minded man surrender to vices as disparate as the smoking of ounce upon ounce of homely black shag and his self-injection with shots of cocaine. Here was the great detective, confidant of Royalty, at one minute as slavishly devoted to a dirty old pipe as any plumber or cabman, at the next dabbling in a drug of exotic association and fiendish potentiality. Holmes was un-married. This alone would have made him attractive to women in times when a good 'match' was the preoccupation of millions because of sharp economic inequalities. In addition he was hand-some and of gallant but not flowery manners. To balance these qualities, which male readers might have resented, Doyle em-phasized the irrevocability of Holmes's bachelorhood. There was a shadow of some lost love, some great sacrifice in the best tradition of Victorian rectitude. Hence, mayhap, the moodiness, the co-caine, even the violin. Sufferers from unrequited love who be-haved oddly were not yet in danger of being saddled with the unromantic label of manic-depressive. Nor, it must be added, was the habit of cohabiting with a male companion in adventure who doubled as biographer regarded as a manifestation of homo-sexuality.

Doyle's final touch of genius in the creation of the ideal detec-tive hero was to put the finished article into the safety of the past. Provided that anachronism was guarded against – and this was not too difficult for a writer whose own earlier lifetime had em-braced the period chosen – adventures related as reminiscence, as history, could have an air of authenticity that would impress younger readers and appeal nostalgically to the older ones. It is unlikely that Doyle looked further beyond his next royalty cheque than any other popular author, but even if he had planned con-sciously to dominate the whodunnit market for the next hundred years, he could scarcely have picked a setting of more abiding fascination than late nineteenth-century London, that curious compound of the homely and the sinister, of sentimentality and terror. It haunts us still, as its most fearful criminal, Jack the

Ripper, is still capable of affrighting a generation that has seen murder put on a production line basis. The Ripper was a reality that stayed in the shadows and became myth; but for millions the world over, the vision of Victorian London is dominated by a myth that became real – the figure in cape and deerstalker, the great autocratic patron of criminology.

Doyle died in 1930. By that time other autocrats of crime fiction had been established and were showing promise of making their authors' reputations. They were so different in temperamental behaviour from Sherlock Holmes as to seem utterly unrelated. This, though, was possibly the result of determination to forestall suspicion of plagiarism; the basic line of resemblance was there, the identity of loyalties and beliefs, and a shared doggedness in following clues.

There was one marked deviation from the Holmesian model. Doyle's hero had dealt with the great and had moved in elevated circles, but only professionally. He himself was a commoner, and it was by sheer power of personality and of intellect that he established parity with, if not superiority over, the Dukes of Holdernesse and Kings of Bohemia who sought his aid. No such feats of character exertion were demanded of the heroes of Buchan and Dornford Yates, of Dorothy Sayers and Margery Allingham, Wallace and Horler, of H. C. Bailey and Anthony Berkeley Cox. That the embattler of crime should enjoy private means was an assumption convenient to authors and apparently acceptable to their readers. In the majority of the standard run of thrillers and detective stories between the wars heroes were depicted as not merely independent financially but what most people would have called rich. They lived, as a rule, in bachelor apartments in the most expensive residential areas of London. Baker Street, most decidedly, did not qualify. They were served not by a landlady but by 'a man'. All were men of influence in useful quarters, many had aristocratic connections, some were directly related to the nobility, a few actually sported titles of their own.

By no means new in 1920 was the device of presenting an apparently foolish, irresponsible young man to readers or audience and then surprising them by revealing his unsuspected depths of intellect or courage. It was a trick that had served authors and playwrights from the earliest times. The fop with the heart of a lion, the bored epicure who became valiant overnight, the cynic who embraced true love: these had been working hard for the livings of Jane Austen, Sheridan, Shakespeare, and others long before them. There continued to exist after the turn of the century a lively desire on the part of readers and theatre-goers to be fooled by appearances – or, rather, *not* to be fooled, for it was not long after Baroness Orczy's debut in 1904 that everyone knew that the weak, lisping Sir Percy Blakeney was really the indomitable and infinitely resourceful Scarlet Pimpernel. The double-living hero was a convention of musical comedy, and the more effete was his ostensible character, the better was everyone pleased when he turned into the Red Shadow or something of the kind in the last act. Crime fiction naturally had its schizophrenic element too. Reputed ne'er-do-wells worked under cover for Scotland Yard, for instance, while young men dismissed by one and all as mental deficients with large bank accounts proved to have been languidly but brilliantly assembling the case for the prosecution.

> 'He came down in Anne Edgeware's car, and the first thing he did when he was introduced to me was to show me a conjuring trick with a two-headed penny – he's quite inoffensive, just a silly ass.' Abbershaw nodded and stared covertly at the fresh-faced young man with the tow-coloured hair and the foolish, pale-blue eyes behind tortoiseshell-rimmed spectacles ... The slightly receding chin and mouth so unnecessarily full of teeth were distinctly familiar.

> (*The Crime at Black Dudley*)

As they should have been, for Albert Campion came of some of the bluest-blooded stock in England. But whose is this disarming chatter?

> 'Why ask, dear old thing? Always a pleasure to assist a fellow-sleuth, don't you know. Trackin' down murderers – all in the same way of business and all that. All finished? Good egg!'

It is the voice of Wimbles, of course, as the chaps at the Foreign Office call Lord Peter Wimsey – or did in 1928 in the days of Trotters, Bungo the cypher man, and old Clumps. And just as Britain's enemies would have paid dearly for underestimating dear old Trotters, it was an unwise murderer who failed to reckon with the hunting instinct of the young man with 'the sleek, straw-coloured hair, brushed flat back from a rather sloping forehead, the ugly, lean, arched nose, and the faintly foolish smile'.

The Silly Ass convention was extraordinarily pervasive in the 1920s and 1930s. It had developed into something quite different from the old dramatic device of dissembling, and was almost a celebration of inanity as such. A universally familiar figure on stage and cinema screen was that of a young man in smart clothes, sickly grin and monocle, whose vocabulary was as limited as his means and expectations were supposed to be substantial. He was generally depicted as having difficulty in understanding the import of what other people said to him. When making his own laboured but idiotically affable contribution to dialogue, he would repeatedly squawk 'eh, what?' and 'don't y'know' and address his companion as 'old bean'. That the public continued to consider this sort of thing enormous fun is proved by the sustained success of the Aldwych farces, in which Ralph Lynn was the perennial embodiment of Silly-Assery; by the popularity of P. G. Wodehouse's Bertie Wooster stories; and, not least, by the politic sense of fashion that prompted writers such as Dorothy Sayers, Margery Allingham and even Anthony Berkeley Cox to endow their detective with an air of fatuity.

It was an American, characteristically, who worked hardest at reproducing the kind of language that precious young Englishmen were believed to employ. S. S. Van Dine used almost as many words to convey the rich, bored and supercilious nature of his investigator, Philo Vance, as to describe the cases he so effortlessly solved. Vance never speaks when he can drawl and his painfully esoteric witticisms are sometimes accompanied by a 'japish smile'. He calls people 'old dear' and expresses his always restrained surprise with ' 'Pon my word'. He chops the G off present participles

– maybe to help compensate Currie, his 'rare old English servant' for missin' the huntin' back home – and eh-whats even New York district attorneys into respectful concurrence. In Vance's manner, Van Dine wrote, 'was an indefinable contempt for inferiority of all kinds'.

'Who was his papa? What was his school?'

This question is asked, in *The Business Minister* by Reggie Fortune. Fortune is the doctor-turned-detective created in 1920 by H. C. Bailey. He is a cheerful, rather garrulous character, obviously well-educated. He has a good address and a manservant named Sam. It should be understood that the inquiry he is making is not supposed to be taken seriously. Henry Christopher Bailey was a classical scholar at Corpus Christi, Oxford, cox of his college boat, a correspondent and leader writer for the *Daily Telegraph*. Such a man would not allow his hero dialogue to invite the scorn of the sophisticated people who, even in England, were beginning to make jokes about native heredity, class and schooling. Reggie Fortune is being fatuous with ironic intent.

'What I want is muffins,' said Reggie – 'several muffins and a little tea and my domestic hearth. Then I'll feel safe.'

Good-natured satirical sideswipes at English class-consciousness, cosiness and love of security are characteristic of Bailey's detective fiction. He was, perhaps, embarrassed as intellectuals tend to be by traditional attitudes, and purged his embarrassment by a little mild fun-poking, but the Fortune stories were never so disrespectful of the established order as to endanger their author's relationship with the world represented by the *Daily Telegraph*.

Edgar Wallace was a good deal less sophisticated than H. C. Bailey and he employed regular policemen to solve most of his mysteries. They were by no means common policemen, though, and it is difficult to envisage the sort of administrative system that would have been needed to accommodate the eccentricities and extra-legal methods of some of his detectives. Perhaps the least likely, if in some ways the most likable, was 'that mild

and middle-aged man' Mr J. G. Reeder. Even his official status,
Detective to the Public Prosecutor's Office, was mythical – not
that his inventor showed himself any more bothered about such
minor matters as authenticity than he did about continuity: a
nonchalance that resulted in Mr Reeder's appearance veering
from 'middle-aged' to 'elderly-looking' in the course of the same
few pages in which his 'slither of sandy side-whiskers' became
'greyish' and 'rather thick', while he shrank from 'tall' to 'of
medium height'. Another characteristic of Mr Reeder, which
would seem to have been at odds with British police procedure
even fifty years ago, was his habit of travelling with a whole trunk
full of ropes, gas mask, extending rods, firearms, a rubber trun-
cheon and a selection of electric torches, pre-dating by nearly forty
years the kill-him-yourself kits carried around by Mr James Bond.
What really mattered was that he had a sufficient private income
to live and be looked after by 'a man' in an elegant apartment in
Bennett Street, Hyde Park – 'a place', Wallace informed his
readers 'where Somebodies live'.

Socrates Smith was another Wallace hero whose relationship
with the Criminal Investigation Department was happily impre-
cise – again perhaps by virtue of independent means and good
address. He occupied (with his 'man', naturally) the first and
second floors of one of the big houses in the outer circle of
Regent's Park. Life had been too full to allow him the distraction
of courtship but in compensation he had seen one woman whom
he might have married pass three times through the Divorce
Court, a feat that had left her with 'a London reputation'. Wallace pointed out that in his early days of studying crime, Smith had
been probably the only policeman in London who walked his beat
by day and spent his leisure hours in one of the most exclusive
clubs in Town. Serving an apprenticeship as a uniformed 'cop',
Wallace explained, was the only way in those days of becoming a
detective. For four years had Socrates Smith pursued this humble
course. Then, having achieved the rank of Sergeant ('an ama-
zingly rapid promotion'), he had resigned in order to study foreign
police methods and also anthropology.

When the fingerprint system was installed, he was called in and
worked with an official status, and it was usual to consult him in
cases where especial difficulties confronted the patient investigators ... He was an acknowledged authority upon finger-
prints and blood-stains, and was the first man to standardize the
spectrum and guaiacum tests for the discovery of blood upon
clothing.

(*The Three Oaks Mystery*)

The British police adopted fingerprint identification in 1901, so
Socrates Smith – 'nearing fifty' in 1927 – could not have been
older than twenty-three when he was called in to share with Scotland Yard his expert knowledge of the system. How long before
that he had spent as a student of anthropology and of foreign
police forces Wallace left unspecified but Smith at the beginning
of his career not only must have lied about his birth date in order
to get a beat to walk, but must have been a clubman at an age that
even Raffles would have deemed tender. Perhaps he looked older
than his years on account of that private income of six thousand
pounds a year his author once casually mentioned.

Margery Allingham published her first crime novel in 1929.
Her detective, Albert Campion, was to become famous in the
course of a dozen of so subsequent mysteries. But who, as Dr Fortune might have asked, was his papa, and what his school?

'Campion – that is your name, I suppose?' 'Well – er no,' said
the irrepressible young man. 'But,' he added, dropping his voice
a tone, 'my own is rather aristocratic, and I never use it in
business ... Listen – do you know who my mother is?' 'No,' said
Abbershaw, with great curiosity. Mr Campion leaned over the
side of the car ... and murmured a name, a name so illustrious
that Abbershaw started back and stared at him in as-
tonishment.

The early Campion was an inane giggler. As a guest he was an
embarrassment and Colonel Gore would have pronounced him an
all-round softie. He could solve a police-baffling mystery, though:

specifically, *The Crime at Black Dudley*. Exactly ten years later, on the eve of the second world war, the giggles had subsided and an altogether more dignified and cerebral detective was suggested by Miss Allingham's observation of him sitting with 'long, thin legs crossed and his pale eyes amused behind his horn-rimmed spectacles'. Furthermore, she was able to report that when urgent matters demanded his attention he would put aside *The Times* *'with regret'* – a clear sign of his having outgrown the silly exuberance of youth. This Campion of 1939 lived in Bottle Street, Piccadilly, kept a manservant and was a member of the Junior Greys. One notes the matter-of-factness of the last piece of information; Miss Allingham had learned how much more effective is cool name-dropping than the girlish enthusiasm of ten years before which had set Campion

> striding jauntily down the street until, to Abbershaw's amazement, he disappeared through the portals of one of the most famous and exclusive clubs in the world.

The change in style suggested confidence that readers could safely be credited with knowing the difference between a London resort of officers and gentlemen and a brand of cigarettes.

To the very end of the Campion saga Miss Allingham's hero remained essentially a patron rather than a practitioner of criminology, even though no more was made of the business of being the son of a mother too distinguished to be named. The pattern had been set and Miss Allingham stuck to it, although there is evidence that as she developed her intelligent and experimental attitude to the writing of fiction she became impatient sometimes with the social scene to which Campion had been committed. The following passage, written in *Mr Campion and Others* (1939), has the ring not of admiration but of satire:

> Petronella was not easy to find. She was neither dancing at the Berkeley nor dining at Claridge's. He looked in at the ballet and did not see her, and it was not until he remembered the Duchess of Monewden's Charity Ball at the Fitzrupert Hotel that he found her ...

Another writer who obeyed the convention of having an aristo-cratic detective – or at least one who was supposedly at home with wealthy and distinguished people – and then felt uncomfortable about it afterwards was Anthony Berkeley Cox. It was in 1925 that Cox, writing as Anthony Berkeley, introduced Roger Shering-ham in *The Layton Court Mystery*. 'An offensive person' was how Cox once frankly described his hero. Sheringham was certainly a little on the loud side, and he associated with characters who made up in volubility what they so patently lacked in social usefulness. But by 1934, when *Panic Party* was published, Sheringham had acquired a more self-effacing manner and a skill – perhaps associ-ated with his success as a bestselling novelist – in provoking his companions to let down their guard of class attitudinizing and reveal human fears and weaknesses. It was only to be expected from an author of considerable insight (Anthony Berkeley Cox was also 'Francis Iles') that he would hasten to produce the kind of detective story which in the words of his dedication to Milward Kennedy, 'breaks every rule of the austere Club to which we both belong'. He had written in 1930 that the detective story was in the process of developing into the novel with a crime theme, 'holding its readers less by mathematical than by psychological ties'. Perhaps it was, but public approval of the change did not show for several more years. Cox's pioneering, his rejection of the stock pasteboard figures of detective fiction in favour of real characters, carefully observed, was not what the commercial whodunnit pur-veyors wanted to sponsor. A leading popular magazine rejected a slightly shortened version of *Panic Party* on the grounds that it was 'lacking sufficient human interest'. 'Life,' commented Cox patiently, 'is very, very difficult' and he went on to write more crime novels that bore a disconcerting resemblance to literature.

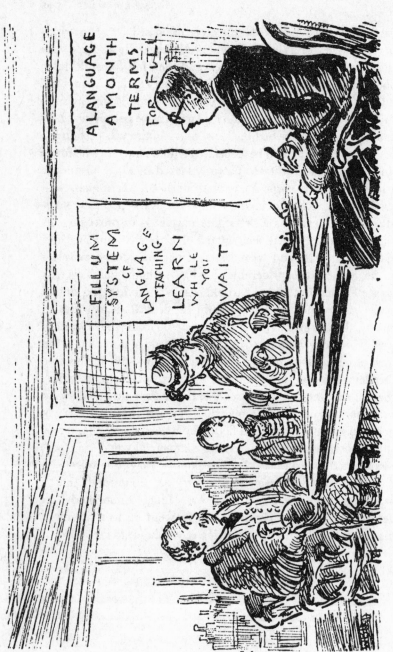

"WHAT PROFESSION WERE YOU THINKING OF FOR THE BOY?"

CHAPTER 15

Smart but not arty

A great deal of crime fiction in the inter-war years was set in London. London and its society fascinated a public which was much more static and more conscious of its provincialism than it is today. In relation to the rest of the country, it was a capital of greater liveliness, more ostentatious wealth and aggressive decadence than the 'swinging' city of thirty years later. Ngaio Marsh came to it from her native New Zealand in 1928 and found the East End streets looking 'drab, broad and bald' on the bright summer morning of her arrival. But Piccadilly smelled of hot bread, coffee, freshly watered pavements, hairdressing parlours and roses. She was surprised by the waist-to-ankle aprons of junior waiters in the restaurants and by an upper-class patois that described people and things as 'shy-making' or 'too delicious, actually' or 'Heaven'. London, alone of the cities of Britain, had all-night entertainment in clubs and restaurants patronized by famous and notorious people. Miss Marsh, in her autobiography, *Black Beech and Honeydew*, recalls how a plump Richard Tauber would go into a reflex rendering of 'You are My Heart's Delight' whenever the band leader at the Hungaria 'flourished up to his table and with an ineffable and excruciating leer, wafted a note or two in the tenor's ear', and how 'an old, old man with a flower in his coat' who sat alone and 'at intervals raised his glass in a frog's hand and touched his lips with it' proved to be Lord Alfred Douglas, once Bosie, the fatefully beautiful young friend of Oscar Wilde.

Ngaio Marsh wrote her first crime story in a pile of penny exercise books after spending a rainy Sunday reading a detective novel – possibly an Agatha Christie, she thought – borrowed from a little library in Pimlico. She named her police inspector after the Elizabethan actor Alleyn, founder of Dulwich College, whose picture gallery she had visited the day before starting the book. Seventeen years later, on a visit to England as a well established author, she was interviewed, broadcast and televised in a country where she was surprised to find 'detective fiction being discussed as a tolerable form of reading by people whose opinions one valued'. In New Zealand, apparently, the form was still suspect in 1950.

Even before Miss Marsh was shown Lord Alfred Douglas sitting in desiccated loneliness at his table near the door of the Hungaria, and heard the black cabaret artist Leslie Hutchinson ('too too, darling, my dear') singing to fashionable women at the night club known as 'Uncle's', the writers of crime fiction were creating their own special image of the capital that would give readers a sense of venturing among the wealthy, the daring, the witty and the wicked. That image was to remain almost unchanged for two decades, although some of its constituents – the Bright Young Things, for instance, and the Jazz Age that had produced 'flappers' and flat chests – were already looking pretty passé by the early 1930s.

Especially faithful to the conception of London as a city where the only life that mattered was nocturnal, confined to the West End, and led exclusively by men and women of impeccable dress sense and a perpetually facetious line in conversation, was the novelist Peter Cheyney. The second world war had already begun when Cheyney published *Another Little Drink,* a thriller of which typical chapter openings were:

Bellamy got up at twelve o'clock. He walked over to the window and looked out on to Half Moon Street. It was a bleak, dull-looking sort of a day . . .

Bellamy went into the Malayan Club at a quarter past nine. He was wearing a dinner jacket. He looked immaculate and happy.

It was a quarter to eight when Vanning went into the Buttery at the Berkeley Restaurant . . .

It was eleven o'clock when the maid awakened Bellamy. He sat up in bed, drank his tea and looked at the front page of the newspaper . . . He got up, wandered over to the window and looked out on to Half Moon Street.

A character in the same book orders the waiter to bring him a bunch of violets, which he then wraps in four five-pound notes and hands to his female companion with 'That will take care of the new frock'. The girl has been telling him how she attached herself to a suspect. 'I was *very* sweet and *very* feminine and *very* comforting . . . in point of fact I was a little too successful because Harcourt got *very* boyish and peculiar all suddenly and tried to vamp me *terribly* intimately.' The frock had been ruined when a half-pint of beer, intended by some third party for the troublesome Harcourt, missed its target.

Being hit by flying beverages was not the only risk one ran in the nights spots of London's West End. There was always a chance that a place would prove that evening's selection by the police for a raid in search of evidence of drug-peddling, illicit gaming or simply contravention of the licensing laws. Bruce Graeme, author of the *Blackshirt* adventure stories, contrives in *Blackshirt Strikes Back* (1940) just such a raid upon the Green Heart Club, which he describes with quite unCheyneylike disapproval as being occupied by a 'bored looking crowd of sleek men and daringly dressed women' who hug each other closely as they dance on the diminutive dance floor to the music of the 'inevitable' dance band or watch the 'usual cabaret turns, more indecent than entertaining'.

Commotion followed the waiter's shout of alarm and the

sudden blacking out. Women shrieked, men shouted. Tables and chairs were overturned: the smashing of crockery drowned even the hammering from the street. Diners, dancers, musicians and waiters stampeded in all directions, cannoning into one another, or against the walls, or falling over upturned tables and chairs. Panic spread causing worse confusion.

The account is remarkably similar to a report by the queen of night-club proprietors, Mrs Katie Meyrick. 'I once had the instructive experience,' she wrote in *Secrets of the 43* (1933), 'of being a visitor at an inferior sort of club at the moment of its receiving a visit from the police, and I have never forgotten the state of frenzy that prevailed. The members of the band vaulted their "fence" and dived through a trap-door to a cellar below ... The women shrieked, the young men blustered, tables and chairs were upset, glasses were smashed wholesale. It was a perfect babel. When the police came marching in, a number of the women went off in a dead faint and one or two young men followed suit, while the rest rushed aimlessly to and fro and babbled hysterically ...'

Mrs Meyrick, who underwent five spells of imprisonment during her chequered and much publicized career, added with commendable loyalty: 'How different was the picture at any of our clubs when we were so unlucky as to suffer a raid! Most of our male members being officers of distinguished regiments, members of the Peerage, experienced men about Town or rich young City magnates, there was never the slightest sign of panic.' It was one of the distinguished military men – a Guards officer – who tried to throw out the 'dirty little Jew' Michael Arlen when he stumbled against the officer's table in a club run by Mrs Meyrick in Golden Square. An experienced man about Town – the sportsman Major Jack Coats – was long remembered in the '43 Club' for his trick of filling a peer's top hat with champagne; the peer, naturally, had 'joined wholeheartedly in the shouts of laughter at his expense'. Also at the '43' had been made the reputation of that rich young City magnate in whose 'moments of overwhelming exuberance' he would call for champagne and large quantities of glasses, each of which he would proceed to drain, throw on the floor and pound to fragments with an empty bottle, ending up the evening with a large pile of ground glass beside him.

Compton Mackenzie recalls in his autobiography that university students in 1929 amused themselves with a game called 'Beaver'. It was played in the street. The contestants, walking in a group, were alert for the sight of anyone wearing a beard. The first to spot such a person and loudly cry out 'Beaver!' scored a point.

The fact that facial hair was a subject for derisive merriment is not simply a reflection on the intellect and manners of some undergraduates in the late 1920s. Beards had associations, real or fancied, that rendered them no less provocative than long hair styles were to prove forty years later. For one thing, they were the badges of vagrancy. Post-war restlessness and economic decline had made the tramp a familiar figure on the highways of Britain. The respectable regarded him and his whiskers as sinister and unsavoury, and he was readily blamed – as many crime fiction plots of the time indicate – for whatever felonies happened to have been committed in his vicinity. For more than a decade it had been a convention of the silent film comedy to identify the knockabout, expendable villain as 'the one with the beard'. Political cartoonists, too, were grateful for a symbol that was so easy to draw; the classic Bolshevik of the period, carrying his precisely spherical bomb with a fuse a-splutter, was as hirsute as a hearth-rug.

But there was another sense in which beardedness was regarded as significant. It was linked in the minds of many with social attitudes and behaviour variously described as Bohemian, cranky, faddist or arty. The beard as a tangible sign of male maturity (not, be it noted, virility, which was considered an indecent concept until popularized commercially in the 1960s) had gone out with Edward VII. George V wore one, admittedly, but as a 'sailor king' he was only observing naval tradition; none would have accused of Bohemianism a man whose hobby was stamp-collecting and for whom, reputedly, the only tolerable aesthetic experience was to hear *In the Shadows*, played by a ship's band. George Bernard Shaw, on the other hand, lacked the excuses both of royal prerogative and maritime custom. Not even old age – he was already seventy-four in 1929 – reconciled the anti-crank public to the great wagging white bush that was flaunted by Shaw. The conservative middle class, to say nothing of the even more conservative section of the working class that had managed to consolidate craft advantages and move to nicer neighbourhoods, regarded Shaw as an argumentative upstart, a scoffer, an irreligious and unpatriotic show-off. It is interesting to reflect that loquaciousness, physical peculiarity and self-confidence, which in combination earned Shaw the active dislike of thousands when he was at the height of his powers as a performer, were the very qualities which a few years later would make the fortune, via television, of any amiable dunce.

Sydney Horler, who regarded 'the acceptance by the English press of Shaw at his own valuation' as 'one of the most remarkable oddities of the present day', left no explicit record of his opinion of beards. He was himself chubbily clean-shaven, however, and what he had to say about hair in another context is possibly significant: 'The truth is that the sight of Miss Gracie Fields' fringe invariably displeases me.' Lieutenant Colonel McNeile naturally disapproved of whiskers in excess of the orthodox military moustache. It was his Bulldog Drummond who habitually applied to a bearded opponent the witty epithet 'fungus face'. Other authors exhibited, in a variety of ways and degrees, what quite clearly was a widespread prejudice in favour of shaving. Apart from Wallace's Mr Reeder and his side-whiskers (which, in any case, he removed in the cause of romance before his career ended) it would be difficult to find a single English detective of the period who had been allowed by his creator to risk being mistaken for villain, crank or artist, otherwise than in the way of disguise.

Feelings ran high. Not, of course, for or against beards as such. They were symbols only. What really engaged the passions of the populace – or of the vocal parts of it – was the affront to 'normality' offered by innovators. The ferocity of reaction to artistic experiment, even of the mildest kind, was in inverse proportion to the interest which the public had previously shown in the particular field of art concerned. Thus sculpture, which for most people consisted solely of the vast bronze tea cosies in the likeness of Queen Victoria that loomed behind drinking fountains or at bus termini, suddenly became the subject of hysterical acrimony with the advent of Epstein.

Those whom John Rhode termed 'artists who draw things as they aren't' were regarded with the sort of furious contempt that not long before had been reserved for Kaiser Bill and the German Crown Prince. 'Ultra-modern' was a term of denigration, as applied to poetry, music and painting, and readers well knew what was meant by Sax Rohmer when he described his heroes, Dr Petrie and Nayland Smith, as being in the guise of 'a pair of Futurists'. The drastic stratagem was the only way in which they could penetrate a certain London club (Prop.: Fu-Manchu).

> 'Coffee being placed before us, we sat sipping the thick, sugary beverage, smoking cigarettes and vainly seeking for some clue to guide us to the inner sanctuary consecrate to hashish ... amongst this gathering whose conversation was of abnormalities in art, music and literature.'

The key word is 'abnormalities'; it expresses the unease, the disgust, the sense of outrage which otherwise harmless and quite tolerant people seem to have felt – with some encouragement from established aesthetic authorities and organs of opinion – whenever departure from tradition was threatened.

Here again is Rohmer making oblique reference to 'modern' art as it existed in the conception of so many of his readers:

> '... she was wickedly handsome. I use the word 'wickedly' with deliberation; for the pallidly dusky, oval face, with the full red lips, between which rested a large yellow cigarette, and the half-closed almond-shaped eyes, possessed a beauty which might have appealed to an artist of one of the modern perverted schools.'

Overtones of immorality are unmistakable. Particularly suggestive is that 'large yellow cigarette'. Yellow was not only the accepted colour of *fin de siècle* corruption, it was the hue of the Eastern hordes poised to overrun the civilized world. Their conquest was being facilitated in advance by artists, or at least by those whose work deviated from standards to which people had grown accustomed. Rohmer clearly considered what he called perverts to be numerous. There were whole schools of them, apparently.

The word 'school' conveyed a hint of disapproval, sometimes of ridicule, when used in popular literature. The implication was that odd people had combined to do odd and undesirable things, their main object being to annoy and scandalize the decent majority. Dorothy Sayers liked to use the weapon of satire against such offenders. 'The cubist poet' was one of her witticisms – a shaft at the subtler end of an armoury of humour that ranged to 'You know Glasgow, where the accent's so strong that even Scotsmen faint when they hear it.' Here is her description of a gathering in 1928 'in a low-pitched cellar' of the kind of intellectuals she found tiresome:

> Ethics and sociology, the latest vortices of the Whirligig school of verse, combine with the smoke of the countless cigarettes to produce an inspissated atmosphere, through which flat, angular mural paintings dimly lower upon the revellers.

The 'Whirligig school' may be a reference to the admirers of T. S. Eliot, whose *Hollow Men* had been published three years before, to the considerable bewilderment of such 'proper' poetry lovers as had survived the shock of his *Waste Land* in 1922.

Agatha Christie, always circumspect in matters of opinion, committed herself to no such censorious view of the new aesthetes as had Miss Sayers. If anything, she seems to have felt rather sorry for them – especially for those who contrived to stray so far afield from their own social milieu as the Royal Opera House, Covent Garden.

He took them to be of the 'arty' class. The girl wore a rather shapeless garment of cheap green silk. Her shoes were of soiled white satin. The young man wore his evening clothes with an air of being uncomfortable in them ... the couple had been joined by a third – a fair young man with a suggestion of the clerk about him ... the newcomer was fidgeting with his tie and seemed ill at ease.

(Thirteen for Luck)

One might note the distinction that readers were invited to draw between the young men and woman here described and the sort of people who would have been perfectly acceptable members of a Covent Garden audience at that time. Opera-going was an approved social exercise for the eminent – opera-going at 'the Garden', that is; not at the Old Vic or Sadler's Wells – and the seating was so arranged that the display of finery in the stalls and boxes could be enjoyed by the patrons of circle and upper circle. Hived off in the gallery and slips – an elevated punishment block of hard, narrow benches on terraced concrete to which admission cost three and sixpence – was the sole section of the audience free to dress as it pleased. The assertion that it comprised the only musical enthusiasts in the building was an exaggeration but not a really wild one. So many ticket holders to the more expensive seats were in the habit of arriving late that it finally became necessary to lock the doors just before the overture and to keep them locked during the whole of the first act. Sir Thomas Beecham, at whose instigation this rule was adopted, followed it up by his famous public rebuke of chatterers in the orchestra stalls as 'savages'.

Merely attending an operatic performance, then, did not carry the stigma of freakishness provided one occupied seats in the better parts of the house. Going to Covent Garden was part of The Season and to that extent obligatory upon both members of and aspirants to Society. *Punch* may have made occasional jokes about opera; it did not joke about opera audiences. That the three characters in Mrs Christie's story were intruders was testified both by clothing and manner. The girl's gown was cheap-looking and ill-cut, her shoes soiled. Her companions wore dress suits as if they were unused to them. The trio's proper place was the gallery, amongst the rest of the 'arty' class.

The contempt and hatred aroused by protagonists of new forms of artistic expression flowed like vitriol through the correspondence columns. Theorists of all kinds were condemned promptly and with a violence that can still chill after forty years. A naval officer who claimed to hold the Distinguished Service Order was inspired by one of Sydney Horler's books to write to him personally: 'There are far too many b.f.s in this world, and a lethal chamber in every parish would be an excellent idea. I am sick of this veneer of so-called culture which goes by the name of education.' Horler's own views were generally expressed with similar forcefulness either by himself or through his character Tiger Standish, but he did manage on one occasion to summarize them temperately: 'The final estimate of anything – art, music, the drama, literature – is invariably made by the man in the street; no reputation worth a twopenny damn can be established without his approval.'

Proclaiming themselves, as always, to represent the interests of that same man in the street, the newspapers of the early 1930s found time in the midst of a circulation war to write in defence of aesthetic decencies. When Epstein's '*Genesis*' was exhibited at the Leicester Galleries in 1931, the *Daily Express* cried out like a poetic spinster who had mistakenly entered a men's lavatory: 'O you white foulness!' In the same year, the *Morning Post* apologized, with elaborate irony, for 'publishing even a photograph of the least objectionable of Mr Henry Moore's statuary'. Poor Epstein again incurred editorially stimulated wrath with his 'Ecce Homo', roundly described by the author of the Father Brown stories as 'an outrage', but at least the Press forbore from inciting the public to violence as it had done, if only obliquely, in 1925. Then the *Daily Mail* had let the condemnation of '*Rima*', Epstein's memorial in Hyde Park to W. H. Hudson, the naturalist, with 'Take this horror out of the Park!' Subsequent defacement of the sculpture had been announced by the *Morning Post* with undisguised satisfaction: 'The inevitable has happened . . . she has been ingloriously daubed with green paint.'

Jacob Epstein and his detractors must have had mutually forgiving natures. Among his commissioned works were portrait busts of Lord Rothermere and Lord Beaverbrook.

Next to 'artiness' in the sins proscribed by middle class orthodoxy and condemned in the parables of crime fiction came 'faddiness'.

By 'fad' is not to be understood preference for rich food, rare vintages, expensive cars, model gowns and so forth. These came under the heading of connoisseurship and were deemed altogether praiseworthy and enviable. Fads were the despicable prerogative of cranks, of queer (the word had not been narrowed then to have an exclusively sexual meaning) and awkward people. A fad was an unreasonable, perhaps even a sinister, partiality. At best, it was excusable on grounds of ignorance; at worst, it was symptomatic of alien loyalties and evil intent.

Crime novelists had considerable fun at the expense of characters credited with odd beliefs or strange tastes. The comic spiritualist was one such stock figure. She – almost invariably a spiritualist was a woman – would talk a good deal about auras, vibrations, and other laughable curiosities to which she alone was sensitive. A variation on the theme was the setting up of a seance in the course of which the plot would be thickened by the mysterious outbursts of a medium. It was not beneath the dignity of Hercule Poirot to fake a 'spirit' appearance in order to trap a murderer. Despite the advocacy of spiritualism by a number of famous people, including the scientist, Oliver Lodge, and the journalist Hannen Swaffer, it never became respectable. Newspapers included it in their list of perennial dependables, along with famous murders, white slavery and 'Was This Man a Woman?' but most of the people who read so avidly about allegedly psychic phenomena were glad of the abiding suggestion of fraud which helped them feel sensible and superior. Writers of crime fiction who permitted a ghost to survive materialist explanation were very rare indeed and were considered to have let the side down pretty badly. Black magic, on the other hand, was sufficiently exotic an affectation to escape ridicule. Dennis Wheatley was later to profit by making it his speciality.

Two of the most doughty champions of 'common sense' as construed by a middle class contemptuous of artiness, fads, cranks and cults, were both writers of detective stories, both converts to Roman Catholicism. One was Gilbert Keith Chesterton, the other, Ronald Arbuthnot Knox, Catholic Chaplain to Oxford University from 1926 to 1939. 'Father' Knox's story, *Solved by Inspection*, is a richly illustrative example of the writing of current attitudes into a piece of popular fiction.

An eccentric millionaire, Herbert Jervison, is found dead in bed, apparently starved to death. Miles Bredon, inquiry agent, investigates on behalf of an insurance company which retains also a doctor called Simmonds. Simmonds says:

> 'This Jervison had pottered about in the East, and had got caught with all that esoteric bilge – talked about Mahatmas and Yogis and things till even the most sanguine of his poor relations wouldn't ask him to stay. So he settled down at Yewbury here with some Indian frauds he had picked up, and said he was the Brotherhood of Light. Had it printed on his notepaper, which was dark green. Ate nuts and did automatic writing and made all sorts of psychic experiments . . .'

'He probably choked on a Brazil nut or something' jokes Bredon, and Simmonds confirms that Jervison was one of 'these people who go in for Oriental food-fads,' adding:

> 'And then he goes and kills himself by refusing his mash. Mark you, I'm not sure I wouldn't sooner starve than eat the sort of muck he ate . . .'

The investigator learns that the millionaire died while locked, with a supply of food, in an old gymnasium, but is assured by Simmonds that

> 'There was nothing queer in that, because he was always shut-

ting himself up to do his fool experiments . . . Probably thought his astral body was wandering about in Thibet.'

A local doctor, Mayhew, refers to Jervison's corpse as

'parked up at the Brotherhood House, ready to be disposed of when it's finished with . . . Yes, they've got to bury him in some special way of their own, tuck him up with his feet towards Jericho, I expect, or something of that sort. Hope these niggers'll clear out after this . . . The neighbours don't like 'em, and that's a fact.'

By discovering clues in the gymnasium, Bredon solves the mystery of how Jervison starved to death (his bed had been hauled 40 feet aloft on ropes by the four Indians). Simmonds tells him:

'Your friends the police have been round, and they've just taken off the whole Brotherhood in a suitably coloured Maria.'

'I am going to do my best to see these four fellows hanged,' proclaims Bredon. 'If I had my way with them, I would spare them the drop.'

CHAPTER 16

Driving like hell

The social historian learns to assess a community's ideas and manner of living partly from the material possessions it is known to have valued. The things themselves are evidence where they have survived, but evidence of a kind that might need to be guessed about, and the guesses even of expert interpreters can be pretty wild. The significance of some objects made less than a lifetime ago can be more difficult to decide than that of relics from households in the Bronze Age; for instance, either personal memory or brilliant deductive powers would be needed to infer musical fastidiousness from a tiny lathe-cum-grindstone marketed in the early 1930s. It was for sharpening the thorns that gramophone enthusiasts used instead of conventional steel needles.

Somewhere in the vaults of the enormous literature of crime there must be a reference to just such a machine. So handy an accessory for the complete blowpipeman cannot possibly have been ignored. Crime fiction has a thoroughgoing objectivity. It may generally be weak in characterization, unconcerned with ideas and sparing of scenic effect, but it must needs accommodate all material things likely to prove useful to the plot. The writers of thrillers and, especially, detective stories, need more props than does the straight novelist. Ivy Compton-Burnett managed to write brilliant if somewhat disconcerting books that gave virtually no hint that their characters had any corporeal relationship with an outside world. What would have become of Sherlock Holmes in her hands, or, for that matter, in those of Virginia Woolf? Neither would have permitted him to hail another hansom, send one more telegram, or ever again to heat a test tube. All he could have expected of Miss C.-B. was an infinitely subtle embroilment with brother Mycroft and possibly some incestuous cousins over a legacy; and from Miss Woolf perhaps an interior monologue (certainly not a monograph) on the one hundred and forty kinds of tobacco ash.

Crime novelists have always written with special care of objects, of possessions. Most crime, after all, is motivated by the desire to possess. Readers recognize such feelings and are anxious to know who gets what, and how. Often there is the question of material clues: these have to be described in some detail. Close attention must be paid to clothing, to furniture, to the layout of rooms, for any or all may prove relevant to the central violent event. In any case, their inclusion in the scene helps to create the realistic, the documentary quality of crime fiction.

Realism, of course, comes in various vintages. Here is a Wallace, 1924:

> In the gorgeous saloon, with its lapis-lazuli columns, its fireplaces of onyx and silver, its delicately panelled walls and silken hangings, Mr Ezra Maitland sat huddled in a large Louis Quinze chair . . . There was a gentle knock at the door and a footman came in, a man of powder and calves.
>
> (*The Fellowship of the Frog*)

An Oppenheim, 1920:

> Dominey and Rosamund dined alone, and though the table had been reduced to its smallest proportions, the space between them was yet considerable. As soon as Parkins had gravely put the port upon the table, Rosamund rose to her feet and, instead

of leaving the room, pointed for the servant to place a chair for her by Dominey's side.

(*The Great Impersonation*)

Both seem at first to be Ruritanian in flavour, but they are not fantasy. Wallace's 'gorgeous saloon' is an accurately depicted example of the sort of dwelling favoured by and constructed for the successful speculator of the 1920s. Oppenheim was permitting his readers – his American readers in particular – to glimpse the admittedly odd but authentic habit of eating at vast distances from one another whereby the more formal English aristocrats still kept their servants exercised in the years immediately after the first world war.

Less concerned to indulge the public's appetite for revelation of how the wealthy lived, ex-engineer Freeman Wills Crofts was one of the few mystery writers of the period who told their stories in terms of routine police investigation. His Inspector French was a plodder, but an observant one. We learn from him that the household of a small London merchant of limited means consisted of father and daughter, two maids, a cook and a chauffeur, all living in a medium-sized house with furniture that had been good but now (in 1924) was shabby. In an apartment in St John's Wood, French found heavy, expensive furniture and fittings; good silk dresses; a carpet worth at least £120; and a half-empty box of Corona Coronas. Several well-bound 'standard works' were in a bookcase in the smoking room but only for decoration. In the sitting-room were several of 'the lighter type of novels, together with a number in French and Spanish with extremely lurid and compromising jackets'. The occupants' income, judged the inspector, would be between two and three thousand a year.

The mention of the large Coronas is significant. Not even the phlegmatic Wills Crofts could resist dropping this rich-sounding name into an otherwise prosaic report. The cigar was to most people in England – which as a nation had rejected it in favour of cigarettes at between fourpence and sixpence for ten – a symbol of opulent success, not always untinged with villainy. Cartoonists and illustrators of comics had a special cigar-image of their own: black and obese and banded with what looked like a Lonsdale belt. The cigar was the epitome of poshness and self-made Phillips Oppenheim never forgot it:

> Argels himself, wearing the clothes of Savile Row, the boots of the Burlington Arcade, and the linen and cravat of Bond Street, wore a red carnation in his buttonhole, and was smoking an expensive Romeo and Juliet cigar.

Lynn Brock's no-nonsense detective, Colonel Gore, could tell a costly cigarette when he saw one but had the self-control to refuse it.

> 'These look about eighteen bob a hundred.' 'A quid', said Challoner laconically. His guest sighed enviously and replaced the cigarette in the miniature silver trunk from which he had incautiously taken it. 'In another, better world, perhaps. In this, not for me. I'll smoke my old dhudeen, if I may.'
>
> (*The Deductions of Colonel Gore*)

Then, as now, the pipe man had certain advantages over the smoker of gaspers. He was more likely to be considered manly, thoughtful, honest and clean-living. Stanley Baldwin probably owed his premiership to that air of calm wisdom and homely reliability which diligent pipe-sucking confers upon the chronically inept. Baldwin's assiduously cultivated ordinariness, incidentally, included a liking for the books of John Buchan, whom he once declared to be 'a ruddy miracle'.

There have been a number of pipe smoking heroes of crime fiction, but most of them are in the adventure-thriller sector where firmness of jaw and good strong teeth are more generally available than in the relatively stuffy, debilitating area of the whodunnit. An exception – a surprising exception in view of his author's drastic demands on his wind – is the appearance of Simon Templar, alias The Saint, among the cigarette addicts. In *The Saint Closes the Case* (1930):

> He lighted a fresh cigarette and hitched himself further on to the

table, leaning forward with his forearms on his knees and the fine, rake-hell, fighting face that they all knew and loved made almost supernaturally beautiful with such a light of debonair dare-devilry as they had never seen before.

But perhaps The Saint's preference was rooted in a desire to be distinguished from those he called

'the birds with the fat cigars and the names in -heim and -stein, who juggle the finances of this cockeyed world.'

Ian Fleming was to echo Charteris with remarkable fidelity a quarter of a century later when he declared of a certain street in Paris:

too many of the landlords and tenants . . . have names ending in -esou, -ovitch, -ski and -stein, and these are sometimes not the ending of respectable names.

His hero, too, eschewed cigars, smoking instead an exclusive brand of hand made cigarettes bearing three gold bands.

The most famous pipe in fiction is unquestionably that of Sherlock Holmes, but nothing suggests that Conan Doyle hoped that it would emphasize his detective's masculinity and bourgeois trustworthiness. It was rather late for that, considering that the man had acquired a violin, addiction to cocaine, and the habit of drawing-room pistol practice. More likely was the intention to add to the impression of Holmes's enigmatic and eccentric nature the extraordinary circumstance of a gentleman electing to smoke black shag, the deadly favourite of coal heavers and lightermen.

One vice Holmes did not embrace and that was alcoholism. Perhaps his example in this respect inspired his successors. Certainly the boozy detective would be difficult, if not impossible, to discover in British mystery fiction of the last fifty years. There is a simple reason for this. The detective is traditionally a somewhat priestly figure, utterly reliable, incorruptible and socially unsmirched. It is permissible for him to be baffled occasionally, to crack a joke, even to stand a round of drinks, in order to show himself related to humanity. But he has only to be seen drunk once and he forfeits the admiration of some of the most right-minded members of the community – the devotees of the murder story.

If inebriation is barred, winemanship has long held honourable place in the English detective novel, while minor bottle play may be found even in the more vulgar medium of the thriller. Bulldog Drummond once specified the inclusion in a motoring 'snack' of half a dozen Mumm 1913. He also was qualified to expose, in his hearty way, the lack of *savoir-faire* in a provincial hotel:

'We will consume one more round of this rather peculiar tipple which that sweet girl fondly imagines is a Martini.'

This kind of cleverness did not reach the same height again in thrillers until Fleming's James Bond began his round of the world's bars and restaurants as vintage selector and cocktail tutor in 1953. By that time, the American tradition of equating hard drinking with toughness, particularly in the fields of espionage and private detection, had crossed the Atlantic. Bond's sixty cigarettes a day were complemented by an average intake of half a bottle of spirits. Even by fairly tolerant medical definition, he was a confirmed alcoholic. So was Philip Marlowe, of course, and to a greater degree, but Chandler's private eye had the excuse of having to cope with the police of Bay City. Compared with them, the operatives of SMERSH were like children on Hallowe'en.

Meanwhile, back in the pure detection belt, Lord Peter Wimsey was offering his guests Balkan Sobranies and exercising 'a palate for wine almost unequalled in Europe'.

'I fancy I could place it within a couple of miles, though it is a wine I had hardly looked to find in a French cellar at this time. It is hock . . . and at that it is Johannisberger. Not the plebeian cousin but the echter Schloss Johannisberger from the castle vineyard itself.'

Albert Campion, Margery Allingham's detective, was another eminently winey chap. His importers, Thistledown, Friend and Son, London, E.C., must have valued him highly. On the very eve of war in 1939 he had the forethought to order twelve dozen of port (Taylor, 1927) to be laid down so that it would be ready for drinking in forty years by his godson, Master Brian Desmond Peterhouse-Vaughn. Neither Wimsey nor Campion, we may be sure, would have behaved as did that Inspector Winterbottom whom Miss Sayers reported for 'emptying his glass rather too rapidly for true connoisseurship'.

Compared with its American counterpart and with such police novels as are published on the Continent, that proportion of the average English thriller devoted to social niceties has always been remarkably generous. Too much happened too quickly in the world of Dashiell Hammett for anyone to notice whether the right ties had been chosen to go with the suits or the right wines with the dinner courses. In any case, it was always Hammett's baddies who had the money to spend on fancy eating and dressing, so to hell with them. Raymond Chandler, despite having been educated at Dulwich College, was of much the same opinion as Hammett. 'Down these mean streets' was the itinerary he set his detective, because he believed that a hero worth writing about should inhabit reality and react to it with 'A lively sense of the grotesque, a disgust for sham, and a contempt for pettiness'. Philip Marlowe would not have swooned with admiration at the sight of a hand-made monogrammed cigarette; he would have marked down its smoker as a likely beneficiary of city hall graft. As for that supremely eloquent testimony to indication of social worth, the motor car, Marlowe characteristically referred to his own as 'the heap'.

No such diffidence has ever been noticeable in the British thriller writers. Their motorized heroes have been tearing around the countryside and through city streets for well over half a century. But not in just any old car. Holmes had been content to overtake malefactors by public transport. The hansom cab ('There's a sovereign for you, my man, if you reach Victoria in eight minutes') and the railway train ('Quick, Watson, the four-twenty-three') never let him down, and readers had sufficient faith in the reliability of institutions in Victorian and Edwardian England not to be sceptical. The motor car aroused new attitudes

entirely. It was excitingly unpredictable, very expensive, sometimes frightening, always enviable. Moreover it was a branded,
identifiable object; and already by the early 1920s, when there
was one car on the road for every 140 people, a motor mythology
had been established. Certain makes were especially admired for
their splendour, size or speed. They were very much 'the thing'
and it was with vehicles from this exclusive category that authors
anxious to impress equipped their characters.

Perhaps the thing-iest automobile of them all was the Hispano-
Suiza. This extraordinary hybrid, with its vast but superbly engineered power unit beneath a bonnet that could be viewed to the
end only on a clear day, was produced in limited numbers but at
unlimited expense. Customers were mostly millionaires and monarchs, of whom Spain's Alphonso – if the assertions of second-hand traders were to be believed – must have changed cars
every other week. A few Hispanos could always be seen on the
Riviera and at other fashionable European resorts, but a car that
needed a hangar rather than a garage (the wheelbase of some
models was fourteen feet and the track nearly five) was hardly a
practical proposition for the ordinary motorist. For the well-connected fictional motorist, on the other hand, it was eminently
suitable, if only by virtue of its resonant double-barrelled name,
and riding around in an Hispano-Suiza became for a while a
convention of the high life novel.

Being himself something of a high life aspirant, that hearty
clubman Lieutenant-Colonel McNeile, alias 'Sapper', overcame
whatever patriotic objections he might have had to a car designed
in Spain by a Swiss and manufactured in France, and gave one to
Bulldog Drummond. Drummond joyfully proclaimed it 'guaranteed to keep in sight anything in England' so it possibly was one of
the racing Boulogne Hispanos with a top speed of something over
110 miles an hour. In that case, however, it is not easy to understand why 'Sapper' described him as driving 'like a man possessed
with ten devils'. Diabolism would have been an altogether
superfluous aid to an eight-litre engine developing some 200
brake-horsepower.

Phillips Oppenheim lived for most of his writing life in real Hispano-Suiza country on the Mediterranean coast. He must have known well the settings used by Michael Arlen in *The Green Hat*, of which the great car was a sort of heroine. And yet when he wanted to convey a sense of luxury awheel, it was a Rolls-Royce that he specified:

> The Scotchman took his place a little gingerly amongst the magnificent appointments of the limousine. He took notice of its wonderful fittings, the cigar-box and match-boxes rimmed with gold, the cigarettes temptingly displayed in a glass case, the tortoiseshell-backed toilet-set . . .

A need for showing the common touch in motoring matters did not find Oppenheim ignorant of the names of cheap, mass-produced models. A financier in *Moran Chambers Smiled* (1932) wishes to make a small gesture of appreciation to his clerk, who has not been looking too well of late. 'Buy,' he instructs him,

> 'one of these new two-seaters tonight on your way home – a Morris Oxford, or something of that sort. A four-seater if you like, of course – anything you like up to three hundred pounds. Engage a chauffeur for a time, and drive to business in the mornings. Put it down to petty cash.' 'You're very good, sir,' the man acknowledged gratefully. 'It will be a great pleasure for me.'

Edgar Wallace was something of a specialist in the production of intrepid characters. Some were virtually indestructible – as was Captain Dick Gordon – and when it was required that he should drive from London to Gloucester with a reprieve for an innocent man about to mount the scaffold, the choice of a matchingly intrepid car was essential. A Rolls user himself, Wallace saw no reason to look further.

> Through Swindon at breakneck speed, and he was on the Gloucester Road . . . He was going all out now, but the road was bad, full of windings, and once he was nearly thrown out of the car when he struck a ridge on the road. A tyre burst, and he

almost swerved into the hedge, but he got her nose straight again and continued on a flat tyre. It brought her speed down appreciably, and he grew hot and cold as mile after mile of the road flashed by without a sign of the town. And then, with Gloucester Cathedral showing its spires above the hill, a second tyre exploded. He could not stop: he must go on, if he had to run in to Gloucester on the rims . . .

Ten minutes later, but not yet quite down to the axles:

'A reprieve, by the King's own hand,' said Dick Gordon unsteadily, and handed the stained envelope to the Governor. (*The Fellowship of the Frog*)

In the decade between 1921 and the eclipse of the firm during the world slump, Britain's Bentley Motors Limited were producing at prices from one-and-a-half to two-and-a-half thousand pounds apiece some of the fastest and most personable cars in the world. Bentley owners constituted an elite only a rung or two down from the clients of Rolls-Royce and Hispano-Suiza. Their machines were not merely testimonials of wealth; they manifested that attribute which in retrospect is hard to define soberly and without sardonic overtones but which, in the 1920s and 1930s, was the most vaunted flower of the British educational system – sportsmanship. For the man-about-town who had won his colours, inherited his father's wealth, and wanted to cut a bit of a dash, the three-litre Bentley open sports car was a *sine qua non* until 1927 when an even more ostentatious model, the four-and-a-half litre, became available to him.

Private detectives, secret agents and adventurers in gallant causes were drawn predominantly from the man-about-town class. What alternative was there? An insurance clerk or a steel erector, whatever his personal gifts and propensities, simply could not get time off to shadow a suspect through Wimbledon; or check a week's purchases of alpenstocks from Harrods. It would be no use – even if he could afford the fare – to rumble down to Folkestone on a slow train when the girl he sought to rescue was in the tonneau of the villain's J-type Dusenberg, seaport-bound at an hundred miles an hour. The inescapable truth was that heroism, like business expansion, required capital as well as flair. Writers who invested, on their leading character's behalf, in a Bentley were simply recognizing this fact and hoping for a prestige bonus.

There were a number of these, including Sydney Horler, in the years when Bentleys either were in production or had not yet acquired second-hand value in a special 'vintage' context. Most tended to refer to the cars simply by name, dropping occasional reference to speeds in the eighties or nineties but not rhapsodizing at length. Such control of enthusiasm, one suspected, was often less indicative of familiarity than of almost total ignorance.

Lord Peter Wimsey, naturally, was a Bentley man – or he was in his younger, more frivolous days. He subsequently switched allegiance to Daimlers, his creator having noticed, perhaps, that Royalty of the time was always conveyed behind that famous fluted radiator.

In 1928, Dorothy Sayers described Wimsey's transport as 'a big open car with an unnaturally long bonnet' which 'had slipped up to them, silent as an owl'. Wimsey wore motoring goggles and when he pushed them up there was disclosed 'a long narrow nose and a pair of rather cynical-looking grey eyes'. The cynical expression was only to be expected from one who had just overtaken two motor cyclists, themselves travelling at seventy miles an hour, in days when there still existed an official universal speed limit of thirty.

Predictably, the motor cyclists, a truculent lower middle-class pair, had their names taken by the police with a view to prosecution whereas Lord Peter was subjected to no inconvenience ('you being who you are', as the local superintendent told him) other than stares of admiration at 'the long sweep of the exhaust and the rakish lines' of his car.

Four years later, Lord Peter was still attracting notice to his means of locomotion. The scene had changed from Eaton Socon, on the Great North Road, to London's Jermyn Street. This time it

was not just the envious comments of bystanders that were heard
but

> the reverent murmurings of a congregation of persons gathered
> in the street to admire its streamlining and dispute about the
> number of its cylinders.

Evidently there had taken place in the interval some
transfiguration so awe-inspiring that religious metaphor was now
in order. Had Lord Peter bought the eight-litre sporting saloon,
that final, two-and-three-quarter-ton gesture of the Bentley
company which in less than a minute could accelerate in top gear
from ten to a hundred miles an hour smoothly and in silence? Miss
Sayers did not say.

No such reticence was to cut short the motor-car lectures of Ian
Fleming, perhaps the last thriller writer to put his hero behind the
wheel of a Bentley. He was very specific indeed. Mark IV engine
... nine-point-five compression ... Mulliners' coachwork ...
painted in rough, not gloss, battleship grey, with black Morocco
upholstery ... Further, it had two-inch exhaust pipes because
Bond 'hadn't liked the old soft flutter of the marque' and the long
grey nose was topped by a big octagonal silver bolt instead of the
winged B.

The car sounded impressive enough and we have the author's
word that 'Bond loved her more than all the women at present in
his life.' But whatever it was that Bond was supposed to be driving
after it had been cannibalized forbearingly by Rolls-Royce at his
request from parts made by them in the first place, it certainly was
not a Bentley.

A quarter of a century before Fleming learned to exploit the
'status' obsession of his times by being airily knowledgeable about
marques and rear axle ratios, Leslie Charteris sent Templar out on
the road in a vehicle of his own invention. He called it the Furillac, implying perhaps that it was a combination of enormous
power and the sort of luxury which the American makers of the
Cadillac were supplying to the few who could still afford to buy
their gadget-laden V-16 monsters in the year after the Wall Street

crash. It seems to have had special advantages for one of the Saint's athletic potentiality:

> The Saint vaulted into the Furillac, and came down with one foot on the self-starter and the other on the clutch pedal. As Patricia gained her place beside him, he unleashed the full ninety-eight horse-power that the speedster could put forth when pressed.

In *The Last Hero* (1930) the Furillac, alas, crashed, but Templar was not at a loss. He took over from a friend an even more extraordinary motor car, somewhat inaptly named Hirondel. There was nothing very swallow-like about that one.

> It was not an inconspicuous car at the best of times, even when sedately driven, that long, lean, silver-grey King of the Road.

This is how The Saint took the tramway-infested road to the north east out of London one night in 1930:

> The Hirondel, as though recognizing the hand of a master at its wheel, became almost a living thing. King of the Road, its makers called it, but that night the Hirondel was more than a king: it was the incarnation and apotheosis of all cars ... a snarling silver fiend that roared through London on the wings of an unearthly wind.

Even on the quite narrow and, as Wallace's Captain Gordon had found to his cost, winding roads of provincial England before the big highway developments of the 1930s, Simon Templar managed a very creditable ninety miles an hour – and after nightfall, at that. The one precaution he did take was to maintain

> a challenging blast of klaxon and snarling stammer of unsilenced exhaust ...

This circumstance was typical of the illegalities that the period's heroes of crime fiction seem to have vied with one another to commit, and it has interest in relation to what Edmund Clerihew

Bentley, author of *Trent's Last Case,* decided as early as 1910 to be an essential ingredient of the detective story. Absolutely necessary, he declared, was 'some fussing about in a motor car or cars, with at least one incident in which the law of the land and the safety of human life are treated as entirely negligible'. By 1940, when he published his autobiography, *Those Days,* Bentley's opinion had hardened even further. He said it was now a 'strict convention' that the detective-hero had to be a driver so idiotically reckless that those in the car with him would totter out of it, pale and trembling, vowing never to entrust their lives to him again, when their destination was reached.

Bentley appealed for an explanation.

'The recklessness is thought to be dashing and attractive, I suppose; risking one's life always has been so; but what I should like to have worked out for me is why risking other people's should be regarded as an activity with something appealing and heroic about it.'

It is ironic that so few people here or in America – where it was first published – realized that *Trent's Last Case* was intended to be a send-up of the conventional detective story, that to this day the book is solemnly indicated as the classic example of something Bentley found utterly absurd.

CHAPTER 17

'With thy quire of Saints for evermore . . .'

As part of the preparation of her thesis, *Fiction and the Reading Public*, Mrs Q. D. Leavis sent out a questionnaire to the most popular writers of the day, including a number of authors of crime fiction. Their answers established, among other things, that substantial and consistent success was always secured by those novelists who reflected and encouraged the habits of thought of the least inquisitive, the least experimental members of the community.

'The general public,' declared one witness confidently, 'does not wish to think. This fact accounts for the success of my stories, for I have endeavoured to make all my descriptions so clear that each situation could be visualized ... with the minimum of mental effort.'

Another ascribed large sales of his books to the fact that he wrote them primarily to please himself, a 'normal man', whose tastes he could assume to be shared by millions of other 'normal' men.

Normality was also stressed by P. C. Wren, soldier turned novelist, whose wildly romanticized accounts of life in the French Foreign Legion fascinated thousands who would not have known a sheik from a shillelagh. 'The bulk of my readers,' claimed the creator of Beau Geste, 'are the cleanly-minded, virile, outdoor sort of people of both sexes, and the books are widely read in the Army, the Navy, the Universities, the Public Schools, and the Clubs ... Although I now make a good many thousands per annum, I still am not a "professional novelist", nor a long-haired literary cove. I prefer the short-haired executive type.'

Whatever undercurrents of sexual motivation may be discerned in this credo, it remains impressive evidence of the quite genuine sense of rectitude that imbued authors of sensation fiction between the wars. A later generation would call them prigs. So they were, but the fact that their priggishness paid off so handsomely acquits them, curiously enough, of the twin charge of hypocrisy. The public, however addled its notions of Algeria, or Chinatown, or Scotland Yard, is wonderfully sensitive to the calculating author, the author who deliberately writes down.

Success strides with sincerity: which explains why some of the most widely read and enduring newspaper and magazine columnists have been humourless, unsubtle and conceited persons with absolute faith in their own platitudes. What P. C. Wren wrote in answer to Mrs Leavis may safely be assumed to express an honest conviction: phrases such as 'cleanly-minded', 'thousands per annum', 'literary cove', 'executive type' – these could have emanated only from a guileless prig or an accomplished satirist, and Wren certainly was not the second.

It was the belief of Mrs Leavis that the pattern of popular fiction in the 1930s had been set by the magazine, the standard formula of which was the avoidance of everything that could possibly cause worry or offence or unease. The magazine had achieved 'readability' not merely by setting itself to amuse and soothe; it was explicitly defiant of other standards and ambitions. 'And by accustoming the reading public to certain limited appeals and a certain restricted outlook, it has spoilt the public for fiction in book form of a more serious nature.' It is true that most magazines became increasingly trivial in content and presentation with every year of the twentieth century. So did newspapers, with which they generally shared common ownership. Both, as Francis Williams has pointed out, were transformed between 1920 and

1940 from instruments 'of information and political persuasion into a branch of the entertainment industry concerned primarily with making the largest possible appeal to readers who wanted to be excited and amused'.

But so long as they were run for profit, in what other direction could they have developed? Today, television has taken the place of magazines as the most often quoted cause of debasement of public literary taste. (Not the least upset by this usurpation are the magazine publishers.) But assertions as to 'taste' are easier to make than to prove. If the process of debilitation had really continued steadily during the past fifty years, it would be reasonable to expect present-day popular fiction to be more superficial, silly and more slipshod, more crude and more vicious than that of the 1920s and 1930s. Many people find it all of those things. But they are applying personal standards and referring to what they consider eternal moral verities. To regard the matter from the Wildean view – that there are no good or bad books, only well and ill written ones – might produce a different verdict.

'I have proved from experience,' Horler wrote in 1933, 'that the reputation of a sensational novelist is more securely placed with the reading public than almost any other form of writer.' With this statement, at any rate, there is no reason for Compton Mackenzie or anyone else to quarrel. Almost every thriller writer of Horler's time testified to the loyalty – the sometimes quite disconcerting loyalty – of his readers. This kind of fan mail has diminished considerably in recent years with the opening of great new channels to draw off the emotions of simple, of frustrated or of easily moved, generous-hearted people; but written fiction still has the special capacity it has always had for sending characters into what might be called the multitudinous affection of society. Television does not have this power. Hard as it tries with repetitive techniques to establish its own folk heroes, all it has succeeded in doing so far is to graft a particular actor's face and mannerisms to some already universally familiar creation of a writer of books. The cinema suffers a like impotence, and this perhaps is poetic justice to an industry which at its commercial zenith regarded

writers as menials to be hired by the squad and drilled into acceptance of the meretricious formulae of semi-literates.

The reason for the failure of television and the great majority of
films to put permanent lodgers into the minds of their audience lies,
paradoxically, in their wealth of means. They can convey so
much, so quickly and with such mechanical expertise, that human
characters slip straight through with the rest of the highly convincing artifacts and do not have to gain entry the hard way
through the imagination. So these same characters can and do slip
out again just as readily, despite the most clamorous promotion
campaigns; indeed the cult of the film star and the TV personality
has itself militated against the establishment of any original hero,
heroine, or even anti-hero capable of outlasting a television series
of a dozen episodes or a half-year's film run.

In the years when Hollywood was riding high – and exceedingly rough-shod – one of its most demoralizing practices was to 're-
make' at regular intervals one or other of a selection of stories it
liked to classify as deathless. The term had a variety of meanings,
of which being out of copyright frequently was one, but its general
application was to anything which on being filmed for the first
time had made a lot more money than had been expected. Apart
from the Bible, to the monopolizing of whose spectacular possibilities Cecil B. de Mille brought a talent trained on pre-Hays
Office pornography, the most favoured material for working over
was historical romance, preferably with religious streaks. To
Victor Hugo, Alexandre Dumas and Leo Tolstoy, the industry
was deeply – and repeatedly – indebted. There grew from this
exploitation of classics a golden goose philosophy. By the 1930s it
had become axiomatic in Hollywood that success could be replica-
ted indefinitely from prototype. Among the more dire consequences were the Andy Hardy family, the Mary Wollstonecraft
Shelley Monster of the Month Club, and the progeny of a sheep-
dog called Lassie. But there was one area in which simple dupli-
cation worked very rarely. It was that of crime fiction.

Several attempts were made to transfer the Holmes opus to the
screen, but not one managed to reproduce whatever it was that

had captured the imagination of the reading public. Perhaps the authentic Baker Street flavour was masked by the unconscionable quantities of swirling vapour wherewith film-makers invariably signified Victorian London (piping it, some said, from that permanent Louisiana swamp set reserved for haunted house B features).

Fu-Manchu was somehow not so much sinister as comical on celluloid, while Edgar Wallace's splendid indifference to probability leaked through into some of the adaptations of his stories and turned them into farce. America's own Earl Derr Biggers was better served. The adventures of his smug, pseudo-Confucian Hawaian detective Charlie Chan formed one of the most durable and popular Hollywood series. It used up three Chan actors, of whom the second, Warner Oland, probably came nearer than did any star of the 1930s to imparting memorable personality to a crime investigator. William Powell's endearing air of hungover courtesy helped to make the *Thin Man* films mildly enjoyable, but they were scarcely identifiable as the work of Dashiell Hammett. The doctoring of original stories to spare the supposed susceptibilities of storekeepers' wives in Illinois was not calculated to leave much that a Hammett or a Chandler would have cared to acknowledge, once the cheque had been cleared. Chandler's script of *The Blue Dahlia* and the adaptation of Hammett's early novel *The Glass Key* were exceptional in their retention of a recognizable degree of their authors' style and concern, while for the film version of *The Big Sleep* the choice of Humphrey Bogart materialized exactly the sardonic, much-damaged but incorruptible Philip Marlowe. Much more closely in line with Hollywood tradition and practice was a dry-cleaned travesty of *Farewell My Lovely*, in which Dick Powell jumped around as Marlowe in the semblance of a pert, over-eager shoe salesman, while written-in lines such as 'She was evil – evil . . .' were declaimed to indicate to the ladies of Illinois what all the shooting had been about.

Film producers in England showed more enthusiasm for the native detective story as potential screen material than might be supposed. The plots, after all, were dauntingly complicated.

Whatever satisfaction they offered could only be attained – like that of guests at a somewhat elaborate dinner – by orderly course-by-course consumption. Cinema audiences did not care to be ruled by the clock, whatever the custom might be in theatres, so it was desirable that films should be as nearly as possible continuously self-explanatory for the sake of those who liked to 'stay round to where we came in'. The detective story, whose very essence was the withholding of explanation until the last minute, might reasonably have been considered a non-starter. Yet a surprising number of whodunnit films was attempted. Some of the least pretentious – *Green for Danger*, for instance, adapted from Christianna Brand's novel, and lent distinction by Alistair Sim as a wonderfully fallible Scotland Yard inspector, came quite near to being successful, but the majority were just standard products of the British film industry's almost psychotic fear of overstraining public intelligence. A notable collector's item among film adaptations of crime fiction is the version of Dorothy L. Sayers's *Busman's Honeymoon* in which Lord Peter Wimsey is played by the American actor Robert Montgomery. Montgomery presumably was chosen in the hope that his fame at that time as a star would make the film attractive to more people. He was a personable, conscientious actor who dressed well, looked clean, and might conceivably have fooled a Bowery doorman into mistaking him for a British aristocrat. Otherwise, he made as convincing a Peter Wimsey as Pancho Villa might have done. The film was a lesson on the essentially static, immutable nature of the detective novel. A trace of New York accent, a certain buoyancy of manner, a suggestion of genuine friendliness in the hearty treatment of menials – these few and so trivial solecisms shattered the image that Miss Sayers had worked so long and devotedly to create, and without which her detection and her books were nothing.

Television failures to transfer crime fiction from print to picture have been less grotesque than those of the film makers and have included some honourable tries. Generally speaking, the older the story, the more nearly satisfying has been the adaptation. Thus Wilkie Collins, Conan Doyle and R. Austin Freeman have fared much better than authors still writing after the second war. The reason is only partly that the earlier work possessed more dramatic content and gave greater scope for characterization. A bigger help to producers and directors was the fact that these pieces came into the category of 'period', which television – in Britain, anyway – always has been able to do extremely well. It was the novels of the more recent 'golden age' of the detective story, the later 1920s and 1930s, which emerged, despite great pains and expense, as fricassees of unlikely behaviour, footling dialogue and forensic absurdities. Much safer was the American contentment to let Perry Mason play out his long television career without leaving the courtroom.

The thriller hero is made of sterner stuff. He need pay no court to the intellect. He can move around, taking his chance with whatever medium he enters. Television does not daunt him, although the probabilities are that it will not accommodate him for long and that even while he stays he will need to defer to certain expectations. One hero there was, though, whose lease of television time had begun to look like a permanent freehold. His name was Simon Templar, alias The Saint.

The Saint of Television existed in the person of Roger Moore, an actor of pleasant voice, athletic build and seemingly imperishable good looks. His manner was casual but aware; it could switch from kindly concern to insouciance, from gravity to lip-curling ferociousness. He was patently a ladies' man, yet a man's man for all that. For he was one of the most devastating balsa-smashers in the business. He looked clean enough to eat your dinner off. And he was one of the very few television characters in relation to whom speculation about toupees seemed indecent.

This latter-day Saint was virile but unmarried, which meant that a not-too-serious touch of romance could be added to each episode. His wealth, evidenced by invariable elegance of apparel and a habit of turning up in expensive places for no better reason than to be met accidentally by an acquaintance in need, was unexplained yet not, somehow, suspect. One felt that it must have accrued from the dispositions of grateful Bohemian monarchs and from daring coups that had left only blackguards the poorer. Wherever he might be, in Tuxon or Maidenhead or Rome or Mombasa, Templar would be whisked to and fro in his big whiter-than-white car. Neither the car nor its owner ever got dirty.

Over the years, one began to feel that the smooth, dependable, inoffensive, sometimes silly but never soporific, Saint series was a projection into drama of all the advertising rituals and assumptions. Most television wears an air of salesmanship somehow; it is, after all, a shop window for talent and ideas as well as things to eat, smoke and wash with, and in the end the patina of commercialism spreads over all. The more expert the programme, the stronger the impression it conveys of trying to sell something. As Simon Templar developed in self-assurance, dress sense, wit and resourcefulness, he became less a representation of good battling against evil than of the victory of the discriminating and deodorized possessor of indispensables.

The Saint's metamorphosis is of particular interest. It provides an opportunity, rare and possibly unique, of making direct comparison in the same persona between the qualities regarded as heroic forty years ago and those which commend themselves to a mass-audience now. Certain of these qualities have been modified scarcely at all. In 1930, Leslie Charteris observed that

> when confronted by an armed man twice his own size, the Saint felt that he needed no excuse for employing any damaging foul known to the fighting game . . .

Karate chops, gouges, trips, and the flailing of opponents with balsa furniture are tactics which a modern television audience accepts with characteristic equanimity. There exists no longer the obligation Charteris apparently felt to justify this sort of mayhem by doubling the odds against the hero. Even the expressions 'foul' and 'fighting game' have a faint mustiness about them, although they will not be altogether unintelligible for as long as sport continues to be ransacked for metaphors by thriller writers, con men and ministers of state.

The vintage Saint books were being written while 'Sapper' was at the height of his popularity. A close relationship between Templar and Bulldog Drummond is apparent at a number of points. Thus the Saint's injunction to a friend to

'Get out your car, fill her up with gas, and come right round to Brook Street. And pack a gun. This is going to be a wild night.'

was a distinct echo of Drummond's cry to Stockton four years earlier:

'Call up your war lore, for we're going to have a peerless night creep!'

The resemblance between the manner in which Drummond addressed an opponent of lower social status and the Saint's approach to his inferiors at that time, is also striking. Here was the Saint, interviewing a petty criminal – or rather a man he suspected of being one:

'Do you talk, Rat Face?' he asked. 'Wotcher mean – talk? Yer big bullies ...' 'Talk,' repeated the Saint patiently. 'Open your mouth, and emit sounds which you fondly believe to be English.'

Again the Saint, his wit now at its keenest:

'. . . the misshapen lump of bone that keeps your unwashed ears apart . . .'

and

'Why haven't you come down before – so that I could knock your miscarriage of a face through the back of your monstrosity of a neck?'

In this mood, Simon Templar was virtually interchangeable with Captain Drummond, author of the felicitous

'Now, rat face, what excuse have you got to offer for living? .. I will break your arm – and that thing you call a face as well.'

But all that was fifty years ago. Drummond never had the chance to learn how to modify his language and behaviour to suit television's heterogeneous audience. He died with the whip of his preparatory school invective at full larrup against unwashed hides and the cringing backs of Bolshy and Dago. His adventures still are read by thousands of consenting Britons, but in private. Their promulgation, unexpurgated, on television would be impossible in a world where Dagos play, and win, at football; where the Unwashed are up to their eyes in enormously profitable detergents; and where Bolshies buy and diligently watch the twenty-six episodes of *The Forsyte Saga*.

The Saint, on the other hand, has adapted himself to new times and a new medium. He still chases evil-doers, but it is unthinkable that he would identify them as simply 'foreign-looking birds with ugly mugs', as he did in *The Saint Closes the Case* (1930), even though his own appearance has remained miraculously unchanged since those days when

> his dark hair was at its sleekest perfection, his blue eyes danced, his brown face was alight with an absurdly boyish enthusiasm.

He is a good deal less homicidal, too. His victims generally recover in time to be handcuffed and led away by representatives of law and order (formerly, it might be recalled, Templar's implacable opponents). Yet in one single encounter in his younger days he shot two men dead, knifed a third in the throat, smashed the jawbone of a fourth, and dropped yet another 'like a poleaxed steer' before concentrating on the last, and most hateful, crook of all.

That knifing, incidentally, is one of the great curiosities of British crime fiction. The convention was very well established by the time the Saint novels began to appear that only foreigners and very low-grade criminals indeed used knives as fighting weapons, although home-bred murderers were allowed to press into service such cutlery as happened to be lying around provided they left it sticking in the victims and did not adopt it as permanent personal equipment. Yet Templar, whom no less reliable a witness than a rival in love once described as 'the whitest man in the world', quite clearly had habitual recourse to this alien practice.

There was a little knife in the Saint's hand – a toy with a six-inch leaf-shaped blade and a delicately chased ivory hilt. It appeared to have come from nowhere, but actually it had come from the neat leather sheath strapped to the Saint's forearm under the sleeve, where it always lived; and the name of the knife was Anna. There was a story to Anna, a savage and flamboyant story of the godless lands . . .

Twenty years were to pass before another fictional hero of like popularity was to be openly credited with carrying a knife. And, like the old time Saint, he was to be an avowed killer.

CHAPTER 18

Licence to kill

The novels of Ian Fleming have been held to represent the watershed between the old-style thrillers that people in the first half of the century were happy not to be able to put down, and the escapist literature of the Pop age. Gone, implies this argument, are the cosy, complicated tales of death at the country house party; departed for ever the aristocratic detective, the homicidal governess, the master criminal audaciously disguised as a commissioner of police, the fiendish Chinese, the mad scientist. Arrived is the daring but irresponsible anti-hero, the hireling of realpolitik. He has in his mouth the radioactive ashes of guilt, but because he is an agent in the struggle between 'us' and 'them' instead of the outdated tournament of good and evil, he is enabled to behave (and, significantly in a society that has heard of something called sadism, to suffer the behaviour of others) in a fashion calculated to give readers more piquant vicarious sensations than ever they could have enjoyed in the pages of Edgar Wallace or Dorothy Sayers, Dornford Yates or G. K. Chesterton.

In an increasingly materialistic social climate, one of the most potent magic words is 'new'. Advertisers use it perpetually, and not only because even they find it easy to spell. People are supposed to be awed by it as once they were awed by the sign of the cross. A 1969 paperback edition of Fleming's *On Her Majesty's Secret Service* had on its cover the heading 'The New James Bond'. The story was then six years old. Whether or not the impending release of a film based on the book justified the use of that word 'new', the publishers clearly thought it a desirable description. Why, after all, should not the book-buying public possess the same commercially conditioned reflexes as the biscuit-and-floor-polish-buying public and salivate on the mention of novelty?

Well, perhaps people do respond in this way. Perhaps they will buy a book on the assurance that it is notably different from or better (or worse) than any other book yet printed. But if so, they are reacting to flattery, to the implication that they have lively tastes and adventurous minds. What they truly are anxious to obtain is not novelty at all, but familiarity. Any librarian will attest that the most commonly voiced request in a working day is for 'another like this' or 'another one by him, or her'. Sought is the reappearance of old friends and enemies, the continuity of recognizable heroism and defined villainy. The readers of sensation literature (and this is no reflection on their intelligence) show a conservatism much more rigid than might be supposed from the extravagance of their fare. Loyalties to specific authors and characters are strong, as are prejudices against experiment, disruption of pattern, and, above all, lapses from seriousness. Such conservatism favours the formula, the series, the stock character, the repeat prescription.

And Fleming, by design, instinct, or great good luck, repeated every prescription in the pharmacopoeia of crime and spy fiction. His thirteen James Bond novels can be seen as a potted history of the twentieth-century thriller.

There was at one time a strong possibility that the argument aroused by the books of Ian Fleming would expand into a minor literary industry. They were attacked as false, decadent and ill-written. They were championed for their readability, their realism and their lack of moral pretentiousness. The dispute continued throughout the 1960's in newspapers and magazines. Several books were published, including an elaborate defence by Kingsley Amis, *The James Bond Dossier*. These, tending as they did to encourage the establishment of Bondology as a spoof science on the lines of the Holmesian discipline, led the debate into even more complicated and, possibly, irrelevant courses. What the contestants often seemed too preoccupied to tackle was the most obviously important question of all. Why had the Fleming stories reached in print and film so vast a public (estimated by the end of the decade to be three times the entire population of Britain) that the name Bond was an international commonplace?

The reasons, one might think, should not have been really difficult to discover. But again and again they were overlooked in the excitement of proclaiming personal views of the literary, moral, political and psychological implications of the Bond saga.

Why the workmanship of Fleming has been so warmly argued about is a mystery. At one extreme, his admirer O. F. Snelling declares the master's skill to be such that he could have rendered a telephone directory fascinating. At the other, Mordecai Richler dismisses him as 'an appalling writer' – stylistically appalling, presumably, not horror-provoking. Neither statement is true. Fleming was a competent storyteller on a journalistic level and within the framework of the formula he adopted for the James Bond novels. Whether he could have done anything successful outside that framework cannot now be proved but the fact that he did not try, despite financial independence and a growing personal weariness with the 007 routine, does suggest that he had nothing else to say.

Fleming's grasp of syntax was reasonably good and it would be ungracious in the post-Hemingway era of buckshot prose not to commend an author who could deliver well-turned sentences. A few of his descriptions are memorable, and not solely by reason of the grotesque elements on which he depended so heavily.

One chronic weakness he suffered was the inability to create characters. All his villains are monstrous puppets, assembled from the rag-bag of childish imaginings. They have no relation to human society and no discernible function other than the indul-

gence of their own unexplained and quite unproductive mal-
evolence. The villains' henchmen are correspondingly bizarre in
appearance and habit; the most distressing from a literary point of
view are certain Americans and Negroes who speak in what Fleming (notoriously 'tin-eared') supposed to be their native vernacular. The only other characters – or character substitutes – of any
importance in the Bond novels are the sexual conquests of 007.
They are distinguishable by name and, in some cases, by slight
physical deformities; otherwise they all are standard issue, breast-
thrusting lingerie demonstrators that pass for desirable sex-pots in
the world of the prep school and, it would seem, British Naval
Intelligence.

Plot structure varies scarcely at all from book to book. Bond is
summoned by his master, 'M', and dispatched upon a mission. Its
object is to thwart a conspiracy, either directly instigated by the
Soviet Union or likely to be to that country's advantage, and to
assassinate the sinister guiding genius. Bond penetrates the villain's stronghold, is captured and tortured. He escapes, with or
without the help of the nymphomaniacal young woman who by
this time has drawn thrustingly abreast of him. He engineers the
destruction of plot, villain and all, fulfilling his personal norm of
three murders per book, and bows out to an interlude of peaceful
fornication until 'M' gets another idea.

With the best will in the world, one cannot pretend that the
phenomenal success of what Fleming once termed, with exploratory false modesty, his 'blatant thrillers' is attributable to
inventiveness, power of characterization, descriptive style, com-
passion, or any other of the literary good mark earners. Critics
have been surprised and disconcerted by this. Some have heard
with relief the rallying cry of Kingsley Amis: 'All literature is
escapist', and approved his contention that the adventures of
Agent 007 constitute reading that is only different from, and not
worse than, 'primarily enlightening fiction'. If what the cautious
call value judgements – by which they mean straightforward personal opinions that may be quoted against them later – are to be
avoided, Amis's conception of literature as a spectrum rather than

a ladder or a class list is useful. Ultra and infra are terms much less committing than top and bottom. But they advance no further the solution of the essential problem: why does Fleming's work sell?

By virtue of passages such as these?

> And after a while his other hand went to the zip-fastener at the back of her dress and without moving away from him she stepped out of her dress and panted between their kisses. 'I want it all, James. Everything you've ever done to a girl. Now. Quickly.'

> ... and of course we were in each other's arms again under the shower and our bodies were slippery with water and soap and he turned the shower off and lifted me out of the shower cabinet and began to dry me lingeringly with the bath towel ...

> The mounded vee of the bikini looked up at Bond and the proud breasts in their tight cups were two more eyes. Bond felt his control going. He said roughly, 'Turn over.'

The sexual encounters in the Bond books are as regular and predictable as bouts of fisticuffs in the 'Saint' adventures or end-of-chapter red herrings in the detective novels of Gladys Mitchell, and not much more erotic. Yet it often has been claimed that these, in conjunction with carefully described scenes of cruelty, form the pornographic core of the Fleming lodestone. At one time this might have seemed a reasonable view. In 1953, when the first of the Bond stories, *Casino Royale*, was published, many people in Britain and America – probably the majority – had inherited and unthinkingly absorbed the notion that merely to read about certain sins was very nearly the same as committing them. The range of such sins was limited, admittedly: felonies such as fraud, robbery, arson and murder were not deemed to contain an element of communicable pleasure, whereas all venereal offences, from bottom-pinching to rape, were. Anglo-Saxons had for so long been more sensitive than other nations to the harm that might be done by 'dirty' books that they were regarded throughout the world as the readiest potential customers for them. The situation was to change radically. With the emergence of what apprehensive people called 'the permissive society', meaning a society less convinced than formerly that morals, like drains, were matters for public administration, the indictment of Fleming as a purveyor of sex and sadism began to sound rather far-fetched. What was wrong, anyway, asked Amis in 1965, with those 'beautiful, firm breasts'? Might not those who affected to deplore Bond's peripatetic copulation really be sublimating into literary criticism their own sexual regrets?

More ingenuous was Amis's attempt to counter the sadism charge by quoting two extracts from 'the real thing' – the works of Mr Mickey Spillane. This is rather like retorting to a diner who complains of having found slugs on his cabbage that he is lucky not to have gone to the establishment next door, where slugs are served as the main course. Fleming's stories do contain liberal lardings of very vicious behaviour. To assert that there never was any element of self-indulgence in his description of torture and beatings is against probability. Unconvincing, too, is the denial of an implicit invitation to the reader to share in the enjoyment.

The third count on which Ian Fleming's reputation has been assailed is snobbery. It arises chiefly from his constant preoccupation with objects and places (not, Amis claims, people) which he supposed to have special merit. He never lost an opportunity of naming an expensive car or specifying a desirable vintage. Brand-named washing aids, or 'toiletries' as their disseminators call them, clearly fascinated Fleming: Bond's almost Holmesian skill in identifying esoteric perfumes is indicated with all the rehearsed nonchalance of a television commercial. But whether this sort of thing really qualified as snobbery is doubtful. Nor is it likely that Fleming the journalist was at the elbow of Fleming the author, prompting him to drop in all those 'free puffs' in hope of being rewarded by some grateful P.R.O. with a Rolex Oyster watch, a couple of bottles of Dom Perignon '46, or, failing all else, a carton of Cadbury's Milk Flakes. The most likely explanation is the simplest – that he just wanted to be thought thoroughly worldly and knowledgeable.

That, unfortunately, is always a dangerous ambition in a writer. A fair semblance of connoisseurship and 'inside' *savoir-faire* can be acquired by an intelligent researcher with time to bother, but just as illusory as the perfect crime is the perfect imposture. One slip (and errors in print sit pat for ever, proclaiming their parentage) is enough to destroy the credibility of all. Consider, for example, Fleming's careful build-up of Bond as the good liver. It is fairly safe to impress the customers with that Dom Perignon '46 and the 'real pre-war Wolfschmidt from Riga', but when Bond confidently doubles his chief's order of peas and new potatoes 'as it's May', the whole edifice of his pretentiousness is demolished by three little words. What he has implied is: *I would not dream of ordering new potatoes and peas if I thought there was a risk of the first having been imported and the second deep-frozen.* If only Fleming had looked into the gardening section of any home cyclopaedia he would have seen that neither fresh peas nor newly dug potatoes can reasonably be expected on an English menu until July.

Where Fleming's snobbery is genuine and not mugged up, it is of a mean order that compares unfavourably with the *haute snobisme* of Wimseyland.

Thus Dorothy Sayers:

> His double-breasted suit of navy blue and his socks, tie and handkerchief, all scrupulously matched, were a trifle more point-device than the best taste approves, and his boots were slightly too bright a brown.

And Fleming:

> ... where elderly couples with Ford Populars and Morris Minors talked in muted tones about children called Len and Ron and Pearl and Ethel, and ate in small mouthfuls with the points of their teeth and made not a sound with the tea things.

Sayers, unselfconsciously employing the authentic speech patterns of the most splendidly odious section of England's gentlefolk:

'What, the intense young woman with the badly bobbed hair and the brogues?' 'Well, she's never been able to afford a good hairdresser ... they're awfully poor, and her mother ought to have some frightfully difficult operation or something, and go and live abroad ... And perhaps Hannah wouldn't be quite so Red if she'd ever had a bean of her own. Besides, you could make it a condition of helping her that she should go and get properly shingled at Bresil's.'

Fleming, describing two men who deserve obloquy because they are Russian agents who film through a false mirror the coupling of a British agent (Bond) with a fourth agent, female, Russian:

And the view-finders gazed coldly down on the passionate arabesques the two bodies formed and broke and formed again, and the clockwork mechanism of the cine-cameras whirred softly on as the breath rasped out of the open mouths of the two men and the sweat of excitement trickled down their bulging faces into their cheap collars.

Sycophantic bluestocking Miss Sayers may have been, but she usually managed to make her characters' expressions of contempt for unmonied people ring with something of the supreme self-confidence of the rich and well-born whom she envied. The reference to Hannah's mother's need of 'some frightfully difficult operation or something' indicates exactly the attitude of bored flippancy with which a socialite of the time would have regarded anyone with the nerve to be ill beyond her means. The certainty of such phrases as 'the *best* taste', '*good* families', discounts the possibility of cavil.

Fleming, by contrast, was unsure and therefore tended to be bad-tempered and petty in his manner of asserting superiority. Having elected as he did to inhabit a world teeming with monstrous villains and evil-minded Soviet satraps, what could he have been thinking of to waste a whole clip of ammunition upon elderly couples sitting in an English tea-room? Compared with the atrocities of SMERSH, the ownership of a Morris Minor and the bestowal of 'common' names upon one's children seem smallish crimes, but Fleming, via Bond, obviously felt very strongly indeed about the genteel affectations of his own country's lower middle class. Was there, perhaps, an element of pseudo-refinement in his own background that embarrassed him?

In the passage about the two spies who are trying to compromise Bond on film, emphasis is laid on certain bodily circumstances. The men's breath 'rasps'. Their mouths are open. They sweat copiously. They are fat, or so we conclude from their 'bulging' faces. And where does their sweat run? Why, into 'cheap' collars, naturally. These few lines epitomize the obsession that is the genuine article lying beneath Fleming's highly publicized but unconvincing epicurism; a simple aversion to human physicality in general and in particular to that of the sort of people who wear cheap collars. It merges sometimes into social snobbery – as when Bond notices that an insufficiently respectful taxi-driver, 'typical of the cheap self-assertiveness of young labour since the war', has a 'foxy, pimpled' face. More often, it inspires an ablution of some kind (Bond is a compulsive washer), or a dissertation on those toiletries, or a swim, or, as an occasional treat, an interlude of love-play in the bathroom. The evidence of friends quoted by Fleming's biographer, John Pearson, suggested that in real life Fleming was disgusted by women viewed otherwise than in the abstract. One said he had refused to have anything more to do with a girl after he had seen her go behind a rock to urinate. Another declared that Fleming would not even have tied a cut finger for her, so extreme was his revulsion from bodily things.

So much, then, for the 'sex, sadism and snobbery' formula which has been held to account for the multi-million sales of the Fleming thrillers. It will not do. Close appraisal reveals no more piquant a combination of these three old ingredients than has been offered by a dozen writers of crime and espionage novels in recent years.

However, the more carefully Fleming's books are examined in relation to the general body of sensation fiction from 1920 onwards, the more striking does one particular aspect of his work become.

It is astonishingly derivative.

George Orwell, as we have seen, compared the work of E. W. Hornung and that of James Hadley Chase in order to support his thesis that popular literature had suffered a decline in moral standards between the two world wars. *No Orchids for Miss Blandish* admittedly is not a text for human improvement, nor even an informed picture of human depravity. It is a calculated, if clumsy, attempt to titillate by projecting its English author's idea of how American gangsters go about being beastly to one another and to their women. Neither Mr Chase nor any of his characters attempts to justify or rationalize this behaviour. The 'Raffles' books, on the other hand, unmistakably invite the reader to approve the assaults and burglaries in the spirit of an onlooker at feats of sportsmanship. Whether this makes Hornung a more moral entertainer than Chase is questionable, but it certainly qualifies him to be considered as a precursor of Fleming.

For Bond, too, is primarily a performer – a sportsman – and our applause is solicited whether the game is murder or seduction or simply card-sharping. He is outside the law, like Raffles, but remains acceptable, as does Raffles, to the sentimental English middle-class world by virtue of two admirable abstractions, loyalty and patriotism. In Raffles's case, the loyalty is to his 'sort'. Bond's is equally nebulous: it is to a mere initial letter, the anonymous head of a secret organization with unspecified and perhaps non-existent limits of responsibility. The patriotism of Bond consists mainly of a willingness to kill or encompass the death of agents of organizations exactly similar to his own except that they have different initials and always lose. It is a more dangerous kind of patriotism but not really much more intelligent than that which prompted Raffles to rob the British Museum of an antique gold cup so that he could send it by post as a personal gift to 'absolutely the finest sovereign the world has ever seen' (his own). The success of such an escapade would be celebrated by Raffles with Sullivans – the special cigarettes he kept for the purpose. A childish indulgence? It might be thought so – or at least its being mentioned might. Yet the later, presumably more sophisticated Fleming permitted himself to go on like this:

> Bond had lit up a Duke of Durham, king-size, with filter. The authoritative Consumers Union of America rates this cigarette the one with the smallest tar and nicotine content. Bond had transferred to the brand from the fragrant but powerful Morland Balkan mixture with three gold rings round the paper he had been smoking since his teens. The Dukes tasted of almost nothing, but they were at least better than Vanguards. . .

Smoking ceremonial changed little over forty years, apparently, among gentlemen cracksmen and secret agents. Nor has the breaking of glass in faces gone out of fashion since Raffles hit his boy pursuer with a torch in *The Wrong House*. Fleming describes two instances: the grinding of a flash bulb into a man's cheek, and Bond's somewhat extravagant use of his Rolex Oyster Perpetual wrist watch as a knuckleduster, so that when

> Bond's right flashed out . . . the face of the Rolex disintegrated against the man's jaw.

A final point of similarity between Hornung and Fleming that might be mentioned is the warmth of feeling generated in both their heroes by delinquent male confederates. Raffles forever had that 'dear old hand' ready for Bunny, his narrator-companion on the burglary rounds. Bond, after only two short encounters with Marc-Ange, the Mafia-style gangster whose specialities included mass murder and organized prostitution, admits readily to having 'developed much love, and total respect, for this man'. He ascribes his feelings to animal magnetism.

The next most prominent character in the Bond album of family likenesses is Uncle Bulldog. Not only was Drummond a great basher of villainous lesser breeds; he was, like Bond, obsessed with cleanliness. His rebukes to adversaries almost always contained such adjectives as filthy, unwashed, foul. Much less taciturn than his nephew, and inclined to idiotic argument,

Drummond nevertheless operated with a dispatch that would certainly have earned him a double-o prefix if such a thing had been
for disposal in the 1920s. He was, for instance, good at shooting
people exactly between the eyes. The amount of time spent by
Drummond in being tied up might help explain Bond's notable
propensity for getting himself trussed, although it is to the younger
man's credit that he offers more intelligible comment on the situation than a muffled oath. Again, the convention whereby any
young woman foolish enough to attach herself to Bond is liable to
be tommy-gunned, staked out as crab food, or otherwise ill-
treated, can be traced to the 'Sapper' canon. One recalls the outsize tarantula sent to Mrs Drummond by Carl Peterson.

The master of the creepy-crawly, of course, was old Fu-
Manchu, the chronicle of whose exploits showers centipedes and
scorpions from every page. If Carl Peterson was the original of
Fleming's Ernst Stavro Blofeld, the fiendish Chinese Doctor was
owed a heavy modelling fee by the creator of Dr No. There is only
one substantial difference between Sax Rohmer's villain and the
Fleming super-sinisters. Dr No, Mr Big, Le Chiffre and the rest
really do get down to cases where torturing is concerned. They
break fingers and whack testicles with great professionalism. Fu-
Manchu was content to make diabolical noises ('My files! My
wire jackets!') without causing anybody actual physical harm – a
matter he deputed to his Burmese assassins or to the centipedes.
Sax Rohmer must have considered that his readers would be
thrilled sufficiently by the mere nationality of the Doctor, con-
stituting as it did that Yellow Peril dread of which was then
politically in vogue. He failed to foresee that shifts of national
commitment and racial attitude would leave works of fiction that
assumed the permanence of such things looking outdated and silly.
Fleming made the same mistake until he tried to redeem it more
than half-way through the Bond series by transferring the onus
for villainy from the U.S.S.R. to the fanciful hotch-potch
SPECTRE.

One more Rohmer–Fleming parallel is afforded by the way in
which the heroes of both have owed their survival on frequent

occasions to the defection of a female associate or servitor of the villain. But whereas the slave-girl Karamaneh's constant shuttling to and fro in her boss's time with warnings or means of escape for Nayland Smith and Petrie was treated by the Devil-Doctor with a degree of forbearance that would have done credit to a Schweitzer, aiding Bond almost invariably had a punitive sequel. Fleming's anti-feminist streak could have been responsible for this difference: Rohmer, by all accounts, was a gentle and chivalrous man, remembered by friends as 'a real charmer'.

No one has ever succeeded in discovering the precise aims of the great Fu-Manchu conspiracy. 'Domination' was the word that Rohmer found sufficient, but he was adept at avoiding definitions and his fog of portentousness remains impenetrable. What the villains were about, how they financed their schemes, by what curious means they had come to be in possession of so much capital equipment, house property and armament (spiders included) in the middle of London – these things were never explained, and most readers have never particularly wanted them to be. Edgar Wallace availed himself of much the same sort of licence in regard to the motives, methods and means of *his* arch-criminals. He loved conspiracies, and in such books as *The Fellowship of the Frog* (1924) and *The Terrible People* (1926), he described in his none too careful but mettlesome way sets of outrageous events engineered in each case by a totally unscrupulous villain and calculated to wreck the security and well-being of the entire community of Britain.

This aspect of Wallace was to be reincarnated in Fleming, of whose novels conspiracy is the essence. Although there is no certainty that either writer deliberately chose the theme as a good 'seller', both were businessmen and firmly in the writing trade for profit. Wallace was astute enough to realize the fascination exerted upon ordinary minds by mysterious clanship such as freemasonry. A person who lacks prospect of gaining power, influence and respect by his own efforts and in his own sphere takes to thinking how he would like to exercise *secret* power. It is a very common form of self-indulgence, as Wallace doubtless knew.

Fleming, on the other hand, must surely have seen something of the usually shabby and often ludicrous reality of plot and counter-plot during his service with Naval Intelligence. If this disenchanted him, he gave no sign in the Bond books. Instead, he postulated conspiracies every bit as bizarre as those invented by Wallace and a technology of knavishness and counter-knavishness that is reminiscent at point after point of the earlier battles against the Frogs, the Terrible People and the rest of Wallace's resourceful undesirables. Even in minor details affinity is obvious. There is, for example, a Wallace precedent for the telephone-gun in Fleming's *From Russia with Love*. It nearly killed that oddly Bond-ish policeman 'Betcher' Long and was 'modelled on the pattern of a humane killer, with a chamber for the cartridge half-way up ...' Again, the report in *Casino Royale* of a Russian agent's suicide 'by swallowing a coat button of compressed potassium cyanide' is an echo of the passing of the formidable Miss Revelstoke, who cheated the gallows (as Wallace was so fond of putting it) by an exactly similar trick. It was Miss Revelstoke, incidentally, whose habit of carrying a 'razor-sharp blade' sheathed between the upper and lower sole of a special shoe she wore gave her a thirty-year lead over Rosa Klebb, Fleming's lethal kicker.

Flamboyance was the quality which, above all others, contributed to the popularity of the books of Edgar Wallace. His plots were outrageous, his continuity was erratic, his 'facts' dubious, his climaxes hasty and carelessly contrived; but always the sheer showmanship of the man made the flaws in his work seem unimportant. Wallace's millions of readers, cheated or not, were satisfied customers. Fleming achieved the same result but more quickly, more spectacularly. It would be easy to conclude that because there are so many similarities between the Bond novels and the books of Wallace, Rohmer, 'Sapper', Oppenheim, Horler, Charteris and the other inexorable bestsellers of their time, then Fleming must simply have studied them and worked out a composite formula for success − a kind of derring-do cocktail. The following random selection of sample ingredients could, with only the slightest modification, be put straight into Bond:

'I took some new Askaris in and they made trouble . . . looted the stores one night . . . I was obliged to shoot one or two and the rest deserted.'

The Great Impersonation – E. Phillips Oppenheim, 1920

'What was the explosive?' 'Dynamite,' said Elk promptly. 'It blew down – Nitro-glycerine blows up and sideways.'

The Fellowship of the Frog – Wallace, 1924

The car responded gallantly and shot forward in a violent swerve across the path of the lorry . . . A space of cigarette-paper dimensions separated the rear wing of the car from the lorry's bumpers, but there was no collision.

Blackshirt Strikes Again – Bruce Graeme, 1940

. . . a blow that shattered teeth in their sockets and smith-ereened a jawbone as if it had been made of glass.

The Saint Closes the Case – Leslie Charteris, 1930

Argels handed the card to the maître d'hôtel . . . 'Serve us with double dry martinis at once – dry, but not too dry, mind. Just a dash of Italian. That suits you, Miss Withers?' 'Perfectly,' she assented. 'You are evidently an epicure.' 'I try to be,' he admitted, leaning gallantly across the table towards her.

Moran Chambers Smiled – E. Phillips Oppenheim, 1932

But what about the flamboyance, the showmanship that is dis-cernible in all these extracts and which enabled Wallace and the others to get away with every literary crime from implausibility to stylistic archaism? Fleming did not possess it. He was a confident story-teller and his books have pace and a certain verve. But Flem-ing used quite different tactics from those of his predecessors to disguise absurdity of plot and paucity of characterization. If Wall-ace and his fellows may properly be compared to ringmasters whose fine airs and whip-cracking distract attention from the mange and lethargy of their lions, Fleming's equivalent is the advertising man, glossing the mediocrity of The Product with pseudo-science and snob-appeal. The old masters of the swash-buckling type of crime and spy fiction did not condescend to try and reconcile the events they described with real life probabilities. Thus did Wallace on one occasion arrange for a bullion convoy to be captured by the filling with carbon dioxide of a hollow in the English countryside through which the lorries were to pass, so that their drivers would be asphyxiated. A wildly impractical scheme if ever there was one, but neither Wallace nor his characters had time to bother with rationalization; another fiendish happening was just around the page.

By their refusal to make concessions to likelihood, no less than by their jingoism and their snobbery, the older writers were asserting personal faith in the stability and moral health of their society. Of course, they seemed to be saying, we all know that such things do not really happen in this well-ordered community of ours: it is only *because* they do not that people find them entertaining as tales.

Fleming and his successors were so to sophisticate the 'shocker', as John Buchan had termed it, that it would become an illusion within an illusion. Into what essentially was still the old-style hokum – the gunplay, kidnapping, chases, escapes and so forth – was elaborately insinuated the proposition that not only were these things happening in very truth, but they were unavoidable, directed to patriotic ends, and approved moreover by that esoteric but admirable minority, the Men in the Know. The process amounted to what is known in the advertising trade as a promotion job.

Admittedly, espionage is in more need of promotion, in that advertising sense, than most human activities. W. Somerset Maugham, who actually did some (its object was only to prevent the Russian Revolution) declared in his preface to *Ashenden* in 1928: 'The work of an agent in the Intelligence Department is on the whole extremely monotonous. A lot of it is uncommonly useless. The material it offers for stories is scrappy and pointless; the author has himself to make it coherent, dramatic and probable.' Malcolm Muggeridge also once had his thumb in the Intelligence pie: tomfoolery was what he thought it. That verdict is not entirely discredited by such record as there is of Fleming's own role in Naval Intelligence which he is supposed to have benefited from by such ideas as freezing clouds to make gun platforms and sinking concrete blocks containing men with periscopes to watch the French coast.

The Bond books romanticize the secret service, but to no greater extent than did *Ashenden*, let alone Buchan's Hannay stories or the old William Le Queux fantasies about dashing Duckworth Drew. Fleming worked harder to achieve verisimilitude than to make sentimental appeal. He chose for his settings real places and took his characters on journeys that could be plotted on maps. He dropped pieces of globetrotter's lore with the persistence of an ageing cocotte letting fall handkerchiefs. His affectation of multilingualism left some pages looking more like menus than accounts of adventure. The apparently obsessive use of brand names may be seen as a further means of boosting credibility. Finally, Fleming set himself diligently to make his hero into The Product for which the circumstances and mood of the times guaranteed a mass sale.

James Bond is a healthy, physically powerful man, with no social responsibilities and no personal ties. He has a zest for life and travels all over the place, drinking and smoking heavily without permanent ill effect. He is enormously attractive to women and a great stud performer. He has no intellectual interests whatever, but is impressively knowing about food and drink, sports, motor-cars, weapons and the appurtenances of high life. He is, when required to be, a ruthless fighter. His political thought is minimal, but would just about turn litmus paper blue. He would not be found dead, if he could help it, anywhere, but least of all in a library, a theatre, a concert hall or an art gallery. He himself kills people pretty often, but they are rotten people, better dead. His job, which is secret and indescribably important, gives him the right to kill people. He is a patriot and unmarried.

The appeal of The Product is considerable. Sales prove it. Most of its qualities, as has been pointed out, are derived from the work of earlier authors in the same area. The exoticism, the fisticuffs, the ingenious hardware, the sinister flora and fauna – these all are variations on old themes; so are the torture scenes and the much over-condemned sex interludes, which have about as much depravity about them as did Sydney Horler's admiration of 'scanties'. But there is another element of the Bond books which, though not an invention of Fleming, was presented by him in higher concentration than the public had ever before shown itself prepared to accept. It is, to use another of the so appropriate metaphors of advertising, his Product's 'Ingredient X', and it is compounded of equal parts of moral abdication and supra-legal arrogance.

Bond is a hero and was intended to be accepted as such. There is no question of his being a tragic or sleazy or pathetic figure caught in political machinery and morally castrated by it. That occupational hazard may await characters in the world of Graham Greene and John le Carré and Len Deighton, but Bond was designed to be both physically and mentally indestructible. By tradition of popular fiction, so enormous an advantage ought to be employed for good and against evil; immortality has always been considered dangerous stuff in the wrong hands. Yet Bond, and all the quasi-Bonds of Fleming's imitators, are depicted as acting entirely without reference to any code other than that curious mixture of bureaucratic nicety and murderous licence whereby, we are assured, the under-cover agents of government everywhere conduct their affairs.

Although the authors of the espionage fiction that has proliferated in the last twenty-five years might have intended otherwise, what they really have fathered is a secret police literature. James Bond has been erroneously labelled 'spy' too long. He is, and always has been, a secret policeman. So are the heroes of James Mitchell, alias Munro, of Deighton and le Carré, of William Haggard and Helen Macinnes. They and others in the same fashionable mould may be supposed to owe their allegiance to M.I.5, to the Deuxième Bureau, to the C.I.A., to this or that or the other currently approved agency of human supervision, but all are as surely secret policemen as were those dour men in belted rain-coats who once sauntered through Europe on the errands of Heinrich Himmler.

It is curious that something of which people throughout the world, and perhaps the English and Americans in particular, have always declared their abhorrence is now an accepted element of their leisure reading. By no means all secret police fiction invites admiration for its central characters in the old sense of cheering the goodies. But the non-committal novel in this field as well as the openly propagandist one finds a public ready to be fascinated by any kind of a tale about political subterfuge, however squalid or vicious. This could be simply a sign of human adaptability. As the number of ways in which we can feel superior to one another is diminished by the erosion of class frontiers, perhaps our repugnance to privily wielded power is being modified by recognition of its incomparable value in the status game.

"Be careful. It's very dangerous this side of the General. This is the arm he invariably brings

Index